THE US MILITARY IN AFRICA

THE US MILITARY IN AFRICA

Enhancing Security and Development?

edited by
Jessica Piombo

FIRST**FORUM**PRESS

A DIVISION OF LYNNE RIENNER PUBLISHERS, INC. • BOULDER & LONDON

Published in the United States of America in 2015 by
FirstForumPress
A division of Lynne Rienner Publishers, Inc.
1800 30th Street, Boulder, Colorado 80301
www.rienner.com

and in the United Kingdom by
FirstForumPress
A division of Lynne Rienner Publishers, Inc.
3 Henrietta Street, Covent Garden, London WC2E 8LU

Library of Congress Cataloging-in-Publication Data
A Cataloging-in-Publication record for this book
is available from the Library of Congress.
ISBN: 978-1-62637-196-5

British Cataloguing in Publication Data
A Cataloguing in Publication record for this book
is available from the British Library.

Any contributions produced by employees of the US government
are works of the US government and are not subject to copyright
in the United States. Non-US copyrights may apply.

Printed and bound in the United States of America

∞   The paper used in this publication meets the requirements
of the American National Standard for Permanence of
Paper for Printed Library Materials Z39.48-1992.

5   4   3   2   1

Contents

Acknowledgments

This book would not have been possible without the dedication and active engagement of a large number of individuals. First of all, I would like to thank the contributors to the book for their patience, persistence, and collaborative dedication to seeing this project through. It has been a multi-year journey, and I have asked a lot from those collaborating on the endeavor. Thank you for working with me to produce what I hope will be a valuable contribution to the growing literature in this field.

The chapters in the book grew out of a project sponsored by the Defense Threat Reduction Agency's Advanced Systems and Concepts Office (DTRA-ASCO). ASCO supported the initial workshop that enabled us to interact with one another in three days of very intense and fruitful discussions. In particular, we would like to acknowledge David Hamon and Jennifer Perry for lending their considerable expertise to the workshop's design, organization, and substantive discussions. As project manager, Ms. Perry shaped the framework of the book, advised us on the selection of cases and contributors, and consistently helped us to refine ideas.

Sandra Leavitt and Alfred Woodson coordinated the planning and execution of the initial workshop. Gustav Jordt (USAF), Jason Neal (USN), and Laura Perazzola (USMC), three former Naval Postgraduate School students, were integral in the execution of the event. These dedicated students and officers served as panel chairs, discussion facilitators, and note takers; they also helped to write significant portions of the report that came out of the workshop.

I would like to thank the faculty of the Department of Political Studies at the University of the Western Cape for their support and fraternity during a five-month sabbatical trip to South Africa; at that time, I worked on editing many portions of the book manuscript. I put the finishing touches on the manuscript while being hosted by the School for Conflict Analysis and Resolution at George Mason University, which was an excellent host. Special thanks to Terrence Lyons at GMU for his camaraderie. Lynne Rienner has been an incredibly patient and supportive publisher, and my sincere thanks go to her for seeing the value in this work.

Finally, I'd like to thank the many individuals who have shared their insights with me over the years. I have been able to participate in planning meetings for many of the programs that are discussed in these pages, and several times have had the opportunity to travel to remote locations in East Africa to learn about the military's activities and engagements. While we may offer critical reflection on the outcomes of these endeavors, one thing that we cannot criticize is the long hours and hard work put into them. Thank you to all these workers for their service, patience, and spirit.

—Jessica Piombo

Acronyms

3D/Three D	Diplomacy, Development, and Defense
AFRICOM	United States Africa Command
AOR	Area of Responsibility
APS	Africa Partnership Station
AQIM	Al-Qaeda in the Islamic Maghreb
CA	Civil Affairs
CDCS	Country Development Cooperation Strategy
CERP	Commander's Emergency Response Program
CEW	Civilian Expeditionary Workforce
CJOA	Combined Joint Operations Area
CJTF-HOA	Combined Joint Task Force-Horn of Africa
CMC	(Office of) Civil-Military Cooperation
CMM	(Office of) Conflict Management and Mitigation
CMO	Civil-Military Operations
CNT	Counter Narcotics Trafficking
COCOM	Combatant Command
COIN	Counterinsurgency
CoM	Chief of Mission
CONPLAN	Concept Plan
CRC	Civilian Response Corps
CSO	(Bureau of) Conflict and Stabilization Operations
CT	Counterterrorism
DATT	Defense Attaché
DCHA	(Bureau for) Democracy, Conflict, and Humanitarian Assistance
DHAPP	DoD HIV/AIDS Prevention Program
DIRI	Defense Institution Reform Initiative
DLI	Development Leadership Initiative
DoD	Department of Defense
DoJ	Department of Justice

DoS	Department of State
ECOWAS	Economic Community of West African States
ESF	Economic Support Fund
EU	European Union
EUCOM	United States European Command
FM	Field Manual
FMF	Foreign Military Financing
FSF	Foreign Security Force
FY	Fiscal Year
GAO	United States Government Accountability Office
GPOI	Global Peace Operations Initiative
GWOT	Global War on Terror
HA	Humanitarian Assistance
HADR	Humanitarian Assistance and Disaster Response
HAO	Humanitarian Assistance Other
HCA	Humanitarian and Civic Assistance
HMA	Humanitarian Mine Action
IMET	International Military Education and Training
INCLE	International Narcotics Control and Law Enforcement
IPCC	Interagency Policy Coordination Committee
IUU	Illegal, Unreported, and Unregulated (Fishing)
MDGs	Millennium Development Goals
MISO	Military Information Support Operations
MoDA	Ministry of Defense Advisor
NDAA	National Defense Authorization Act
NGO	Nongovernmental Organization
NSC	National Security Council
ODA	Operational Detachment-Alpha
OECD	Organization for Economic Cooperation and Development
OEF-TS	Operation Enduring Freedom-Trans-Sahara
OFDA	Office of Foreign Disaster Assistance
OHDACA	Overseas Humanitarian Disaster and Civic Assistance
OMA	Office of Military Affairs

OSC	Office of Security Cooperation
OTI	Office of Transition Initiatives
PKO	Peacekeeping Operations
PREACT	Partnership for Regional East Africa Counterterrorism
PRT	Provincial Reconstruction Team
QDDR	Quadrennial Diplomacy and Development Review
QDR	Quadrennial Defense Review
SADC	Southern African Development Community
SCRAT	Sociocultural Research and Advisory Team
S/CRS	Office of the Coordinator for Reconstruction and Stabilization
SDA	Senior Development Advisor
SJSR	Security and Justice Sector Reform
SOCAFRICA/ SOCAF	Special Operations Command, Africa
SOCOM	Special Operations Command
SPP	Strategy, Plans, and Programs
SSA	Security Sector Assistance
SSR	Security Sector Reform
SSTR	Security, Stabilization, Transition, and Reconstruction
TSC	Theater Security Cooperation
TSCTP	Trans-Sahara Counterterrorism Partnership
TSOC	Theater Special Operations Command
UN	United Nations
USA	United States Army
USAID	United States Agency for International Development
USG	United States Government
USN	United States Navy
WTO	World Trade Organization

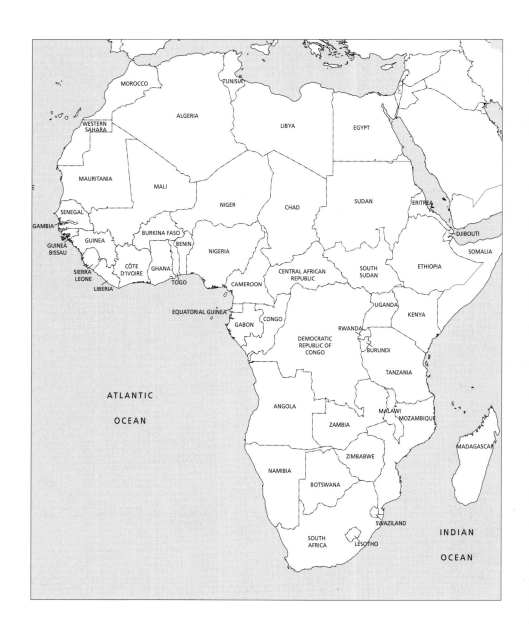

1

Addressing Security Threats in Africa

Jessica Piombo

How can a defense organization address security issues in an environment where insecurity often stems from challenges of governance and development? The traditional toolkits of defense institutions and actors are not designed or intended to address concerns related to governance and development, challenging these agents to devise novel approaches. The need to adapt is especially strong when military actors are tasked with addressing insecurities that stem from areas outside of traditional, interstate consideration: politically closed systems, state-dominated economic opportunities, and widespread poverty, food insecurity, and vulnerability. These unstable areas are often rife with multidimensional security challenges such as armed conflict, terrorism, illicit trafficking, communal violence, resource competition, and problems associated with significant population displacement. A true response that aims to resolve rather than manage these issues requires attention to governance and development, as much as it does to traditional security institutions like militaries and police forces. The relationship among governance, security, and development defies simple causality, and means that efforts to address any single side of the triangle must take into account the other two.

As has been widely argued by academics, international organizations such as the United Nations Development Programme (UNDP), and even the US Department of State, Africa's security challenges largely relate to deficient levels of good governance (including effective democratic governance and the active inclusion of minority and marginalized ethnic groups in the business of governance), as well as socioeconomic equality. Armed insurrection, lawlessness, and terrorism have predominantly emerged in Africa in response to this state of affairs.[1] To respond to these challenges, the United States Department of Defense (DoD) has experimented with a wide range of approaches and programs to respond to the nature of the security environment in sub-Saharan Africa.

Particularly since 2001, these efforts have raised many questions and generated fierce debates about the proper role of the US military within the "whole of government" approach to security; whether the US military was attempting to assume a developmental role in Africa; and whether US foreign policies within Africa have become militarized and/or securitized. In this volume, we analyze the first two of these debates by asking what blend of civilian, military and private programs and activities can help to produce outcomes that work on all three aspects of the security-governance-development dynamic to reduce insecurities in sub-Saharan Africa. The authors in this volume interrogate the activities of the US military and the broader Department of Defense as they have experimented with novel approaches to dealing with nontraditional security challenges.

Collectively, this volume assesses the changing role of the US Department of Defense in sub-Saharan Africa as it has become involved in activities outside its traditional toolkit of military training and equipment programs, the two cornerstones of traditional theater security cooperation. The first question the authors investigate is how these programs operate, the degree to which they involve civil-military cooperation, and how the differential capabilities and resources of the various US government agencies affect programs that attempt to take a broad view of security. The second broader, and ultimately more important question, is what role the US military can play in helping to reduce the nonmilitary sources of insecurity and to create more stable and secure environments for the citizens of African countries?

The authors review a selection of US security programs in Africa, investigating a set of initiatives where government actors attempted to create programs that brought together a range of actors outside the normal military toolkit, addressed issues beyond military-training, and which considered both the causes and manifestations of complex security challenges. Most of these initiatives moved the US military out of its traditional roles such as kinetic operations (i.e., military action using lethal force) and military training, and brought the Defense Department into direct interaction with counterparts in the State Department, the United States Agency for International Development (USAID), and a range of nongovernmental organizations (NGOs).

The Complex Nature of Security Challenges in Africa

The mutual relationship between state-based and human security problems in Africa, as in much of the global south, means that programs to counter insecurity must address both individual- and state-level drivers.[2] In these environments, not only must our conceptualization of security shift, but the focus and responses of states must also adapt to new realities. Traditional approaches in which human security issues are treated as distinct from physical (state) security ones are not sufficient to address and resolve security challenges at either level. "The state-based security architectures of the twentieth century cannot address twenty-first-century vulnerabilities. We need to make a core shift from focusing on traditional threats to focusing on conditions-based vulnerabilities."[3] These "conditions-based vulnerabilities" often lie outside traditional national security considerations and defense capabilities, and have in turn led governments like that of the United States to adopt discourse and policy in which development issues should be considered part of the arena addressed by the national security establishment.[4]

Fundamentally, national security problems tend to emerge as a result of deeply rooted human security issues, including those that are economic or social in nature. Once those forces take hold, and an identifiable national security problem emerges, the effects of that national security problem are not limited to political or security-related concerns within a state government or governments. A national security concern can also, in turn, fuel insecurity at the group or individual level, particularly if the state can no longer provide security guarantees (assuming that it could ever provide them). These insecurities can be social or economic in nature. Therefore, a cyclical pattern can emerge where a local security challenge fuels a national security challenge, which then creates additional local security issues, and so-on.

As a brief example to demonstrate this relationship, consider the challenge of small arms and light weapons proliferation and use in Africa. Poverty, inequality, and lack of opportunity can lead to desperation. In this condition, if an opportunity to serve as a middleman in trafficking presents itself, individuals who would not normally engage in the activity would be more likely to do so in order to address their social and economic insecurities. Whether the trade is in small arms and light weapons, contraband goods, drugs, or humans, trafficking offers high payoffs and can, in certain contexts, help those who are otherwise desperate to gain status as others begin to view them as powerful and successful individuals. Thus, individuals or a group may engage in cross-border arms trafficking as a way to address personal insecurity.

Since trafficking networks generally involve multiple groups, individual attempts to address personal insecurity can feed into to a complex and networked state-level security problem. Collectively, the members of a trafficking network can contribute to the movement of massive weapon supplies either within a country or across state borders, depending on the security situation at play. Systemic factors, such as the presence of closed, authoritarian, or corrupt political systems, can allow small-time trafficking activities to generate (or contribute to) increasingly insurmountable arms proliferation activities and perhaps facilitate a widespread sharp increase in violence, the emergence of cross-border conflicts, and civil wars.[5]

Of course, the emergence of war and conflict can also provide additional opportunities for arms trafficking operations to occur due to an increase in supply and demand of arms. Increasingly unstable economic and social security situations, resulting from the conflict, may make arms trafficking more enticing to other individuals whose lives have been shattered as a result of widespread violence and uncertainty. As trafficking operations grow and violence continues without an end in sight, nearby states, including those not directly impacted by the conflict, may soon become sites for violence, and their leaders may become increasingly concerned about the real potential for "conflict spillover." This, in turn, impacts the nature of bilateral and multilateral relationships among the state governments. If a spillover occurs, it will cause additional human security concerns in a more widespread area, and the cycle of insecurity will linger but at a grander scale.

More than one security dynamic is likely to influence the security situation in a given area at any given time. In extending the small arms and light weapons example, it quickly becomes apparent that increasingly severe population displacement and health and food insecurity situations can emerge when conflict erupts. At the same time, these very factors may have contributed to the violent conflict in the first place, as Liberian refugees in northern Côte d'Ivoire did in the early 2000s (when a steady stream of refugees-turned-migrants later became a source of tension that fed into the outbreak of war in 2003). The dynamics are a causal analyst's tautological nightmare. Depending on the situation, terrorism and maritime security crises can manifest in situations of extended conflict, as they have in both the Niger Delta and Somalia. The confluence of these factors is nearly always complex and context-dependent, but understanding how they intersect with one another is imperative to gain a holistic picture of any security situation, particularly if one hopes to develop and execute engagement activities to address it (the focus of Chapters 9-11 of this book).

Working to promote security and stability goals in this type of environment means attempting to reduce the sources of insecurity, addressing the cyclical relationship between different drivers, and operating at the individual, community, state, and interstate levels. Simply working to disrupt smuggling and trafficking networks will not eliminate the factors that drive individuals into these networks in the first place. Eliminating income from illicit trafficking without developing alternate livelihood and income opportunities may even make people *more* vulnerable and insecure. These dynamics necessitate a different approach to reduce insecurity than found in traditional interstate oriented security programs.

Multidimensional Responses to Complex Security Issues

In the early 2000s, as the international security environment shifted and the United States began to prioritize issues of ungoverned spaces, vulnerable populations, and poverty as threats to national security, Africa and challenges to security in Africa became higher priorities for US foreign policy. The US government created multiple security programs that explicitly attempted to combine the efforts of agencies traditionally involved in foreign assistance with those of the US military. These programs have been variously described as "interagency," "whole of government," "3D" (diplomacy, development, and defense), and "smart power" approaches, and have been used across the globe to address multiple causes of security and insecurity. In Africa, three flagship initiatives attempted to build bridges between the security and development communities: the Combined Joint Task Force-Horn of Africa (CJTF-HOA), the Trans-Sahara Counterterrorism Partnership (TSCTP), and the Africa Partnership Station (APS).

Each of these blend civilian and military actors in different ways, and address specific development-security dynamics within the scope of their programs. The TSCTP, with a mission to counter violent extremism across the Sahel region, is the most comprehensive of the three. The Department of State coordinates all activities of the TSCTP to ensure that the programs of specific agencies complement each other. Concrete initiatives are undertaken by the Department of State (DoS) in the diplomatic and public information realms; USAID engages in education and development activities to counter extremism; and the DoD provides education and training to regional security forces to increase their ability to fight and eradicate extremist groups. In most circumstances the actors in the TSCTP do not work directly with each other, rather the coordination is high-level.

The CJTF-HOA is directly managed by the United States Africa Command (AFRICOM)—in 2002-2007 by the United States Central Command—and has fewer interagency partners directly involved in its structure and processes than does the TSCTP. CJTF-HOA does have a significant focus on civil-military engagements throughout the Horn of Africa, utilizing naval engineers (the Seabees) and Civil Affairs groups to dig wells, and build and refurbish schools and healthcare facilities. There are a range of other activities that involve providing medical, dental and veterinary care, as well as more traditional military training activities. CJTF-HOA also provides fora and training programs to help regional militaries build their own civil-military and disaster response capabilities.

The management of the APS, like the CJTF-HOA, is also entirely within the military, as it is run by US Naval Forces, Africa (the Navy component command for Africa). APS focuses on enhancing maritime security in the Gulf of Guinea, includes maritime civil affairs groups, and also works with nongovernmental organizations and other government organizations on education in the maritime realm (fisheries development, education for coastal management, and other nontraditional, development-oriented security activities). Within Africa, these three initiatives have raised a great deal of controversy about the role of the US military in promoting "developmental" solutions to security challenges.

Efforts to integrate security and development efforts peaked with the creation of AFRICOM in 2007. Based on experiences and lessons from the TSCTP, CJTF-HOA, and APS, the US government had come to realize the difficulties of adopting cohesive security strategies in Africa. The Bush administration initiated a reorganization within the DoD in February 2007, announcing plans to create a geographic combatant command dedicated to Africa that would organize all defense programs on the continent under a single command, rather than the existing three commands. Launched between February 2007 and October 2008, AFRICOM assumed responsibility for the design and execution of DoD programs on the African continent, taking over programs previously administered by US Pacific Command, US Central Command, and US European Command.

As it combined the administration of the DoD's efforts in Africa under one structure, AFRICOM also announced that it intended to operate differently than traditional combatant commands.[6] The vision for AFRICOM reflected the nature of insecurity in Africa, where challenges stemming from problems of governance and development often posed indirect threats to the national security of the United States. Military solutions that focused on kinetic operations would do little to change the nature of the threat environment in most African countries. Therefore, working to protect US security interests within Africa meant attempting to reduce the sources of insecurity and helping to strengthen African security capabilities, as well as assisting vulnerable communities to protect themselves against threats.

Not only was AFRICOM's scope of activities conceived more broadly than that of other combatant commands, but also the manner in which it would operate differed from traditional notions of military operations. As originally planned, AFRICOM was meant to operate in a highly interactive manner with civilian government agencies such as the DoS and USAID. The initial vision reflected the emerging belief that in regions of the world like sub-Saharan Africa, an interagency approach was necessary to address complex security challenges and bridge work in development and security. AFRICOM had initially been conceived as a fundamentally interagency organization, with large numbers of non-DoD personnel in significant positions of responsibility, rather than as a defense organization to which a small group of interagency partners provided advice.

The United States Southern Command (SOUTHCOM) had already adopted a similar approach to US security engagements in Latin America and the Caribbean, but SOUTHCOM had been designed and structured as a traditional command. Civilians could play advisory roles in SOUTHCOM, but not hold implementing posts. AFRICOM's planners attempted to design a military structure that would place civilians in important functional and decision-making positions. These civilians were to come from various government departments, such as the Department of State, USAID, the Department of Justice, and the Department of Treasury. The purpose was to bring the insight of these organizations into the daily workings of AFRICOM and to orient it towards greater interagency cooperation.

On the ground, programs were designed to reflect this interagency perspective. As AFRICOM's mission and operating concept took shape, its scope of activities grew to include the three flagship programs previously discussed, as well as a range of more traditional military activities such as theater security cooperation (training and equipping African militaries) combined exercises, and peacekeeping training programs. Military efforts would work in tandem with governance programs, so that a security sector reform program would integrate defense reform with justice programs that focused on the rule of law. Security force capacity building would unfold in countries where democratic reforms had already been enacted, and where civilians had been teaching their African counterparts how to democratically and responsibly control and utilize their security agencies. Counterterrorism programs were meant to encompass educational and development initiatives, as well as skills training for military and police forces. Some of these programs were already underway, and AFRICOM was supposed to help push the coordination even deeper into the planning and implementation process.[7]

AFRICOM thus inherited a range of programs that include significant elements of capacity building, humanitarian and civic assistance, natural disaster response, and "stabilization" activities. In 2007-8 AFRICOM's proposed mission encompassed a significant number of projects and programs modeled on the civil-military development projects of the TSCTP and CJTF-HOA that looked like small-scale development programs (human capacity building, institutional reform, and economic assistance). AFRICOM's transition team planned to build on these programs to help support and sustain African capacity for non-kinetic and limited military missions, emphasizing humanitarian assistance (HA), disaster relief, medical assistance, security cooperation, and capacity building. The command would prioritize theater security cooperation and be capable of only limited military operations; it had no dedicated forces and would require external support to launch any kinetic military operations.

AFRICOM has evolved significantly from this initial vision: the crucible of the Libyan intervention in 2011 led AFRICOM's second commanding general (then, Carter Ham) to realize that the command's operational structure was not suited to running a military campaign. Since 2011, AFRICOM has reduced its emphasis on the interagency approach and increased its focus on traditional military training, security sector reform, and other theater security cooperation activities. The nontraditional activities still exist across the continent, though traditional military engagements have assumed more prominence.

Scope and Plan of the Book

It has been more than thirteen years since the establishment of the CJTF-HOA in Djibouti (2002), and eight since AFRICOM was created. There is now a significant record and set of experiences in the realm of nontraditional security initiatives in Africa. In this volume we assess these efforts to work across the development-security divide, examining their impacts on the African security environment, as well as the process and outcomes of US security engagement in sub-Saharan Africa. The contributions cover a range of programmatic areas and initiatives and consider the debates that these engagements have created.

Chapters 1-3 look at how US government agencies have evolved to operate in rapidly changing security environments where nontraditional security threats outnumber traditional threats. The authors analyze the military's changing role in "nation building" and the development-security divide and situate the creation of AFRICOM within this context.

Chapters 4-7 focus on specific types of security challenges and how the US either works directly or with African partners to address them. Some of the chapters are conceptual, analyzing overall approaches, while others present case studies of particular initiatives, assessing how these programs affect the security environment in Africa. These analyses also explicitly address coordination across multiple US and nongovernmental actors and condider the role of the US military in these programs. The authors evaluate programs that variously work to strengthen weak security sectors, address cultures of corruption that create insecurities, attempt to counter terrorism through civil-military affairs, or enhance the maritime security of partner countries. Each of the chapters asks a set of questions about the creation of the programs, the actors involved, and the effectiveness of both the interagency process and the efforts to improve the African security environment.

In Chapters 8-11, the authors assess the record of these whole of government efforts to address insecurity and promote a more stable and secure environment in sub-Saharan Africa. They also propose avenues for improvement.

Notes

Note: All opinions expressed in this chapter are my own and do not reflect official positions of either the Naval Postgraduate School or the United States government.

[1] Lamb, "Parading US Security Interests as African Security Policy," 50-52.

[2] Beebe and Kaldor, *The Ultimate Weapon Is No Weapon*. The geographic reference in this volume is primarily sub-Saharan Africa; for convenience we will also refer to it as "Africa."

[3] Beebe and Kaldor, *The Ultimate Weapon Is No Weapon*, 4.

[4] For example, the 2001 National Security Strategy identified statelessness (a governance deficit) as a major national security consideration, and in 2010 President Barak Obama issued a Presidential Policy Directive on Global Development. "The directive recognizes that development is vital to U.S. national security and is a strategic, economic, and moral imperative for the United States" and called for "the elevation of development as a core pillar of American power and charts a course for development, diplomacy and defense to reinforce and complement one another in an integrated, comprehensive approach to national security." The first quote is from www.whitehouse.gov/the-press-office/2010/09/22/fact-sheet-us-global-development-policy, accessed September 26, 2012; the second from www.state.gov/ppd, accessed December 15, 2014). These are discussed in more depth in Chapters 2 and 3.

[5] See, for example, Houngnikpo, "Small Arms and Big Trouble," 165-186.

[6] For more on the history of these developments, see Ploch, *Africa Command: U.S. Strategic Interests*.

[7] Much of this information is derived from conversations with multiple officials at AFRICOM in November 2007 and over the course of 2008.

2

The Military's Role in Development

Andrea Kathryn Talentino

Understandings of development have changed in the last two decades, as the concept of what is often described as a security-development nexus has come to dominate academic and practical discourse. That nexus is based on a recognition that underdevelopment can contribute to instability and can lead to a commitment, at least in rhetoric, to improving the lives of others as a way to enhance international security. The nexus is also characterized by a gap between the meager resources nations devote to development efforts and the ambitiousness of their stated goals. The UN Millennium Development Goals (MDGs) are emblematic of both aspects, since they link nations to an ambitious agenda to improve the developing world but remain under-realized in all cases, particularly the eighth goal concerning a global partnership. Nonetheless, the language of development is much different than in the past, and the change was driven primarily by three factors: (1) the changing conceptions of security enabled by the end of the East-West rivalry; (2) the growing attention to a variety of international problems, notably poverty, civil conflict, human rights, and economic development, and their connection to state failure; and (3) the increasing use of international intervention as a conflict resolution tool.

Few areas of the world illustrate the conundrum of weak states and faltering development more thoroughly than sub-Saharan Africa, which has struggled to progress on many social and economic indicators over the last several decades.[1] It is also the area with the greatest concentration of conflicts in the world paired with endemic crises of political instability and overall insecurity.[2] In 2007-2008, the new US Africa Command (AFRICOM) was explicitly created with the goal of serving both local development needs and US security interests. AFRICOM was designed to be a regional military headquarters, with the mission of "sustained security engagement through military-to-military programs, military-sponsored activities, and other military operations as directed to promote a stable and secure African environment in support of US foreign policy."[3] At its creation, the Bush administration described AFRICOM as a humanitarian undertaking and aligned AFRICOM's mandate more closely with peacebuilding operations than with traditional military commands, tilting its goals toward development. At the same time, the US and international observers questioned whether the military was an appropriate vehicle for pursuing development objectives and raised concerns that its involvement would effectively securitize all interactions.

This chapter examines the role of the military in development in order to assess the potential role that military actors can play. It asks specifically whether AFRICOM can serve development and if so, how. Africa is a fitting place to undertake this examination precisely because the continent is an important focus for US counterterrorism strategy. Moreover, Africa demonstrates the wider problem of the link between underdevelopment, civil conflict, and failing states. Both the chronic crisis of underdevelopment and the threat of terrorist activity are ever-present concerns on the continent, and recognizing these twin challenges is important because both development and security can be valid goals. The fact that the United States might attach security interests to its pursuit of development does not negate that it also attaches development interests to its pursuit of security. The question is really whether development has been wholly securitized, or whether security has also been developmentalized.

Development and Security

Though development and security have always been closely linked, in most eras development was considered the purview (or problem) of each individual state, and of value only insofar as it served security. The nineteenth century scramble for Africa, Germany's two agendas of expansion in the twentieth, and the economic and scientific aspects of the Cold War were all driven by states' concern that they must develop or lose ground to their rivals. The colonial empires and conquering armies had little concern for the welfare of the individuals or regions they controlled. International operations were undertaken exclusively to serve the needs of the expansionist states, in spite of rhetoric (depending on the era) pertaining to civilizing or improving the areas affected.

The concept that development and security might be mutually reinforcing did not receive serious attention until the end of World War II. The Marshall Plan is perhaps the best example of a policy whose primary objective, ensuring US security, was achieved through the pursuit of development. Similarly, the Alliance for Progress under John F. Kennedy sought to improve economic and social conditions in Latin America as a means of shoring up US influence there and strengthening America's position vis-à-vis the Soviet Union. Though the Marshall Plan and Alliance for Progress identified economic factors as important for stability, they did not necessarily envision prosperity for the target areas. Instead, they aimed to encourage enough capacity for states to be reliable allies and resist communism. The Peace Corps, too, was born of a primary interest in security. For all these security initiatives, development was a means to that end.

Academics also described a link between development and security during the Cold War, particularly as it became clear that development was not a simple and linear process but one that seemed to generate conflict and upheaval. Modernization theory analysts championed the concept that development entailed not simply economic changes but also corresponding shifts in political organization, social norms, and habits (thus distinguishing it from development economics).[4] Those theorists' basic definition of development was similar to contemporary views, though they paired it with an imperial perspective that juxtaposed modern/good with primitive/ bad, and defined modern as "those types of social, economic, and political systems that have developed in Western Europe and North America."[5] Contemporary critics might argue that the imperial flavor remains pervasive today: the link between democracy and modernization theory has be seen clearly in the strategy of liberal peacebuilding, a form of regime change undertaken by international actors to enact political and economic liberalization in target states. Although liberal peacebuilding is intended to be a collaborative effort with local governments it also has a strong tendency to promote international preferences at the expense of local ones and to enforce subjective notions of good government.[6] Importantly, however, modernization theory implied a link between development and stability that fueled further debate and has been further operationalized through peacebuilding.

During the Cold War era development initiatives increasingly showed that instability and conflict were frequent components of transition, leading Samuel Huntington to examine the concepts of political order and security as essential considerations in development.[7] He argued that institutions were crucial to the process of development in order to contain social and political conflicts. Thus, he concluded that capacity-building should precede democratization, a point reinforced nearly 40 years later by Roland Paris.[8] The social aspect was further explored by academics who focused on civil society and the more visceral aspects of change, such as political identities, desires for revenge, and mechanisms of opposition in society.[9] Even scholars who focused almost exclusively on economics as the sum of development agreed that the major powers would be better off and more secure if they helped to develop peripheral states both economically and politically.[10] The various strands of development theory thus converged on certain basic principles, notably that development meant recreating Western models, was inherently desirable for citizens of the primitive states, and would benefit all states, directly or indirectly. More stable economies and less political upheaval would be the result, and thus development efforts would redound to the benefit of the entire international system.

One significant change in the contemporary period is the use of military forces as a vehicle for development, which is now commonplace if still somewhat controversial in the context of peacebuilding. In 1994, the UN Development Program made an explicit link between development and security in its *Human Development Report*, a connection that was reinforced by UN Secretary-General Boutros Boutros-Ghali in his 1995 *Supplement to an Agenda for Peace*.[11] At the same time, conceptions of conflict resolution and the uses of intervention were changing, leading to development of the complex peace operations that are so familiar today. Although international actors initially focused primarily on conflict, they soon expanded their writ to include postconflict rebuilding and statebuilding efforts, which necessarily entailed some attention to development.

The understanding of development as an essential aspect of security became a key feature of all postconflict operations, leading Bjorn Hettne to suggest that the rise of international intervention securitized the concept of development.[12] I would argue that the converse is also true—intervention developmentalized the concept of security. By introducing statebuilding as an important partner of security and blurring the lines between where one began and the other ended it opened the door to expectations that security cannot be fully realized without effective state capacity. But exactly what role the military can or should play in assisting development remains ambiguous and somewhat controversial.

Though North Atlantic Treaty Organization (NATO) forces initially tried to draw a strict line between military tasks and broader civilian development tasks in Bosnia in the mid-1990s, they quickly discovered that any such division was both artificial and unsustainable. Neither half of the operation, military or civilian, could succeed without progress in and assistance from the other, forcing a reassessment of the cooperation within two years of the operation's deploying. NATO subsequently made peace operations support an essential part of its mission and went on to provide military assistance in the broader service of state development in Kosovo and Afghanistan. Other traditional military actors, notably the US Army, have also made development in both the political and economic arenas a central part of their objectives.[13] Of course, development does not mean the same thing to all organizations, and the brand the army pursues is geared toward attaining specific security objectives. At the same time, the fact that development strategies are considered as central to the army's mission as defense indicates the extent to which such ideas have permeated and shaped understandings of security. This is not simply a one-way street, where security transforms development, but one where the opposite trend occurs as well.

But the context of peacebuilding provides both a relatively clear role and a clear justification for the use of military force, while it simultaneously includes civilian reconstruction efforts that focus on a panoply of social, political, and economic tasks. This stems from the fact that international peacebuilding operations are generally deployed in or after a period of conflict, when the state has eroded and a sovereign entity may be compromised either in practice or in conceptual legitimacy. In these contexts, peacebuilding initiatives attempt to prevent further strife and create the conditions for stable political and economic development. Establishing a secure environment is as central to the mission as is establishing the structure of government.

The role of military forces as a tool of development in less urgent contexts, where widespread conflict and humanitarian crisis are not part of the equation, is far murkier. On the one hand, weak state environments, even if lacking conflict, are likely to share a set of characteristics found in peacebuilding environments, notably porous borders, ineffective security forces, rampant corruption, and weak or absent rule of law, all of which fall at least partially into the ambit of military concerns. On the other hand, such states are also characterized by functioning if limited governments, often a strong institutional presence for the local military, and the absence of the variety of factors that give peacebuilding operations a semblance of legitimacy as they intrude on or even assume the responsibilities of state sovereignty. Thus, peacebuilding in the African context, outside of an explicit postconflict scenario, rests on shakier principles than in its initial conception in the seminal *Agenda for Peace.*[14]

AFRICOM's Creation: The View from Both Sides

The Department of Defense (DoD) raised the possibility of a unified command for Africa over a decade ago but no strategic imperative existed to give the idea force. The US government's new priorities after the terrorist attacks of September 11, 2001 made the need more evident, and the initiative also fit squarely within the George W. Bush administration's broader emphasis on Africa. Though he did not make the issue a major part of his public relations agenda, Bush tripled the amount of humanitarian aid going to Africa over his two terms and made a concerted effort to address issues related to poverty and health, particularly HIV/AIDS.[15]

The precise role of AFRICOM in US policy is unclear. The DoD pushed for its creation based on the perceived imperatives of the global war on terror combined with other crises in Africa, notably in Somalia and Sudan. Navy Rear Admiral Robert Moeller, the director of the planning and implementation team for AFRICOM, noted that one motivating factor was the need to consolidate DoD activities in Africa as a result of the continent's increased importance.[16] Counterterrorism is not noted in his comments but is clearly a subtext, since that is one of the primary factors that made the African continent more important to US interests. Also present from the beginning were plans to partner with African governments and to pay attention to those governments' particular challenges. The DoD described AFRICOM as a "combatant command plus;" the "plus" referring to soft power elements aimed at building the foundations of stability through a broader focus on civilian development.[17] That is also a subtext in the position of the executive branch, which under both Presidents Bush and Obama has focused on AFRICOM as a means to strengthen African capacities and emphasize the soft power elements of partnership and development. Obama has also deployed AFRICOM in many traditional ways, notably by deploying combat-equipped troops to assist regional forces in Uganda, Libya and Mali.

The twin pillars of AFRICOM's genesis were reflected in the diverse group of voices from both sides of the political spectrum, including Democratic senators, US Agency for International Development (USAID) officials, and Heritage Foundation analysts, who endorsed its creation. Not surprisingly, the objectives of these disparate voices differed. Senators such as Russell Feingold (D-WI) argued for a coherent US presence mainly because of concerns about the prevalence of civil conflict and the attendant humanitarian and development crises, while the Heritage Foundation defined the issue in terms of US interests and strategic needs.[18] Nonetheless, the record is clear that nonmilitary entities of the US government strongly supported AFRICOM and viewed it as a means to pursue both the coordination of US policy and the emphasis on development more broadly.

On the opposite end of the spectrum, congressmen, foundations, and civilian government employees opposed AFRICOM because they feared security concerns would co-opt development and resisted the military's involvement in traditional arenas of the Department of State (DoS).[19] Though General William Ward, AFRICOM's first commander, described its mission as one of empowerment for African governments, members of Congress questioned the wisdom of using the military as a tool for pursuing development objectives. The controversy led AFRICOM to retreat from the original description of its role in development and meant that its alliance with civilian agencies did not fully materialize.

Subsequent mission statements have been more restrictive, and the level of civilian involvement has been limited. Embedded civilians constituted only 1 percent of the staff when AFRICOM reached operational capacity in late 2008, and to date they remain under 2 percent.[20] Initially AFRICOM's objectives had been focused on assisting the training and professionalization of partner militaries, a mission that fit with traditional military activities as well as the perceived capabilities of the command itself. After General Carter Ham assumed command in 2011 the concept of capacity building became a more central part of the command's objectives, as did the connection to initiatives pursued by nonmilitary organizations of the US government, such as the Department of State. The pendulum seems to have swung back more recently, however, with AFRICOM de-emphasizing interagency efforts and defining partnership in more limited ways.

Outside of the United States, most obviously in Africa but elsewhere as well, AFRICOM has been criticized as a blatant attempt to gain control of Africa's resources, notably oil, and to dominate its governments to suit US interests. AFRICOM is portrayed as essentially a means of de facto colonization. In this view, the US government was motivated to form AFRICOM to pursue counterterrorism, resource extraction, and overall strategic dominance, and in particular to counter the potential for other countries such as China to exert power in Africa.[21] US policymakers voiced all of those strategic interests at one time or another, which helped generate concerns in Africa that domination rather than development might be the real US agenda.[22] The most vocal African critics of AFRICOM's birth tended to be countries with higher growth rates and less aid dependency. Those countries that were most aid-dependent, particularly on the United States, tended to be more supportive of AFRICOM. Thus, Carl LeVan argued that "external economic dependence serves as a source of leverage over African countries."[23] The countries most closely financially tied to the United States, such as Liberia and Rwanda, were vocal in support, with Liberia even offering to host AFRICOM's headquarters.

Concerns lingered, with some observers describing AFRICOM as a modern effort at colonization. At a congressional hearing in 2008, several representatives expressed the fear that AFRICOM was simply "going over there to protect oil and fight terrorists."[24] Although the voices of dissent vary in their emphasis, they all focus on the drive to control resources, the need to combat incursions into Africa by other major or growing powers, and the desire to create forward basing for counterterrorism activities as the primary purposes of AFRICOM.[25] The most extreme critics suggest that the attempt to involve civilian agencies is window dressing rather than a serious interest in development and "does not camouflage its primary militaristic thrust."[26] Conspiracy views of AFRICOM still abound on the internet. The African view is encapsulated by the belief that AFRICOM "is a Trojan horse through which the US will pursue and defend its key interests in Africa."[27] The fact that some of AFRICOM's most concrete tasks are inherited ones oriented to battling Islamic extremists merely solidifies the belief that it is about fighting wars rather than preventing them.

There is yet a third view of AFRICOM, and US African policy in general, that suggests something quite different. David Chandler does not examine AFRICOM specifically, but he describes the fanfare about development in Africa, particularly the focus on development and security as a twin package, as an "anti-foreign policy." Anti-foreign policy refers to the absence of any framework or policy consensus directing US actions and reflects a concern for self-image rather than a considered mechanism for commitment.[28] Indeed, Chandler suggests that the focus on the development-security nexus is simply a way to make a grand statement while essentially disengaging from the continent. It is a means to "evade responsibility for strategic policy-making" and has been undertaken without any kind of strategic framework or effort to reorganize policy-making mechanisms to reflect new objectives.[29]

Similar views are expressed by Nicholas Van de Walle, who argues that the adjustment of US policy toward Africa has been at best partial and inconsistent. Although the packaging of security and development initiated during the Clinton years gained favor under the Bush administration due to the seemingly obvious connections between the two in Afghanistan and Somalia, it led to an increase in aid without any change in conception, design or purpose. In addition to echoing Chandler's critique about the lack of coherence in policy, Van de Walle also notes that the increased aid masked a corresponding drawdown in diplomatic presence and institutional organization.[30] While the aid paired with the creation of AFRICOM seemed to herald a major shift and a potential strategic plan, Van de Walle concludes that, to the contrary, Africa policy became more haphazard and less of a priority.

Between 2002 and 2010 focus on Africa coalesced somewhat due to oil, though that focus was also highly dependent on demand. President Bush increased oil exports from Africa to the US, and in 2006 twenty-two percent of all crude oil imported into the US came from Africa.[31] Nigeria has consistently been one of the top five exporters of oil to the US, and during that period Angola also ranked in the top 10.[32] After 2010, however, the US reduced the amount of oil it imported from Africa by 90 percent, largely because shale oil discoveries in the US produced the same kind of light sweet crude that was the signature of African oil production.[33] The current US policy strategy toward Africa reflects the same kind of widespread focus on everything from security to health to elections that has defined previous eras, which suggests that whatever impetus may have existed for greater coherence is no longer relevant.

In 2012, the Obama administration articulated a new strategy for sub-Saharan Africa based on four pillars: strengthening democratic institutions, spurring economic growth, advancing peace and security and promoting growth and development.[34] The pillars and the rhetoric suggest that the conceptual mission of AFRICOM might be swinging back to incorporate more development, as even the focus on peace and security referenced those states in terms of "the basic security needs" of the people.

AFRICOM's own rhetoric, however, continues to privilege more unilateral security needs. For example, after a change in command in April 2013, General David M. Rodriguez presented AFRICOM's new posture statement to Congress a year later, leading with the assertion that "United States Africa Command is adapting our strategy and approach to address increasing US national interests, transnational security threats, and crises in Africa."[35] Although he also mentioned the importance of building more effective institutions and rule of law, the statement ties those goals directly to US economic and security interests, not to African development more generally. AFRICOM's website consistently highlights four goals that relate more directly to US security interests than African development: "Deter and Defeat Transnational Threats," "Prevent Future Conflict, "Support Human-itarian and Disaster Relief," and "Protect US Security Interests." One interesting change, however, is the emphasis placed on partnerships "with countries that have the greatest potential to be regional leaders and influencers in the future."[36] Although this too is primarily to serve US ends, it also has the potential to serve development goals as well by linking US support to partners that have the political will to both reform their own institutions and influence others to do so, as will be discussed below.

Although these accounts suggest that overall policy coherence has not changed, or has even deteriorated, Carl LeVan argues that AFRICOM's creation did represent an important shift in how the US does business. He suggests that the increased aid to Africa corresponded with "a weakening of traditional organs of diplomacy and development," with the DoD's aid disbursement dramatically increasing over the last decade while that of the State Department and USAID fell.[37] While the traditional levers of diplomacy and soft power may have been declining somewhat, the ebb and flow in DoS and USAID budgets seem to remain within a consistent continuum that does not necessarily suggest a decline in their overall impact.[38] At the same time, the DoD's budget for Africa has likely increased as a result of both AFRICOM's creation and heightened counter-terrorism activities, and reflects the reality that some of the development role has shifted to that body and made it a central player for US involvement with Africa. While the discussions above suggest that the criticisms of the command (and to some extent the support as well) are far overblown, they also suggest that AFRICOM does represent a potentially important shift in rhetoric and attitude. The objectives articulated by General Ham and the good partner emphasis of General Rodriguez suggest a potential for AFRICOM to forge new ground if operationalized.

The Development Africa Needs?

"Development" is accepted as an urgent necessity in Africa in particular, but the term covers a huge variety of tasks and initiatives. In addition, the concept that security and development are tied is accepted as a truism, but with little consideration as to what development means in that context or how it should be pursued. Indeed, some commentators have cautioned that the connection is false because seeing the two as entwined obscures the ways in which security initiatives might undermine development and vice versa.[39] It is important, therefore, to consider what kind of development is so urgently needed and how it might serve security.

The lessons of the 1990s showed that development is intimately related to security in terms of a country's capacity to survive because political, economic, and social weakness can lay the foundations for civil conflict.[40] The attention to and labeling of failed and failing states were indicators of this realization, as was the development of complex peace operations throughout the 1990s. Importantly, however, although international efforts to resolve civil conflict have achieved the primary goal of ending violence, they have been much weaker when measured by their impact on development, whether political, economic, or social.[41] An apparent failure to improve the development of weak states has persisted, in spite of international attention. Moreover, the terrorist attacks of September 11, 2001 (9/11), demonstrated that development is also intimately related to the dangers each country might pose to others, even those at a considerable geographic distance, because of the apparent link between weak states and terrorist activity.[42]

Taken together these two issues, the perception of underdevelopment as a cause of conflict and as an enabling factor for terrorism, led rather quickly to the belief that development and security must be considered together, with the latter attained by focus to the former. The Bush administration, which prior to the 2001 terrorist attacks had derided such tasks as nation building, joined with academic voices to argue that development was not only beneficial in its own right but was also an essential tool of counter-terrorism.[43] That understanding was the basis for the "transformational diplomacy" Condoleezza Rice endorsed as secretary of state, which focused on democracy building, and the military operations in Afghanistan and Iraq.[44]

In some ways this was not notably different from previous US foreign policy except to the extent to which development as an end in itself was explicitly tied to security. That was a subtle and important shift in rhetoric. The primary lesson the US government drew from 9/11 was that the lack of development in Afghanistan led directly to the growth of Al-Qaeda and its capacity to harm the United States. Importantly, however, the lesson focused on political development, with the Taliban in Afghanistan seen as irresponsible political actors primarily because of their willingness to support and implicitly endorse terrorist activities and Al-Qaeda. Although people decried the orthodox and repressive policies of the Taliban on Afghan society, the Bush administration's motivation to remove them from power stemmed from their political embrace of terrorists, not a desire to see social development flower in Afghanistan. And that highlights the fundamental problem with the rise of attention to development in general and the linking of it with security in particular. Development still tends to be narrowly conceived as tied to a security end rather than to the broader and deeper state- and peacebuilding efforts that are usually required as the partners for security and development. The result is generally that neither end is achieved.

One reason for the failure of development approaches to date is that they tend to focus on the symptoms of state fragility rather than its causes. This is true both in US approaches and international approaches, particularly those taking place under the peacebuilding label. The May 2010 US *National Security Strategy* (the most recent available at this writing) accurately pointed to the "underlying political and economic deficits that foster instability" and enable extremism as central concerns, and a variety of UN studies have noted the same problems.[45] In spite of that attention, however, few initiatives at any level have been able to address the problem of weak institutions that is a hallmark of most states that are behind in the development race.

This focus on symptoms instead of causes is most glaring in the case of states emerging from civil conflict, where international initiatives tend to struggle with the complexity and scope of the challenges faced. In a triumph of form over function, international actors often privilege the act of voting more than the capability of institutions and at times seem to be driven more by the need to check off accomplishments than to measure their actual value. Political milestones are often window dressing and give the appearance of liberalization without its benefits; they often do little to improve economic and social factors and are negotiated without adequate involvement of or responsiveness to local actors.[46] Haiti provides a particularly poignant example. Despite two international peacebuilding operations, Haiti remains mired in misery and in 2011 saw the return of a once disgraced dictator. Democratic structures are not synonyms or proxies for institutional developments.

Numerous scholars have emphasized the need to build effective political institutions in order to achieve stable peace, but translating that into policy is extremely difficult.[47] Providing the continuing support for those structures to actually function is far harder to achieve and much less of a priority, in part because donors care most about the creation and in part because maintenance support would require an extended and intrusive commitment that few have the stomach for. International actors' failure to really understand and engage with local systems and needs is also increasingly noted as an obstacle to effective state building.[48] The problem is compounded in cases that are not postconflict, where development takes place in partnership with an existing government. In such cases, it is harder for international actors to ignore local preferences but also easier for competing efforts and interests to stymie progress. Where initiatives are not part of a larger program of transformation and where the existing government might have strong ideas both about what development is required and what external actors can contribute, it becomes much more difficult.

The problems caused by emphasizing stability over development are reflected in the outcome of peacebuilding programs to date; these efforts provide an important lesson regarding the type of development that is really needed. Particularly in the case of Africa, analyst Mohamed Salih notes that development efforts in the context of peacebuilding have failed to address issues of poverty, exclusion, and justice and have thus created tensions that actually make underdevelopment and continued conflict, whether violent or not, more likely.[49] His critique is part of a larger set of commentaries that focus on the failure of peacebuilding efforts to provide the kind of development that is most essential, notably the social and economic initiatives that are consistent with local interests and affect how people live, their access to levers of power, and their relationship with others in their community.[50]

This critique is important to consider within the wider context of security because the report card for peacebuilding operations suggests that they often perpetuate the social problems that lead to violence rather than ameliorate them. Moreover, peacebuilding efforts tend to be afflicted by a strong disjunction between the interests of international and local actors and the perceived lack of respect shown from the former toward the latter.[51] In general, the development part of peacebuilding proceeds from the concept that the society in question simply needs to be given the tools to function well and that its existing tools are to blame for the current problems.[52] This harkens back to the weaknesses of modernization theory and corresponds to what Mark Duffield describes as the "monotonous" rediscovery of poverty as a "recruiting ground for the moving feast of strategic threats that constantly menaces the world order."[53] Poverty is viewed as a fault of technique rather than an outcome of structural problems, and one that can be fixed when the proper tools are applied.

The importance of social and economic causes as a source of both conflict and underdevelopment is also captured in the literature on insta-bility and resources in Africa.[54] While much of the attention goes, quite properly, to the role of resources and predatory elites in creating incentives for conflict, two underlying problems are largely forgotten. The first problem is weak governments, which create the conditions that allow the looting of resources, and the second is the desperation of regular individuals, which creates a willing work force for illegal activities. Many, though certainly not all, of the problems that afflict weak states are rooted in economic crisis and the inability of the country's citizens to feel secure in an economic sense. To note that is in some sense foolish, as it suggests that underdevelopment is caused by underdevelopment. But the important point is that the development that matters most for security revolves around the comfort of the citizenry and their ability to fulfill basic needs. If they have that comfort, they are more likely to engage with the government and less likely to seek other sources of authority. That in itself is not a recipe for success, but it is a necessary condition for building the legitimacy that a government so desperately needs, and requires, from the beginning, to create capacity.

A number of important considerations come out of the above discussion of development. As Dustin Sharp discusses in Chapter 4 of this volume, many African countries are gripped by a culture of impunity and law-lessness that enables the illegal and terrorist activities that cause the most concern for the US government. Criticisms of AFRICOM point to the exploitation of resources and dominance of the populace, but these problems are already happening and in many cases are perpetrated by local rather than US actors. The primary means for addressing those problems should not be by applying Band-Aids to weak governments, but by focusing on facilitating socio-economic development that would strengthen rule of law, link citizens to their governments, and create both accountability and connection between governments and citizens.

First, development should be viewed primarily as a social and economic initiative rather than a political one. Second, less attention should be paid to macro political and economic factors, and more attention should be paid to grassroots needs. Third, efforts to give citizens access to and a stake in their governments are essential. Fourth, individual security matters most, and may have nothing to do with personal safety. Although in some cases security may refer to safety, in others it may simply pertain to the ability to provide for one's basic needs and a perception of social security. Finally, to be effective, any initiative must be part of a considered framework of policy that links different types of approaches (military, diplomatic, and economic) into a single strategy. The coordination of policy is essential, as discussed elsewhere in this book, and no single entity no matter how well-intentioned can succeed outside a whole of government approach. Ad hoc efforts are likely to yield little benefit and are largely a waste of money. The evidence suggests that neither political stability nor international security can be improved without focusing on the panoply of socio-economic crises that afflict states in Africa. AFRICOM was intended to address that problem, but the evidence suggests that it has evolved toward a more traditional and narrow approach, discussed below.

AFRICOM: Continuity or Difference?

AFRICOM bills itself as a different kind of command, but how different is it? It is clearly driven by US security needs but the development aspect of its mission has been less clear. The command's first Posture Statement (2010), focused on AFRICOM's unique role as an interagency command and its emphasis on capacity building among African states. Then-Commander William Ward emphasized that AFRICOM's theater strategy would "enable the work of Africans to marginalize the enemies of peace and prevent conflict, thereby enabling the growth of strong and just governments and legitimate institutions to support the development of civil societies."[55]

While AFRICOM's activities remained explicitly military, the 2012 Posture Statement's tone suggested an effort to diversify AFRICOM's objectives. The simple reality is that US security interests are a priority and AFRICOM is a military command. But even by pursuing these more traditional interests, AFRICOM could still make a significant contribution, and it seemed to be positioning itself to do that by changing the framing of its involvement in Africa. Though the 2010 Posture Statement mentioned partnership it did not mention African viewpoints on security or the causal factors that create the security challenges relevant to the United States.[56] The 2011 statement, by contrast, included a section titled "Listening to Our African Partners," which outlined four defense-oriented goals articulated by African states. The 2012 statement seemed to take that a step further by weaving references to regional interests as well as DoS interests throughout its discussion of objectives and mechanisms for attaining them. Perhaps most notably, in 2012 General Ham clearly positioned AFRICOM within a broad US approach and implied that all parts must be coordinated in order to achieve success.[57] Although specific goals of capacity building were not mentioned, as they were in 2011, the overall impression was of a command pushing for partnership on all fronts rather than one conceiving of security in an insular and exclusively military form.

Between 2010 and 2012, therefore, the positioning of AFRICOM shifted subtly from simply developing partnerships to actually listening to African states' articulation of problems and working with them to address challenges. The 2014 statement was quite different. The new commander, General David Rodriguez, did not speak the language of partnership, nor focus on much beyond strict US security interests. The consequences of weak government were presented solely in the context of US security, with no reference to the overall impact on African states or regions. Connections to African states were also discussed solely in terms of military-to-military efforts. This much narrower focus likely reflected the practical realities of what AFRICOM has been able to affect and accomplish thus far. It represented, nonetheless, a disappointing retrenchment from the broader language and concept of whole of government efforts and partnership. One piece that was important, however, and a potential change, was the concept of partnering with countries that have potential to lead or influence others.[58] It represented a return to the concept of "lead states" that dominated the Clinton-era engagement with Africa, and if this were to imply greater selectivity regarding with which partners US works, it could change the value of AFRICOM significantly.

One of the most interesting initiatives AFRICOM has pursued throughout is the State Partnership Program, which links a US state's National Guard with an African nation for the purposes of training and relationship building, and replicates a program used with Eastern Europe after the collapse of the Soviet Union. The program has the potential to encourage development through military linkage and AFRICOM's success as a development actor will rest in large part on its ability to inculcate certain norms of behavior for African militaries as both institutions and individual actors. Learning mechanisms are one way to diffuse norms and work just as they sound—norms are adopted in the target country because policymakers develop new ways of thinking based on information they receive through a variety of sources.

The State Partnership Program thus created a clear teaching and modeling structure through which AFRICOM could impact African states while leaving the power of change in their hands. Evidence shows that security institutions can be effective at promoting normative change across a broader spectrum than simply security issues.[59] By modeling institutional norms, military actors are able, under certain circumstances, to reinforce political and social shifts, as happened in Eastern Europe after the collapse of the Soviet Union. This is a valuable role that AFRICOM can both play and facilitate in the region while also ensuring the autonomy of its partners.

Some observers believe AFRICOM's military approach inhibits any real benefit for development. I suggest, based on the above, that there are small but important mechanisms by which AFRICOM can emphasize the development side within the context of military tasks. One challenge, however, is the lack of specificity in AFRICOM's and broader US perspectives. Robert Berschinski suggests that the US tendency to "aggregate" extremist actors by lumping all security challenges into a single conception of global threat is not only dangerous but counterproductive. First, it elides different objectives and interests among extremist actors and creates a single policy of counteraction that may not always be appropriate. Second, it prevents any consideration of the grievances and issues that may lie at the heart of extremist activity.[60]

United States policy shows evidence of these tendencies, and they inhibit a critical prerequisite for making AFRICOM matter beyond security: a broad understanding of local interests and dynamics. The 2014 Posture Statement provided detail on the extremist groups it prioritized but only a brief and general comment on regional instability. There is ample evidence that the two are closely linked, however, whether directly through operations in a particular state or indirectly through unrest as a fertile ground to transit goods, make money, or gain adherents. In spite of these limitations, it is clear that AFRICOM's activities have been heavily focused on the sort of norm diffusion noted above in a direct military context. The AFRICOM website profiles a variety of activities, from large scale exercises with troops from the Economic Community of West African States (ECOWAS), to sharing expertise in settings from medicine to forensics.[61] Though all clearly military tasks, these programs also serve the dual purpose of training and professionalizing African militaries, just as

African states seemed to have requested and as is urgently needed for both internal and external benefit.

AFRICOM's primary weakness is that its military approaches do not address the root causes of weakness and may actually perpetuate them. As Ndlovu-Gatsheni and Ojakorotu argue, "the weak African state is not an innocent political formation requiring humanitarian rehabilitation. It is a dangerous phenomenon if conceptualized from a security perspective."[62] In their view, leaders of weak states are cunning in their effort to use securitized approaches by outsiders to consolidate their rule and gain benefits for themselves while at the same time continuing to ignore the needs of the population they represent. This phenomenon is also precisely why Salih argues that peacebuilding efforts in Africa have reinforced the culture of the Big Man and personalistic rule. His view accords with the arguments of other scholars who suggest that African politics are dominated by self-interest and the conception of public service as a means to personal gain.[63] Critiques of AFRICOM have hinged on this concern, as some observers believe that securitizing development has perpetuated the corrupt and weak governments that were a familiar fixture of Cold War politics and laid the groundwork for many of the weaknesses Africa now experiences.

AFRICOM is not equipped to assist with statebuilding, nor should it be. But this area is precisely where AFRICOM can forge new ground. If it could serve as the point agency for the coordinated, integrated, whole of government approach that informed its development, AFRICOM could significantly change the effect of US policy in Africa, and elsewhere. Clarence Bouchat explores this idea further in his contribution to this volume. Security sector reform is an essential piece of development and the area where AFRICOM has a clear value, but that should be the beginning, not the end, of the focus on stability.

As Berschinski argued, "AFRICOM must divorce itself from the model of US military engagement in Africa since 9/11 in order to achieve its ends."[64] I suggest that means mobilizing entities like the Department of State and USAID to identify areas of joint activity and use their concentrated resources to effect broader change. The latest posture statement and its neglect of the interagency language thus suggests a step backward in achieving long-term benefit for the US, not forward. AFRICOM's work with partner militaries might help identify broader political issues that are the provenance of the DoS and thus catalyze development on multiple fronts. Corruption is an essential part of the story, as are accountability and transparency. Most of all, governments that are responsive and responsible to their constituencies are sorely needed, and development efforts will need to take place at multiple levels in order to achieve results.

AFRICOM's Possibilities and Potentials

AFRICOM is in a position to make a significant contribution to under-standings of development and security. If it focuses solely on military tasks as its endpoint, it will remain a very familiar example of US approaches to the world. But if it can use military tasks as a means to fuel other change, then it really could be different. This shift would be particularly important in light of AFRICOM's recent involvement in military operations in Libya, which reignited concerns that it is "business as usual." A key task ahead, therefore, is to rededicate AFRICOM to a "steady operational partnership" focused on improving African abilities by both increasing its efforts and evaluating its impact specifically as a development command thus far.[65] A candid assessment of AFRICOM's development impact would be useful, and could further identify areas of partnership with the DoS. Which way AFRICOM evolves, however, is dependent on the larger policy machinery of the US government. AFRICOM has the potential to model how security can be developmentalized so that the two approaches serve and shape each other. But that can only happen within a broad and conscious policy effort, involving many parts of the US government, which targets complementary programs that reinforce and sustain each other.

So how can AFRICOM live up to its potential? The first priority is to change the haphazard approach currently employed in choosing states to work with and to define what states AFRICOM should be working with and how it should be working with them. Hints of this appear in the 2014 Posture Statement, though it is not clear whether Rodriguez truly means choosing partners more likely to support norms like accountability and transparency or merely those that are larger in terms of population and GDP.[66] As Stewart Patrick points out, not all weak states are the same. Even though in some general ways the roots of weakness may be similar, the response to and capabilities of states in that condition vary widely. Patrick defines four categories of weak states: (1) those that have the will and the way, (2) those that have limited means but are willing to change, (3) those that have the means but not the commitment, and (4) those with neither the will nor the way.[67] These different categories indicate important considerations for entities seeking partnerships. Only the first two cases provide the opportunity for change; working with states in the latter two categories might result in little more than endless frustration and a waste of resources.

To consider some existing examples: Liberia is likely a second category state that has few institutional resources of its own but at least a solid commitment to building more effective political and social interactions. In that context, AFRICOM's initiative of mentoring the Liberian military makes sense and could yield benefits for both parties, particularly when paired with political and economic programs. AFRICOM's previous program to train the Armed Forces of the Democratic Republic of the Congo (DRC) made much less sense, since the problems within the armed forces are part of an endemic culture of impunity that is supported at all levels of government and rests on collusion between the army, political elites, and illegal actors.[68] The DRC is a third (possibly fourth) category state that is theoretically in the midst of a democratic transition but is bedeviled by the deeply entwined problems of both predatory elites and abundant resources. Given these challenges, training of the armed forces is somewhat like the little boy who stuck his finger in the dike: it does not alter the overall institutional weakness or incentives for corrupt and predatory behavior. AFRICOM's current focus on multi-state activities and exercises may be helpful in avoiding bad partnerships but probably also limits the impact of the positive modeling.

The problem, of course, is that the decisions regarding with whom AFRICOM works are political. In some cases, AFRICOM's commander may be able to make contacts that lead to a successful partnership with a military that is interested in learning and ready to make the commitment to do so. Norm diffusion can take place through security institutions teaching alternative behaviors, and is most successful when the "students" clearly identify as such and invest in the learning process.[69] Carefully choosing which countries to work with can thus extend the role of the military to include norm modeling that can encourage social and political shifts. But there are many times when the command is simply told to partner with another military, for reasons that have little to do with real compatibility and everything to do with US agendas, UN agendas, the personal interests of policymakers, and even perhaps media coverage of world events. Even so, if US policymakers want to benefit from AFRICOM, they need to develop a more effective means of selecting promising partners. Linking DoS and USAID programs to AFRICOM initiatives may be particularly helpful in this regard, as it would help clarify what states would benefit most from partnerships.

Being selective means that there will be areas where AFRICOM simply chooses not to work, and those areas could be relevant to US counter-terrorism interests. Such cases can be dealt with by other, more standard military means, but should be beyond the purview of AFRICOM for several reasons. First, nothing beneficial is likely to come of intervention in those areas. Limited initiatives in hostile environments will not lead to the outcomes sought by the United States. Second, by avoiding such areas and focusing instead on countries where engagement, broadly conceived, could have an impact, AFRICOM can reinforce its value to development efforts, support political and economic initiatives, and pull in other US government agencies. Such a positive role could enhance AFRICOM's legitimacy in places where it does operate and demonstrate that its objectives are not solely tied to US strategic needs.

Third, a clear selection process could introduce conditionality into US policy. International and nongovernmental organizations increasingly follow such a standard procedure whereby assistance is based on local actors' willingness to work for common goals. Conditionality also introduces linkage between different categories of action, such as social and political, and identifies clear roles for other US agencies. Finally, it creates a means of rewarding willing actors and maximizes the potential for success. By choosing to work with some rather than others, the US government can acquire leverage in its Africa policy and get involved in environments where change is more likely. Right now the command works relatively indiscriminately across the continent, but that may not be the most effective approach.

In addition to choosing its partners more carefully, AFRICOM can achieve its development potential by ensuring that it acts based on concerns expressed by African leaders. This concept was not mentioned in the 2014 Posture Statement, but it should be the command's top priority. The African Union (AU) has expressed a variety of initiatives and needs, notably in a 2010 report by the AU Panel of the Wise. That report focused on elections and election-related violence as two essential issues for African states and stated a need for assistance with election monitoring and observation, and assistance in increasing the AU's military capacity, notably its standby force.[70] Both activities seem tailor-made for AFRICOM, with the second in particular falling under its stated theater objective to help African states and organizations develop capacity to execute peace operations.[71] Both also relate very specifically to efforts to catalyze and consolidate democratic government and accountability in African states. AFRICOM's current initiative to support the AU mission in Somalia illustrates how it can work in partnership with and build the capacity of local actors, and such programs should be expanded to other areas. Its training program with ECOWAS represents a positive step but will only prove useful if AFRICOM is open and responsive to the preferences and needs of that organization as well as the US government.

In addition to helping with elections and building military capacity, AFRICOM should be fostering a dialogue regarding civil-military relations. At present, most of AFRICOM's initiatives concerning military activities take place at the military-to-military level. Whether AFRICOM personnel have been conducting training exercises or breakfasting with the Djibouti Air Force, the focus has been on military exchanges. An essential problem in many African countries, however, is the power of the military vis-à-vis civilian actors and the lack of trust between the military and society.[72] By fostering dialogue at the civilian level, AFRICOM could focus on norm diffusion, notably standards of accountability and restraint, and give civil society the tools to begin to redefine the relationship between the military and the populace. Conversations at the military level will be ineffective in many contexts unless there is an extremely responsive commanding officer. But pitching the conversation at the civilian level introduces expectations in society and gives civil society the means by which to push for change. That dialogue serves not only the direct goal of improving the military-civilian relationship, but also builds the foundations for more effective civilian participation and demands for desperately needed accountability.

Engaging in civil-military dialogues would also serve as a way for AFRICOM to integrate more thoroughly with its civilian counterparts across the US government and other parts of the DoD that do explicitly work to foster conversations about civil-military relations. AFRICOM has undertaken this type of initiative in northern Nigeria, where it worked in 2012 to enhance interaction between military personnel and civilians, complementing DoS programs in the area. This project was a small but very welcome example of both the type of constructive engagement AFRICOM can make vis-à-vis military affairs, and the ways in which it can help drive the whole of government approach. Creating the means by which military personnel and civilians can interact may help break down the fear factor and build a sense of agency among the citizens. The exclusive 2014 focus on military-to-military connections represents a missed opportunity. Military-civilian interaction introduces an important element of accountability by suggesting that the ruling regime is not the military's only constituency. If the DoS efforts can build on those trends in civilian development programs, they could significantly transform the relationship between military and civilian (nongovernmental) groups.

Conclusions

One common worry about development is that it will become securitized, and that can certainly be seen in numerous contexts. But AFRICOM has the potential to show that security can be developmentalized. As noted above, the problems faced in weak states are not only political, but social and economic as well. Security problems often derive from economic and political weakness. Recognition of that could give AFRICOM the chance to affect the ways in which African citizens interact with themselves and their governments, notably through initiatives to give a society access to its military or efforts to inculcate norms of accountability and transparency.

Three rules of thumb should guide AFRICOM's future operations: (1) make African nations true partners, (2) choose those partners carefully, and (3) link its efforts to broader US political initiatives. Unfortunately it seems to have retreated on all three measures. AFRICOM seems to have moved away from the concept of interagency coordination, partnership, and local development and defined its mission more squarely in the context of unilateral US security. It does not sound like it wants to be the kind of different command that shaped its creation, though it could become one if it seeks on its own and within the wider US policy establishment to develop a coherent approach to its mission. As peacebuilding examples have shown, shutting out local voices and dismissing their preferences are not successful strategies, nor are narrowly focused approaches that do not integrate and coordinate the efforts of different agencies.[73]

AFRICOM has tinkered around the edges thus far, but it needs to develop a vision of action that links its military capabilities to a larger process of norm diffusion. Training partner militaries, for example, is valuable when conceived as part of the means to a larger end, but less valuable when conceived as an end in itself. Without pushing to create a broad approach, whatever successes it may have will be short lived. Conceiving of projects more broadly would allow AFRICOM to move closer toward a model of developmentalized security and create a new standard for security involvement.

Notes

[1] United Nations, Millennium Development Goals Report 2014.

[2] Hewitt, et. al, *Peace and Conflict 2012*; Center on International Cooperation, *Annual Review of Global Peace Operations 2013*; Chabal and Daloz, *Africa Works*; and Salih, "A Critique of the Political Economy of the Liberal Peace."

[3] As cited in its 2010 Fact Sheet, www.africom.mil (2010 fact sheet no longer available).

[4] See, for example, Lerner, *The Passing of Traditional Society*; Huntington, *Political Order in Changing Societies*; and Przeworski and Limongi, "Modernization: Theories and Facts."

[5] Eisenstadt, *Modernization: Protest and Change*, 1.

[6] Autussere, *Peaceland*; Newman et al., eds., *New Perspectives*; Richmond, ed., *Palgrave Advances in Peacebuilding*.

[7] Huntington, *Political Order in Changing Societies*.

[8] Paris, *At War's End*.

[9] See O'Donnell and Schmitter, *Transitions from Authoritarian Rule*; Linz and Stepan, *The Breakdown of Democratic Regimes*.

[10] Hirschman, *The Strategy of Economic Development*.

[11] United Nations Development Program (UNDP), *Human Development Report*; Boutros-Ghali, Supplement to *An Agenda for Peace*.

[12] Hettne, "Development and Security: Origins and Future."

[13] Department of the Army, *Stability Operations*.

[14] Boutros-Ghali, *An Agenda for Peace*.

[15] Fletcher, "Bush Has Quietly Tripled Aid to Africa;" van de Walle, "U.S. Policy Towards Africa;" and Morrison and Cooke, *U.S. Africa Policy Beyond the Bush Years*.

[16] Wood, "Africa Command Will Consolidate U.S. Efforts on Continent." See also Moeller, "The Truth about AFRICOM."

[17] Ploch, *Africa Command: U.S. Strategic Interests*.

[18] United States Senate, "Exploring the U.S. Africa Command;" Schaefer, "Creating an Africa Command."

[19] LeVan, "The Political Economy of African Responses."

[20] LeVan, "Political Economy of African Responses;" AFRICOM, "Fact Sheet."

[21] Nhamoyebonde, "AFRICOM—Latest U.S. Bid to Recolonize Continent;" Keenan, "U.S. Militarization in Africa."

[22] Ploch, *Africa Command: U.S. Strategic Interests*; Pham, "AFRICOM Stands Up."

[23] LeVan, "The Political Economy of African Responses," 16.

[24] Tuckey, "Congress Challenges AFRICOM."

[25] Keenan, "U.S. Militarization;" Berschinski, AFRICOM's Dilemma;" Issa and Faraji, "Revisiting and Reconsidering AFRICOM;" Shabazz, "Africa Continues to Reject U.S. Military Command;" Associated Press, "Africans Wary of AFRICOM, U.S. Motives."

[26] Issa and Faraji, "Revisiting and Reconsidering AFRICOM."

[27] Associated Press, "Africans Wary AFRICOM, U.S. Motives."

[28] Chandler, "The Security-Development Nexus."

[29] Ibid, 365.

[30] van de Walle, "U.S. Policy Towards Africa."

[31] Allgov, "U.S. Foreign Policy in Africa."

[32] U.S. Energy Information Administration, *Petroleum and Other Liquids*.

[33] Phillips, "U.S. Oil Imports from Africa Are Down 90 Percent."

[34] United States Africa Command, "Fact Sheet: The New Strategy toward Sub-Saharan Africa."

[35] Rodriguez, "Posture Statement of U.S. Africa Command."

[36] Rodriguez, "Posture Statement of U.S. Africa Command," 2.

[37] LeVan, "Political Economy of African Responses," 7.

[38] Congressional Budget Justification, assorted fiscal years.

[39] International Peace Academy (IPA), *The Security-Development Nexus.*

[40] Hewitt, et. al., *Peace and Conflict.*

[41] Autussere, *Peaceland*; Newman et al., eds., *New Perspectives*; Pickering and Kisangani, "Political, Economic, and Social Consequences of Foreign Military Intervention;" Paris and Sisk, eds., *The Dilemmas of Statebuilding.*

[42] Hewitt et al., *Peace and Conflict*; Patrick, "Failed States and Global Security."

[43] Rotberg, *When States Fail*; Fukuyama, *Statebuilding*; The White House, *National Security Strategy 2006*; Bush, "2004 State of the Union Address;" Bush, "2005 State of the Union Address 2005."

[44] Rice, Remarks at Georgetown School of Foreign Service.

[45] The White House, *National Security Strategy 2010.*

[46] Autussere, *Peaceland*; de Mesquita and Downs, "Intervention and Democracy;" Mansfield and Snyder, *Electing to Fight*; Pickering and Kisangani, "Political, Economic, and Social Consequences."

[47] Paris, *At War's End*; Chesterman, *You, the People*; Fearon and Laitin, "Neurotrusteeship and the Problem of Weak States."

[48] See Richmond, ed., *Palgrave Advances in Peacebuilding*; Newman et al., eds., *New Perspectives.*

[49] M Salih, "A Critique of the Political Economy of the Liberal Peace."

[50] See Autussere, *Peaceland*; Richmond, ed., *Palgrave Advance in Peacebuilding*; Newman, et al., eds., *New Perspectives*; Paris and Sisk, *Dilemmas of Statebuilding*; Englebert, and Tull, "Postconflict Reconstruction in Africa."

[51] Autessere, *The Trouble with the Congo.*

[52] See Newman et al., eds., *New Perspectives on Peacebuilding*; Richmond, ed., *Palgrave Advances in Peacebuilding.*

[53] Duffield, "The Liberal Way of Development."

[54] See Reno, *Warlord Politics and African States*; Herbst, "Economic Incentives, Natural Resources, and Conflict in Africa"; and Collier et al., *Breaking the Conflict Trap.*

[55] Ward, "AFRICOM Posture Statement" (2008).

[56] Ward, "Posture Statement of U.S. Africa Command," (2010).

[57] Ham, "Posture Statement of U.S. Africa Command."

[58] Rodriguez, "Statement of General David M. Rodriguez," 2.

[59] Gheciu, "Security Institutions as Agents of Socialization?"

[60] Berschinski, *AFRICOM's Dilemma.*

[61] See www.africom.mil/Newsroom (accessed July 8, 2014).

[62] Ndlovu-Gatsheni and Ojakorotu, "Surveillance Over a Zone of Conflict."

[63] See Chabal and Daloz, "Africa Works"; Salih,"A Critique of the Liberal Policy"; and Reno, *Warlord Politics.*

[64] Berschinski, *AFRICOM's Dilemma*, iv.

[65] Stevenson, "AFRICOM's Libya Expedition."

[66] Rodriguez, "Posture Statement 2014."

[67] Patrick, "Failed States and Global Security."

[68] International Crisis Group (ICG), "Congo: A Stalled Democratic Agenda."

[69] Gheciu, "Security Institutions as Agents of Socialization?"

[70] African Union Panel of the Wise, *Election-Related Disputes and Political Violence.*

[71] Ham, "Posture Statement of U.S. Africa Command," 10; Rodriguez, "Posture Statement 2014."

[72] Houngnikpo, *Africa's Militaries.*

[73] See Newman et al., eds., *Liberal Perspectives.*

3
Evolving Civilian and Military Missions

Jessica Piombo

The previous chapter discussed the debates sparked by the securitization of development, the "developmentalization of security," and the increasingly prominent role assigned to Africa in US national security considerations. The debates are not new, however; AFRICOM's creation merely gave them added importance and a concrete focus. AFRICOM's creation marked one end-point in an evolution of US military doctrine and programs in the security and stabilization field. The fierce debates over AFRICOM, along with attempts by the civilian governmental and nongovernmental (NGO) communities to keep up with the changing role of the military in statebuilding and development, laid bare critical tensions in the policy community that have influenced the content and design of security programs.

Various communities approach the component tasks embedded in the security-development nexus differently. They have divergent under-standings of both the definitions and the activities involved in working on "development," "humanitarian assistance," and "stability operations," and correspondingly different approaches to each of these. Understanding these different perceptions of basic concepts frames the ongoing debate about the appropriate roles and responsibilities of the US military in Africa, and more broadly in any developmentalized security arena. In the first section of this chapter, I analyze these postures and review the types of programs and authorities that the US military utilizes to conduct nontraditional security initiatives. In the second half of the chapter, I situate these military programs within broader evolution of how the United States conducts statebuilding and postconflict recovery.

I argue that, contrary to popular arguments, the military does have longstanding experience in "nation building" and similar activities; what is new is the scale of the military's involvement in these statebuilding initiatives.[1] In recent years, particularly since the wars in Iraq and Afghanistan, civilian actors have struggled to keep up with their military counterparts in terms of resources and operating posture; as a result, military actors have undertaken some development tasks. While recent changes in the civilian agencies involved in stabilization and reconstruction have the potential to shift the imbalance between military and civilian agencies in these endeavors, it remains to be seen how these new initiatives will survive the circumscribed budget climate that has curtailed government spending since 2011.

Development, Postconflict Stabilization, and Humanitarian Assistance: Contrasting Definitions

As Andrea Talentino discussed in the prevous chapter, when the US military expanded its activities in conflict response, postconflict recovery, and statebuilding, it began to operate more directly in fields of activity traditionally considered the purview of development and diplomatic agencies. These organizations use similar terms, but they often refer to vastly different activities, which can lead to both conceptual and operational confusion. The organizations hold divergent understandings of both what development, humanitarian assistance, and relief operations mean, and what it takes to work in each of these arenas.[2]

Development versus Humanitarian Assistance

For the DoS, USAID, and most NGOs, development and humanitarian assistance are distinct enterprises. Development involves long-term engagement to produce economic, social, and even political changes within a country.[3] By contrast, humanitarian assistance is a response to a precipitating event, such as a natural disaster, drought, or political upheaval, often short-term in duration. Development programs are often tied into larger national political agendas, while humanitarian assistance programs are meant to be impartial and without overarching politicization.[4]

The distinction between politicized development and non-politicized humanitarian assistance has been drawn since the 1970s when reactions to the crisis in Nigeria over the Biafran war led to the foundation of Doctors Without Borders (Médecins Sans Frontières, MSF). When Bernard

Kouchner established MSF, he embedded within it two central principles that led the way to create a new form of "rights-based" humanitarianism: freedom of criticism or denunciation and the right of intervention for purposes of humanitarian assistance (the "without borders" component of MSF).[5]

According to these principles, assistance should be given to any person in need, regardless of the larger circumstances or situations that have caused the problem, and whether or not parties in the conflict consider that issues of sovereignty should protect them from humanitarian intervention.[6] Emergency humanitarian assistance should never be politicized or denied to those in need because of their political affiliations, and such aid should never be part of a larger political or military strategy. All humans have a right to assistance without being judged for why they might require it. Moreover, humanitarian assistance must be impartial in order for organizations to be granted entry into difficult situations; theoretically, this impartiality would protect NGO workers. The most traditional humanitarian assistance organizations that work on these principles focus primarily on a human rights solution to meeting immediate need. Many of them also resist being incorporated into, or affiliated with, any military operations, even those run by the United Nations.

Development organizations, in contrast, may be part of a larger political program, and they are often aligned with, or directly supported by, national governments. Assistance programs may be targeted towards countries that are strategically important, rather than those more "objectively" in need of development assistance. Not all development assistance is politicized, but it is more acceptably used for political ends than humanitarian assistance. Development NGOs and government agencies also take a longer-term perspective to their work than do humanitarian or disaster response NGOs. Development agencies are often not prepared to see displacement (refugees/internally displaced persons/returnees seeking relief) as a development challenge, nor are they usually equipped to work and respond to immediate crises.[7]

The distinction is important, because the decision whether or not to provide aid and/or assistance is often tied to high-level international politics. The humanitarian NGOs decry this politicization of aid, and their responses to AFRICOM and the securitization debate find root in a long history of opposition to manipulation of aid and assistance. In the 1970s and 1980s, for example, the Carter and Reagan administrations faced the moral and political dilemma of how to assist people in Ethiopia, who were in desperate need, without strengthening the hostile Ethiopian government in the process. Carter administration officials favored assistance for emergency purposes only, and they specifically opposed giving development aid to a regime that they accused of grave human rights abuses.[8] The Reagan administration, in contrast, provided development assistance to governments that were cooperative in the fight against communism regardless of their human rights records. Similar issues cropped up during the ongoing Global War on Terror following the September 2011 attacks when once again, the US government provided assistance to Ethiopia in the face of criticism about the Ethiopian government's oppressive tactics.

Finally, aside from the distinction between development and humanitarian (i.e., emergency) response, some analysts further divide types of humanitarian assistance. These analysts argue that postconflict and postdisaster situations call for very different types of responses, capabilities, and programs.[9] The logic is the same as that used by the NGO community and others who draw a sharp distinction between humanitarian assistance and disaster relief, on the one hand, and development, on the other.

Stabilization, Reconstruction, and "Humanitarian and Civic Assistance"

The military uses a different lexicon for this range of activities, and the differences go beyond mere semantics. The terms "stabilization" and "reconstruction" as commonly used by US government agencies and programs blur the boundaries between development and humanitarian assistance. They also blend the emergency postconflict or postdisaster response (i.e., stabilization) with longer-term economic recovery and development components (which fall under reconstruction).

The conflation is not universal across US government agencies, but within the government these concepts are tied more closely together than in the nongovernmental world. The conflation of concepts also manifests in how the tasks of stabilization and reconstruction are grouped and ordered. The Center for Strategic and International Studies (CSIS) and the Association for the US Army produced one of the early and foundational works on stabilization and reconstruction, outlining four pillars of reconstruction: security, justice and reconciliation, social and economic well-being, and governance and participation.[10]

This framework blends emergency response, long-term development, and political assistance into an integrated approach. When State Department officials set up the Office of the Coordinator for Reconstruction and Stabilization (S/CRS) in 2004, they adopted a modified version of the CSIS framework, restoring the distinction between humanitarian assistance and longer-term economic programs. S/CRS (now, the Bureau for Conflict and Stabilization Operations, CSO) worked under a framework that divided stabilization and reconstruction activities into five areas: security, governance and participation, humanitarian assistance and social well-being, economic stabilization and infrastructure, and justice and reconciliation.[11]

Stabilization and reconstruction operations further divide into chronological phases: initial response, transformation, and sustainability. These phases are akin to the conceptual distinction between emergency response (humanitarian assistance) and developmental programs, adding a component that considers which types of actors are best suited to responding in each phase. During the initial (emergency) response, international military involvement plays a critical role in protecting life and property because this is when assets and people must be quickly brought to the area that requires assistance. The initial response often focuses on providing security to the area and to the individuals assisting those affected by the natural disaster or conflict; these responses constitute traditional humanitarian assistance.

During the transformation phase, projects must develop local legitimacy and foster sustainable indigenous capacity, and thus the focus shifts from security to economy, governance, and justice – projects in the realm of traditional development programs. This is when military and civilian organizations often work in close contact with one another. Long-term recovery efforts constitute the sustainability phase and ideally witness the withdrawal of most of the international military effort as military assets are replaced with civilian agencies trained in economic development, governance assistance, and the provision of social welfare.

Despite these well-articulated frameworks adopted by the Department of State, the Department of Defense groups all of its engagements, whether disaster response, refugee assistance, or well-drilling, under the rubric of "humanitarian assistance." Humanitarian assistance falls within the larger ambit of stability operations, which also include any operation that aims to stabilize a country politically, militarily, and/or economically. Stability operations have also been called "military operations other than war," or non-kinetic operations. Stability operations are the activities that take place after a military victory or before a military action as "shaping operations" —activities intended to avoid conflict altogether, reduce the threat in an environment, or prepare a battleground before conflict.[12] Thus, when the military trains for stability operations, it can be training for disaster relief, traditionally defined humanitarian assistance, and development activities all at once—plus a few kinetic components as well. From an NGO and aid-worker standpoint, this mixing of different types of assistance and activities is highly problematic.

When explicitly addressing "security, stabilization, transition, and reconstruction" (SSTR) operations (what others call stabilization and reconstruction), the Department of Defense collapses the subject areas into just three issue areas: security, economy, and governance.[13] The economy issue area incorporates both humanitarian assistance/disaster relief and development programs into the same category. To the US military, humanitarian assistance refers to a set of five distinct programs, which are incorporated within the realm of "security assistance." Only one of these is the same type of humanitarian assistance as the phrase is understood by the nongovernmental community: disaster response ("humanitarian assistance and disaster response," HADR). The US military runs programs under the humanitarian assistance rubric that include: (1) Humanitarian Demining Assistance; (2) Humanitarian Assistance–Excess Property Program (HA EP); (3) Humanitarian and Civic Assistance (HCA); (4) Humanitarian Assistance Other (HAO); and (5) Overseas Humanitarian Disaster and Civic Assistance (OHDACA), which includes the HADR programs.[14]

Of these, OHDACA projects are the most prolific. They are funded directly through regional combatant commanders to enable them to respond to disasters and promote postconflict reconstruction through "unobtrusive, low-cost, but highly efficacious" projects.[15] Within its first year, AFRICOM developed an internal document that described these programs, their statutory authorities and funding cycles, and instructed how each should be utilized within the command's area of responsibility.[16] There are also two US government/DoD programs designed specifically for natural disaster response: the Foreign Humanitarian Disaster Response Program and the Commander's Emergency Response Program (CERP).

Government and economic reconstruction efforts are funded separately; they fall within the 1206, 1207, and 1210 programs that fund the provincial reconstruction teams in Afghanistan and Iraq and support the training of foreign militaries worldwide.[17] Each of these programs has distinct goals, requirements, and funding streams. Section 1206 covers "train and equip" programs, established under the National Defense Authorization Act (NDAA) to provide the Secretary of Defense with authority to train and equip foreign military forces for two specified purposes: (1) counter-terrorism and stability operations, and (2) counterterrorism operations carried out by foreign maritime security forces. Section 1207 funds were a two-year program designed to help establish the S/CRS within the State Department and to promote a "whole of government" approach to security sector assistance.[18]

Also called the Integrated Security Assistance Program, Section 1207 authorized the Defense Department to provide up to $200 million directly to the State Department. When the 1207 program was re-authorized (through fiscal year 2010) in the 2008 NDAA, the funds were authorized in section 1210, and thereafter the program was associated with both 1207 and 1210 funds. In contrast to 1206 funds, which have been administered solely by combatant commanders, 1207 funds were interagency: DoD monies allocated and spent by the State Department, with USAID representatives on the technical advisory board.[19]

Together, these various programs have authorized and financed projects that the DoD has undertaken in countries worldwide to help counter instability by training and equipping foreign militaries, providing support to vulnerable communities in an attempt to reduce or eliminate conditions that lead individuals into radicalization (i.e., counter-terrorism programs that attempt to address communities and individuals considered to be at risk), responding to natural and man-made disasters, enhancing maritime security capabilities, combating illicit trafficking, and addressing a range of other issues.

In conducting these programs, the DoD has significantly blurred the lines between (economic) development, humanitarian assistance, and statebuilding activities. The approaches have been developmental—building human and institutional capacity, constructing infrastructure—as well as emergency-response oriented. Some activities fall within the traditional realm of security assistance as practiced by the DoD for decades, and others took the DoD far beyond its usual roles. All of the programs have incited a heated debate and close analysis of program design and execution, as well as attention to whether the programs reproduce those already provided by other assistance agencies.

Military Involvement in Stability and Humanitarian Operations

Though these endeavors have never been a central focus of military doctrine, strategy or priorities, the military has conducted "nation building" activities for over a century.[20] The US military first undertook fully-fledged nation building in Japan, Germany and Europe after World War II, but there are many other examples of the US military supporting development and statebuilding activities.[21] These infrastructural and governance tasks are similar to today's stabilization and reconstruction duties. Likewise, classic counterinsurgency tactics include efforts to shape the political environment, which can encompass anything from either shoring up or eroding support for a domestic government to building goodwill towards the United States and its allies. In these counterinsurgency efforts, US military forces promoted judicial reform, improved public health and education, and increased honest governance. They have employed these strategies in places as diverse as Cuba, the Philippines, Korea, Vietnam, and various countries in Central America.[22]

The US Army first established explicit civil operations units during the Vietnam era, but they were subsequently de-emphasized and dismantled in the post-Vietnam backlash against nation building. Since 2001, there has been renewed interest in increasing the civil affairs capacity in the US Army, which in the mid-2000s developed an active duty component. Prior to this, all civil affairs personnel had been reservists. Even the US Navy has developed civil operations units, beginning with the creation of "maritime civil affairs" groups in 2007.

As the national and international security risks posed by failed, failing, and weak states began to manifest in the late 1990s and early 2000s, US national security policy increasingly prioritized support to threatened states. Addressing new national priorities and responding to the exigencies of US engagements in Afghanistan and Iraq, the US government, in particular the Defense Department, has steadily attempted to revitalize SSTR activities in doctrine, training, force structure, and interagency processes. Most of the ensuing doctrine, directives, and studies focused on postconflict situations or complex emergencies, during which reconstruction involves statebuilding and economic recovery. The military role became firmly entrenched well beyond just providing humanitarian assistance and disaster response.[23]

In December 2003, the Defense Department began to consider creating a military force dedicated to stability and reconstruction operations. Navy Vice Admiral Arthur Cebrowski, at the time the chief of DoD's Office of Force Transformation, declared that the September 11, 2001, terrorist attacks on the Pentagon and the World Trade Center forced planners to consider conducting stability operations in places where the US military had not previously engaged in military activities. The stability force that Cebrowski envisaged would include some of the military's best people and equipment and would require combined arms combat capabilities, as well as military police, civil affairs, military intelligence, psychological affairs, engineers, and explosive ordnance teams. It also would be a joint force and draw on the entire "interagency," i.e., nonmilitary components of the US government.[24] At the time, however, little was done to turn Cebrowski's vision into a reality.

The Defense Science Board's *2004 Summer Study* called for the creation of stabilization and reconstruction capabilities in the US military. The *Summer Study* noted that the United States was engaging in stabilization and reconstruction operations more frequently than in the past: board members noted that since 1989, the US military had begun new stabilization and reconstruction operations every 18 to 24 months. The study recommended that the US military increase its capabilities in four principal areas, two of which related to stabilization and reconstruction: (1) stabilization and reconstruction capabilities; (2) strategic communication;

(3) knowledge, understanding, and intelligence relating to stabilization and reconstruction; and (4) identification, location, and tracking for asymmetric warfare.[25]

The study suggested that stabilization and reconstruction operations tended to last longer than major combat operations. Such operations typically stretched anywhere between five and eight years, and required a skill set different from that required in a combat operation with a kinetic focus. In the board members' view, the US military needed to begin to train explicitly for SSTR operations. The *Summer Study* noted that SSTR operations were necessary because of the changing nature of warfare and implied that stabilizing societies in the wake of war was the key to eliminating the conditions that foster terrorism around the world. This logic also implied that the US military should become more involved in natural disaster relief, both to stabilize vulnerable societies and to win hearts and minds in the global struggle against Islamic terrorism.

Why did these directives call for new roles and capabilities for the US military? The Defense Science Board's *Summer Study* envisioned a transition from military to civilian activities in stabilization and reconstruction operations, with the military footprint being heaviest in the initial phases and then gradually giving way to a more civilian-focused effort. In the board's estimation, the military has unparalleled management and planning capabilities that the civilian sector cannot reproduce:

> While the military has deep experience in operational planning and execution, other parts of the U.S. government seldom demonstrate comparable management discipline, and plans are often poorly prepared. Their ability to prepare and validate plans is not comparable to that of the U.S. military. Even when seemingly sound plans are prepared, the failure to test and challenge them makes success problematic.[26]

While the *Summer Study* authors argued that the military would be more appropriate as the lead in short-term postconflict stabilization efforts, it was not the best agent to lead long-term development and rebuilding, the reconstruction phase.[27] The *Summer Study* therefore proposed that the State Department should take over operations once it was able to mobilize personnel and funding. During long-term reconstruction activities, the Defense Department should function as a supporting actor. Since each organization has a distinct set of skills and operating timeframes, each is suited to handle specific tasks at particular points in the conflict and postconflict cycle.

Recognizing this assessment of capabilities, and on the direction of then-President George W. Bush, in late 2004, the State Department set up the Office of the Coordinator for Reconstruction and Stabilization (S/CRS). S/CRS was meant to coordinate, lead, and integrate interagency efforts to prepare and conduct stabilization and reconstruction activities across the whole of government. In essence, it was designed to reproduce what the National Security Council should have been coordinating, as emphasized in 2005 in National Security Presidential Directive 44 (NSPD-44). NSPD-44 stipulated that all other government agencies involved in these stabilization and reconstruction activities were to report to S/CRS, including those agencies operating within the DoD establishment.[28]

On the DoD side, the first major policy directive to implement the recommendations of the 2004 *Summer Study* was the US Defense Department's Directive 3000.05 of November 2005.[29] In issuing this directive, the DoD was motivated by the emerging realities of engagement on the ground in Afghanistan and Iraq, where occupation had pushed the United States back into nation-building projects of the kind that had been avoided since the Vietnam era. The United States established the first provincial reconstruction teams (PRTs) in Afghanistan by early 2003, and while ambitious and diverse in their goals and accomplishments, most of the teams were affected by challenges related to interagency coordination and cooperation.[30] DoD Directive 3000.05, therefore, not only attempted to place stability operations on the same footing as major combat operations, it also assigned the Department of State as the lead in SSTR operations, and gave the DoD a supporting role.

Pursuant to the Directive, stability operations were now defined as military and civilian activities conducted during times of peace and conflict to establish or maintain order in states and regions. SSTR activities included Defense Department activities that support US government plans for stabilization, security, reconstruction, and transition operations and lead to sustainable peace while advancing US interests. In defining the term "SSTR," DoD Directive 3000.05 expanded the scope of stabilization and reconstruction to include a wider gamut of activities, further blurring the lines between development, humanitarian assistance, security, and state-building. Because of this, DoD 3000.05 spurred the intense debates about roles and responsibilities, which in part motivated this volume.

DoD Directive 3000.05 serves as a landmark in how the US government regarded stabilization and reconstruction activities. The directive increased the priority of these activities, while also identifying specific duties and benchmarks to be met by each of the Under Secretaries of Defense, combatant commanders, and other officials.[31] Interagency coordination problems continued to confront the PRTs, then operating in

Iraq as well as Afghanistan, and the directive was an to attempt to address these problems and enforce a "whole of government" approach to stabilization and reconstruction.

In 2006, both the US *National Security Strategy* and the *Quadrennial Defense Review* (*QDR*) emphasized the non-kinetic, stabilization, and reconstruction operations that the US military was conducting. The *National Security Strategy* once again highlighted the problems caused by failed and failing states and directed the US government to anticipate and respond to state failure where appropriate This response could include initiatives designed to strengthen democracy, improve the rule of law, support market economies, and enhance the legitimacy of governments. The *QDR* also emphasized the importance of humanitarian concerns in the war on terror. Based on US experience in Iraq, Afghanistan, the Indian Ocean tsunami, and the South Asian earthquake, it argued that forces needed to prepare to undertake irregular warfare and humanitarian operations.[32]

Within the Department of Defense, the SSTR rhetoric was beginning to find expression in practice. In May 2006, the Chairman of the Joint Chiefs of Staff issued a notice (3245.01), which appointed the Joint Staff as the office with primary responsibility for "matters pertaining to stability operations, security assistance, technology transfer, and the Office of the Coordinator for Reconstruction and Stabilization (S/CRS)."[33] The notice designated a specific office to oversee progress on these matters and created the Department of Defense Stability Operations Executive Council and Stability Operations Working Group. Both groups were to be composed of all the Defense Department components assigned responsibilities pertaining to SSTR operations.

A new Army field manual (FM 3-24, 2006) further endorsed the importance of interagency coordination within postconflict stability operations in order to effectively pursue counterinsurgency objectives.[34] This was followed in 2008 by the first Army doctrine explicitly on stability operations, the *Stability Operations* Field Manual (FM 3-07).[35] The motivation for this new document, General William S. Wallace explained, was that "we recognize that in a contemporary operational environment in the 21st Century, conventional military operations, offensive and defensive, will be conducted simultaneously with stability operations."[36]

Lieutenant General William B. Caldwell, IV, then the commanding general of the US Army Combined Arms Center, argued that this document was necessary because nation-building efforts would increase in the future, existing independently from combat operations. According to Caldwell, "America's future abroad is unlikely to resemble Afghanistan or Iraq, where we grapple with the burden of nation-building under fire. Instead, we will work through and with the community of nations to defeat insurgency, assist fragile states, and provide vital humanitarian aid to the suffering."[37] The *Stability Operations* Field Manual would serve as the guide for the US Army—and, Wallace argued, hopefully the NGOs with whom the Army works—in these endeavors.

Civilian Efforts to Engage in Stabilization and Reconstruction

At the same time as the US military was organizing to conduct these operations, the civilian side found itself unable to fully participate in the "whole of government" approach because of lack of personnel and staffing procedures. The small Office of Transition Initiatives within USAID has been able to rapidly deploy personnel since the early 1990s, but the Department of State and other offices of USAID had much slower procedures and could not compel their employees to work in difficult areas or those that posed security risks. This proved particularly challenging when State and USAID attempted to send sufficient numbers of personnel to Iraq and Afghanistan in the early to mid-2000s.[38] Without these civilians, the military found itself in the position of conducting tasks in governance and reconstruction for which its personnel were not trained or prepared.[39]

S/CRS had been created specifically to help overcome some of planning the bottlenecks experienced in the more traditional bureaus within the DoS and USAID. Other initiatives, discussed below, attempted to address the personnel problems. S/CRS also attempted to promote greater interagency collaboration within stability and reconstruction operations. The office had a difficult beginning, however, as initially it had no independent budget or hiring authority, and relied primarily on secondments (temporary transfers) from other DoS entities to staff the office.

In its early years, S/CRS focused mainly on conceptual issues and on working with interagency partners to develop processes and organizational structures for whole-of-government stabilization and reconstruction operations. S/CRS, together with US Joint Forces Command, produced a number of frameworks and handbooks that were meant to guide SSTR efforts and provide guidelines for interagency cooperation. These included the "Draft Planning Framework for Reconstruction, Stabilization and Conflict Transformation" (2005); an Interagency Management System to coordinate the management and execution of operations (2007); and an Interagency Conflict Assessment Framework (ICAF, 2008).

S/CRS did little operationally in this timeframe. In fact, the first coordinator, Carlos Pascual, resigned in protest over what he considered the hamstringing of the office due to the lack of the finances or personnel to make its role effective.[40] Former Secretary of State Colin Powell and Richard Armitage commented that in retrospect, they "felt as if they were set up for failure.... at its inception, S/CRS was only given a pittance of $17 million with a 37-person staff, compared to the 80 personnel requested, inviting magnanimous offers from DoD to fork over bodies and funding."[41] In 2008, S/CRS gained more stable footing, when Title XVI of the fiscal year (FY) 2009 National Defense Authorization Act codified S/CRS into law, expanded its functions, and authorized the creation of a deployable civilian force, which came to be called the Civilian Response Corps (CRC).

The civilian agencies, particularly USAID and the Department of State, continue to face challenges in being able to deploy personnel to crisis response situations in a timely fashion. For one, the two agencies are chronically understaffed for the range of responsibilities, so there are few personnel to spare when crisis situations develop. Second, the structures of the agencies for the most part still do not allow for rapid deployment of personnel to emerging crises. This has created and sustained a systematic bias in stabilization and reconstruction activities towards a higher military than civilian presence. Despite all the doctrine and studies, military actors still tend to dominate across the range of postconflict activities, because the civilian agencies do not have the financial or human capacity to match.

The Civilian Response Corps was meant to address the structural constraints that USAID and the Department of State faced in rapidly deploying civilian personnel into conflict and postconflict situations. The initial plan for the CRC was to recruit within USAID a cadre of civilian personnel who would be available to work with the military in SSTR programs like the provincial reconstruction teams in Iraq and Afghanistan. The CRC was formally established in July 2008, and began building a three tiered system of active duty civilian responders and reserve units which could be called up for deployment in the short-, medium- and long-term timeframes.[42]

The vision was short-lived, however: the CRC was never developed to its full initial vision due to budget cuts and partisan disputes in the ensuing years, and has since been officially dissolved. USAID retained some of the initiative, and transformed the office that had been developed to oversee the CRC (the Office of Civilian response) into the "Office of Crisis Surge Support," CS3, in late 2009. This office "rapidly deploys highly qualified technical experts providing critical development skill sets in support of USAID operations worldwide."[43] It represents the spirit of the Civilian Response Corps, but is fully funded from within USAID's budget.

Despite continuing pronouncements of high-level DoD officials (including Secretary of Defense Robert Gates) that the civilian agencies needed to be properly resourced if they were to fulfill their roles in postconflict situations, the DoS and USAID have continued to struggle for both financial and human resources. When the Section 1207 program was established in 2006, the DoD was given legal authorization to help finance State Department efforts to enter into stability operations, which helped, but this was a short-term program and not something that could be counted on in the future.

In late 2008, President Barack Obama finally announced that the DoS and USAID would be given additional funding to hire more personnel. Unfortunately this came at the same time as a budget battle within the US Congress that threatened to de-fund USAID entirely, while also questioning spending on all foreign assistance programs and agencies.[44] While there were repeated setbacks in funding the CRC, the administration was able to support the Bureau of Conflict and Stability Operations (CSO), the successor to S/CRS, "to provide rapid responders to crisis regions, support conflict prevention efforts, and stabilize crises and set the conditions for the transition to long-term peace."[45]

The FY2013 budget also allocated an additional $75 million "to address emergent national security challenges;" directing $50 million to the existing Complex Crisis Fund and $25 million to a new Global Security Contingency Fund, which had been introduced in FY2012 to integrate DoD and DoS resources to address security crises.[46] The CRC itself suffered from lack of funding, lack of executive action to establish its governing structures, and never really moved beyond its embryonic state. Despite rhetoric supporting initiatives like these, however, the Obama administration's record has been disappointing to those who wish to try to balance civilian and military capabilities.

The disappointment in the lack of movement to concretely enhance civilian capabilities was even keener given the emphasis on development as a national security concern during the Obama administration and other policy commitments made during the administration. In the May 2010 *National Security Strategy*, President Obama identified development and the reduction in global inequality and poverty as national security issues for the United States. Obama called for civilian units to be strengthened and to take their rightful place alongside military compatriots. He argued that

> to succeed, we must balance and integrate all elements of American power and update our national security capacity for the 21st century. We must maintain our military's conventional superiority, while enhancing its capacity to defeat asymmetric threats. Our diplomacy and development capabilities must be modernized, and our civilian expeditionary capacity strengthened, to support the full breadth of our priorities.[47]

The May 2010 *National Security Strategy* laid the groundwork for the re-invigoration of the State Department and USAID that then-Secretary of State Hillary Clinton had been planning. In July 2008, Clinton had initiated a process within State Department and USAID that would attempt to mimic the DoD's *Quadrennial Defense Review*. The *Quadrennial Diplomacy and Development Review* (*QDDR*) would attempt to take a similar hard look at the operations of the DoS and USAID—their programs, policies, and priorities—and to rationalize all of this in a document that would critically assess the agencies. In so doing, the hope was that the *QDDR* would make recommendations internal to the organizations and help them to lobby externally across the US government.

The *QDDR* process was difficult, since it had never been attempted before. Led by Anne-Marie Slaughter, at that time the Director of Policy and Planning for the DoS, the *QDDR* participants took over a year to conduct their analysis and release a report. When the report finally launched in December 2010, Clinton proclaimed:

> The QDDR provides a blueprint for elevating American "civilian power" to better advance our national interests and to be a better partner to the U.S. military. Leading through civilian power means directing and coordinating the resources of all America's civilian agencies to prevent and resolve conflicts; help countries lift themselves out of poverty into prosperous, stable, and democratic states; and build global coalitions to address global problems.[48]

The *QDDR* recommended several reorganizations within the State Department and USAID, including folding the Office of the Coordinator for Stabilization and Reconstruction into a new bureau, the Bureau of Conflict and Stability Operations (CSO).[49] The new bureau would be able to command a greater share of the budget and personnel, and hopefully to elevate the State Department's role in the stabilization and reconstruction of countries after conflict.

CSO became functional in November 2011, with the mandate to support the State Department's ability to anticipate major security challenges, drive an integrated response to conflict prevention and stabilization, and leverage partnerships with nongovernmental and international organizations. CSO's mission is to help prevent conflict, address the drivers of conflict, build on existing initiatives, and promote "burden-sharing."[50] CSO assumed control over the Civilian Response Corps and developed a Training and Education Division to support the ability of the CRC, US government civilians, and military personnel to plan and implement stabilization and reconstruction activities.

In terms of division of labor between the State Department and USAID, the *QDDR* recommended that the DoS be designated as the lead agency for political and security crises, while USAID would be given responsibility for leading responses to "humanitarian crises, resulting from large-scale natural or industrial disasters, famines, disease outbreaks and other natural phenomena."[51] This replicated the existing division of labor, as the Office of Foreign Disaster Assistance within USAID had already been the government's lead agency on disaster response and humanitarian issues. This division of authority between agencies has been criticized because it fails to recognize that many disasters, such as famine, are inherently political, which thus circumscribes the realm of activities in which USAID could truly lead.[52]

The *QDDR* drafters aimed to address the perceived gap between development and diplomacy, on the one hand, and defense, on the other. They believed that, if the civilian agencies were provided enough funding and personnel, there would be no cause to engage in the debates that consumed so much of AFRICOM's early days: the military would have civilian counterparts that were able to respond to crises, operate in complex situations, and promote their policies and programs at the same pace and depth that the DoD was able to. Whether the infusion of resources will create this parity of operations remains to be seen, but money is only part of the issue.

Debates Over the Military's Involvement in Statebuilding

One might ask why the critics of this imbalance between military and civilian capabilities and involvement in postconflict reconstruction are so strident. Debates over the US military's involvement in non-kinetic missions were initially driven by the reconstruction efforts in Afghanistan and Iraq, but they reached a peak in the mid-2000s as assessments of the "hearts and minds" programs of the CJTF-HOA began to surface.[53] The creation of AFRICOM brought out the allegations about securitizing development and US foreign policy in Africa. AFRICOM provided new impetus to vehement debates about the appropriate roles of military, government civilians, and nongovernmental actors in supporting security in Africa and elsewhere.[54]

What were the bases of these critiques? First of all, many believed that AFRICOM would bring more "boots on the ground"—an increased US military presence in Africa. Critics also proclaimed that AFRICOM would militarize the substance of US foreign policy in Africa.[55] By this, they meant not only that the budget of the Department of Defense would eclipse development and governance efforts, but also that the very substance and focus of US policy would become fixated on security concerns, much as they had been during the Cold War.[56] The potential militarization of US foreign policy was only one component of the debates that AFRICOM's creation stimulated. Other disputes re-energized concerns over the ability and effects of US military activities that touched on economic development and governance (reconstruction operations) and a separate set raised the alarm about how the military's involvement in humanitarian assistance would compromise humanitarian goals and affect the nongovernmental communities operating in the same space.

In the previous chapter, Andrea Talentino analyzed the highest level of debate: over whether military actors can bring about effective interventions to enhance African security by adopting a perspective that development is a necessary precondition for security. In this chapter, I consider more concrete debates about how these military interventions can or cannot bring about capacity building and sustained development; and how military activities impact the humanitarian space. Together, these two chapters lay down the terrain that many of the case studies in this book explore in one way or another.

Critiques of Reconstruction Operations

The first and most encompassing set of concerns challenged the capabilities of the US military to conduct reconstruction operations.[57] These critics argued that the US military was not trained to engage in developmental work—whether this is the development of human capacity or socio-economic development—and yet many of its projects touched on these realms. Additionally, critics raised concerns over the design and execution of these projects: the military's approach was not designed to create local ownership of projects; the military could not devote personnel to a project on a long-term basis; and the time horizon of military engagements was considered woefully short and therefore unable to produce truly developmental outcomes. Better, critics argued, to put more resources into the agencies whose personnel know how to develop human capacity, state institutions, and economies: the United States Agency for International Development and the Department of State.

Capacity concerns were voiced related to the planning process, implementation, monitoring, and evaluation; and critics questioned how the security motivation of the programs would influence their ability to bring larger-order improvements to the host nations. In the planning arena, questions arose as to how projects were selected and then planned. Given the security objective of the programs, host nation needs and priorities were often not the top priority when planning these projects. Reconstruction and development programs were often conducted in areas of strategic importance, regardless of population density or economic connection to the rest of the country. The process for nominating and accepting projects was based on complex military regulations that required justification of the security impact, not on developmental logic or goals. Needs assessments were secondary to security payoffs (and here, the global war on terror imperative often dominated). This, as the CJTF-HOA experience will show, affects the distribution and type of projects that are pursued.

On the implementation front, questions arose about the criteria for choosing who implements the projects. The two main humanitarian assistance programs (Humanitarian Assistance Other [HAO], and Humanitarian and Civic Assistance [HCA]) are officially intended to train US service people. Delivering humanitarian or developmental assistance is a tool for training, and increasing the skills of US military is the main objective of the programs. Overseas Humanitarian Disaster and Civic Assistance (OHDACA) programs and provincial reconstruction teams tended to utilize either military construction units or contractors, not necessarily of local origin. Local populations contributed little to project implementation in the main humanitarian assistance programs; thus these programs provided few opportunities to transfer skills and build capacity in the local populations.

As a result, the development-oriented humanitarian assistance projects violated one of the fundamental lessons learned from over 50 years of development projects: community participation, ownership, and buy-in, together with local capacity building, are the only ways to make projects sustainable and to have a long-term impact. Because local populations are rarely involved in implementation, the US military typically misses an opportunity to develop ties with them, and should the projects require maintenance, the population may not have gained the necessary skills. Most of the OHDACA and HCA projects utilized the US military in order to train US uniformed personnel, or they brought in local or international contractors. Training of local tradespeople has not been a component of the programs.

Traditionally there has been little to no provision for monitoring and evaluation built into military humanitarian assistance and reconstruction efforts. The projects have not developed a metric to evaluate whether they have actually contributed to the US security goals in the short term, nor have they systematically measured their long-term strategic or developmental impact. A great deal of money has been spent on the CJTF-HOA, provincial reconstruction teams, Africa Partnership Station, and Operation Continuing Promise (in South America), yet little is known about the impact of these projects.

If they were built into the projects, what would be the appropriate criteria to measure their impact? The goals are explicitly not developmental, so evaluations would not use the standard measures of development found in indices like the Human Development Index or the Millennium Development Goals. The strategic goals that the projects were meant to achieve are often extremely vague, which means that the standards against which to measure them have not been established beforehand. Without pre-established goals, there really is no way to test their impact. For example, in 2007 when I asked the leader of a civil affairs team in Kenya how he knew whether or not his projects in the Lamu Bay area had any impact, he responded, "sure … if there's a decrease in terrorism."[58] His response indicates a blunt measurement tool, to say the least.

Finally, regarding motivation, an important set of critiques notes that security concerns dictate projects' locations and thus could limit the projects' broader impacts in terms of economic progress or social services. Military reconstruction projects are selected for reasons that often have only tangential relationships to the host nation's interests. Instead, the United States selects projects to deliver high visibility and "quick impact" results in areas of strategic importance. If the goal is counterterrorism, for example, then projects are selected in geographical areas of a country that the US deems vulnerable to terrorist recruitment or operation, regardless of population density or the need for development assistance. This selection process can create a set of programs that look developmental but have little economic impact and, without careful monitoring, deliver only speculative security benefits. The traditional development goals of high-leverage projects—community participation, ownership, self-sufficiency, and sustainability—do not factor into the motivation for or planning of most of these securitized projects.

Critiques of Humanitarian Operations

A second set of concerns focuses on the US military's involvement in disaster relief or complex emergencies, rather than military involvement in reconstruction/ development-type activities. Here, the criticisms are often articulated by nongovernmental organizations. The NGO community has a diverse set of opinions about the involvement of any military force in HA programs. Some consider the military a valuable operating partner, while others refuse to participate in any project in which a military force is involved, however remotely. Given this range of opinions, the following summary will not represent the position of each and every individual NGO, but is a compilation of the most prominent critiques.

One set of concerns centers on the capacity and experience of military actors in providing humanitarian assistance, and how these constraints could undermine the effectiveness of the operation. In this, the critiques mirror similar apprehensions regarding military involvement in developmental programs. Because the military does not have the training and expertise to effectively carry out humanitarian assistance, and because military actors often lack sufficient knowledge of the local population to effectively deliver aid, military actors do not have policy guidance to help them navigate in such exigencies.[59] They may therefore deliver aid to people who do not need it, or may deliver inappropriate supplies without knowing it. They also can make the situation worse by delivering supplies to local actors who will then use these resources to bolster their own power. NGO actors feel they are locally grounded enough to avoid these problems, while military actors are not.

A second set of critiques is both conceptual and practical: military involvement in humanitarian assistance is highly political, and therefore threatens humanitarian principles such as neutrality. As a consequence, the safety of true humanitarian aid workers has become compromised, while the effectiveness of the assistance is curtailed.[60] Critics charge that the potential blurring of the lines between diplomacy, development, and defense could put NGO workers at risk, particularly if NGO activities are confused or associated with US military activities.[61] Humanitarians believe that they can operate in insecure environments without military protection, because they are protected by their humanitarian principles of neutrality, impartiality, and independence (creating the "humanitarian space").

The function of the humanitarian space is to allow NGO workers to operate without fear for their personal safety, because all sides to a conflict (if it is a conflict situation) respect their mission and the fact that they deliver aid to all who need it. Military humanitarian assistance is fundamentally different, and military involvement can threaten the integrity of the humanitarian space. As a result, the mission itself could become compromised, which then threatens the safety of individuals working in the mission, even if they are not military.[62]

The missions and principles underlying NGO and military interventions differ, the goals of an operation are not the same, and desired outcomes will vary. The essence of the humanitarian mission is to provide help to all who need it, regardless of their culpability in the situation at hand. Humanitarian NGOs, therefore, do not discriminate between combatants and noncombatants when they provide aid.

In contrast, military operations are framed by a political agenda, not by a humanitarian imperative; thus, many NGO workers feel that military involvement in HA compromises the objectives of the mission.[63] The sponsoring government wants to achieve a political objective through the assistance, a position antithetical to that of the impartial humanitarian motivated purely by need. Because military HA places security and stabilization at the core of its mission, many fear that it would be denied to needy populations if they pose a security risk, or if they are considered to be enemy combatants.[64] A corollary to this objection is that military HA would be delivered on a partisan basis, and the military might only intervene in crises when intervention would serve its own national interests.

A final concern is that military forces often fail to consult NGOs in the planning process when designing a humanitarian intervention. Often, the US military has been unaware of, or unappreciative of, the role of HA organizations during relief efforts (and the same is often said of the longer-term development and reconstruction operations as well). This short-sightedness can lead to the military either duplicating NGO efforts or acting in a manner that may be detrimental to the long-term development of the people being helped.[65] The military doctrine on HA is minimal and often insufficient to foster significant collaborative efforts between the military and HA organizations.

This creates coordination problems when interaction with NGOs becomes necessary. The lack of consultation can lead the military to inaccurately assess the root causes (if a conflict situation) or real needs of the population (both during natural disaster and conflict responses). It is for this reason that USAID stations a representative from the Office of Foreign Disaster Assistance (OFDA) within most combatant commands: the OFDA representative is the authority for any disaster response that a command undertakes. In the African arena, before AFRICOM was created, there had been a tendency for the CJTF-HOA and troops stationed in the Sahel region to conduct disaster assistance without USAID oversight. AFRICOM created an NGO office in its outreach branch to help address these issues, an initiative analyzed by Teresa Crawford and Trina Zwicker in chapter eight of this volume.

The bottom line of the critique is that there is an unavoidable blurring of the lines between humanitarian actors and military actors when the military becomes involved in humanitarian assistance, whether responding to natural disasters, conflict situations, or complex emergencies. "Sharing the space" can therefore compromise the operations and safety of the humanitarian NGOs and their workers, and compromise the integrity of HA overall.

Conclusion

Military involvement in stabilization, humanitarian assistance, reconstruction, and statebuilding has a long and contested history. Whether or not the US government will engage in "nation building" once the Iraq and Afghanistan interventions have finally and completely ended is open for debate, but smaller-scale developmental interventions (couched as stabilization activities) are likely to remain common in the future. These interventions are likely to increase as the military becomes more involved in world regions where security cannot be improved without addressing root causes, which are likely to reside outside the realm of state-based, traditional security. Thus, attempts to enhance African security, for Africans and not just the United States, means that international actors like the US military are bound to become involved in an ever increasing range of activities.

Will the US military be able to accomplish its goals of enhancing African security? Will it be able to pursue these objectives in a manner coordinated with other actors, civilian and nongovernmental? Many of these efforts push military actors into roles outside the realm of their military training and into activities outside their traditional focus, which means that in order to be effective, military actors and organizations will need to work with civilians and organizations that do have these competencies.

Yet, as Caroline Earle has argued, there are "no standardized operational structures for civilian interagency participation or civil-military integration in stability operations other than the existing country team platform. This challenges the ability of the government and military to train on civil-military integration during stability operations."[66] Consequently, sustained civil-military coordination necessary to successfully address developmentally driven security problems will remain circumscribed. While there is more latitude and ability to create this cooperation in "steady state" activities as opposed to crisis-response ones, there remains little strategic- and operational-level guidance on how to effectively integrate the diplomatic, development, and defense instruments of the US government into one cohesive effort. Because of this, the fierce debates about whether the DoD has been militarizing US-Africa policy have had the opportunity to grow and take root.

Notes

Note: All opinions expressed in this chapter are my own and do not reflect official positions of either the Naval Postgraduate School or the United States government.

[1] While the US government tends to use the term "nation building" for these types of activities, what they are really referring to are activities to build a government, which are the components of statebuilding. In academic discourse, nation building refers to the creation of a unified national identity. Throughout this chapter, I use the term "statebuilding," as this more accurately captures what these programs attempt to do.

[2] The US military labels all noncombat operations "non-kinetic" activities. These include civil affairs, public outreach efforts, "hearts and minds" campaigns, etc. Combat operations span the range of aggressive, "traditional" military activities.

[3] Lele, "Sustainable Development: A Critical review," 609. See also Sen, *Handbook of Development Economics*.

[4] This is the traditional vision of humanitarian assistance; there is also a more politicized version that includes humanitarian assistance as part of a postconflict toolkit, in the field referred to as "new humanitarism." See Duffield, et al., "Politics and Humanitarian Aid"; this is the introduction to a special issue that focuses on the changing relationship between politics and humanitarian assistance. Modern humanitarian assistance often is not apolitical, though the actors involved in the endeavor attempt to keep it so.

[5] See Chandler, "The Road to Military Humanitarianism."

[6] See Chandler, ibid., 685.

[7] Ferris, "Addressing the Gap Between Relief and Development."

[8] Kissi, "Beneath the International Famine Relief in Ethiopia." For a larger review of these issues, see Chatterjee and Scheid, eds., *Ethics and Foreign Intervention*.

[9] Piombo and Malley, "Beyond Protecting the Land and the Sea."

[10] CSIS, "Post-Conflict Reconstruction: Task Framework." For the website of the Post-Conflict Reconstruction project of CSIS, see www.csis.org/isp/pcr/ (accessed April 11, 2007).

[11] Department of State, "Post Conflict Reconstruction Essential Tasks."

[12] For more on this, see particularly Chairman Joint Chiefs of Staff, *Joint Operational Planning,* Joint Publication (JP) 5-0; the description of the phases of operations falls on pages III-37-38.

[13] DoD Directive 3000.05.

[14] These are the categories created by the Defense Security Cooperation Agency. For more information, including specific guidance, statutory authorities, and directives for each of these programs, see www.dsca.mil/programs.

[15] Griffin, "A Working Plan." The other HA programs are administered and overseen by the Defense Security Cooperation Agency, and information about them can be found at www.dsca.mil/programs (accessed June 24, 2011).

[16] "FY08, Humanitarian Assistance Program Standard Operating Procedures."

[17] The numbers refer to the authorizations for these programs. For more on the 1206 program, see Serafino, *Security Assistance Reform: 'Section 1206'.*"

[18] See the United States Institute for Peace website for a comprehensive review of the 1207 program. In 2008, USIP conducted a review of the 1207 program. Also see Perito, *Integrated Security Assistance.*

[19] For an evaluation of these programs after their first four years, see Government Accounting Office (GAO), *DOD and State Need to Improve Sustainment Planning.*

[20] Dobbins, et. al., *America's Role in Nation Building.*

[21] For example, as the US Army explored the western region of the United States in the nineteenth century, it built roads, compiled scientific records, improved river transportation, delivered mail, and supported new governmental institutions such as police forces and the agricultural extension service. See Tate, *The Frontier Army in the Settlement of the West.*

[22] Irish, "A 'Peace Corps with Guns.'"

[23] The World Health Organization (WHO) defines complex emergencies as "situations of disrupted livelihoods and threats to life produced by warfare, civil disturbance and large-scale movements of people, in which any emergency response has to be conducted in a difficult political and security environment." WHO, *Environmental Health in Emergencies and Disasters.*

[24] Stone, "DoD Considers Creating Stability and Reconstruction Force."

[25] Defense Science Board, *2004 Summer Study on Transition to and from Hostilities.* For an analysis of the report see Miles, "Defense Science Review Board Report."

[26] Defense Science Board, *2004 Summer Study on Transition to and from Hostilities*, 36.

[27] Stabilization activities normally refer to those designed to halt military hostilities and return a country to a peaceful civilian government—to stabilize the political situation.

[28] The White House, "NSPD-44: Management of Interagency Efforts." Not all welcomed the creation of S/CRS, concerned that there was little funding or political for statebuilding to be undertaken effectively; that the duties S/CRS would take on were already covered in other parts of the government bureaucracy; and that S/CRS would become an organization in search of missions, pushing the U.S. government into more of these efforts. See Logan and Preble, "The Case Against State's Nationbuilding Office."

[29] Updated in 2009, the directive can be found at www.dtic.mil/whs/directives (current as of August 2013).

[30] Hernandorena, "U.S. Provincial Reconstruction Teams in Afghanistan."

[31] In the initial directive, Section 4.1 of Directive 3000.05 (on DoD policy) read: "Stability operations are a core U.S. military mission that the Department of Defense shall be prepared to conduct and support. They shall be given priority comparable to combat operations and be explicitly addressed and integrated across all DoD activities including doctrine, organizations, training, education, exercises, materiel, leadership, personnel, facilities, and planning." In the 2009 revision, this was scaled down to "Stability operations are a core U.S. military mission that the Department of Defense shall be prepared to conduct with proficiency equivalent to combat operations."

[32] Crawley, "Pentagon Emphasizing Humanitarian Aid, Reconstruction Work."

[33] Combined Joint Chiefs of Staff. "Military Support for Stability, Security, Transition and Reconstruction (SSTR) Operations," 1.

[34] Department of the Army Headquarters, *Counterinsurgency*.

[35] Department of the Army Headquarters, *Stability Operations*.

[36] Harlow, "Army Unveils New Stability Operations Manual," 105. At the time, Wallace was the head of the U.S. Army Training and Doctrine Command.

[37] Harlow, "Army Unveils New Stability Operations Manual."

[38] Subsequent changes to personnel management and career progression have helped the Department of State and USAID to deploy a sufficient number of civilians to fill positions in postconflict countries.

[39] Kelly, et. al., "Stabilization and Reconstruction Staffing."

[40] Price, "The Future of S/CRS—What's in a Name?"

[41] Ibid.

[42] Serafino, *Peacekeeping/Stabilization and Conflict Transitions*. In its first year, Congress appropriated approximately $75 million for the program ("U.S. Launches Civilian Rapid Response Force"). For an account of the establishment of the corps, see Farr, "From Idea to Implementation."

[43] USAID, "The Office of Crisis Surge Response Staff." For a more optimistic read of the CRC, see Earle, "Taking Stock: Interagency Integration in Stability Operations," 40.

[44] The FY 2011 budget called for an additional 410 hires at the State Department and 200 at USAID, with a stated aim to hire 1,600 foreign service officers by 2014. Most of these positions were intended for overseas posts, to augment the civilian presence. Miller, "Obama Pushes More Hires at USAID, State Department." For a discussion of the Republican effort to defund USAID, along with a host of other programs, see Rogin, "165 House Republicans Endorse Defunding USAID."

[45] Department of State, State and USAID FY 2013 Budget.

[46] US Department of State, Office of the Spokesperson, "Fact Sheet: Overview of Obama's FY2013 Budget for State and USAID."

[47] The White House, *United States National Security Strategy 2010*, 5.

[48] Clinton's comments appear on the front webpage of the *QDDR* on the Department of State's website, www.state.gov/s/dmr/qddr/ (accessed February 14, 2012).

[49] US Department of State and US Agency for International Development, *Leading Through Civilian Power.*

[50] The Stimson Center, "State Department Establishes New Bureau."

[51] *QDDR* Executive Summary, www.state.gov/documents/organization/153635 (accessed March 1, 2013).

[52] See, for example, Unger, "Opinion: The QDDR: Following Through on Civilian Power?"

[53] Bradbury and Kleinman, *Winning Hearts and Minds?*; Lischer, "Winning Hearts and Minds in the Horn of Africa."

[54] See, for example, Lamb, "Parading US Security Interests as African Security Policy," 50-52; Nathan, "AFRICOM: A Threat to Africa's Security." This entire issue of *Contemporary Security Policy* debated the establishment and implications of US Africa Command.

[55] For instance, many feared that overly securitized foreign assistance would prioritize security assistance, particularly in the effort to combat global terrorism and build strong African militaries to counter terrorism and help engage in peacekeeping. In turn, this would end up supporting the illegitimate and corrupt political regimes that created many of Africa's security problems in the first place. See Pincus, "U.S. Africa Command Brings New Concerns," 13.

[56] This concern was not limited to AFRICOM's establishment. See Bessler and Seki, "Civil-Military Relations in Armed Conflicts."

[57] GAO, *Defense Management*, 14.

[58] Civil affairs lead at the US Embassy in Nairobi, Kenya, interview with author, May 2007.

[59] Pugh, "The Challenge of Civil-Military Relations in International Peace Operations," and Pugh, "Military Intervention and Humanitarian Action."

[60] Rietjens et al., "Co-ordinating Humanitarian Operations in Peace Support Missions."

[61] Author's interview with Linda Poteat, at the time a director at the umbrella NGO InterAction,Washington, D.C, July 2007; and GAO, *Defense Management*, 14.

[62] Byman, "Uncertain Partners: NGOs and the Military," 104; Abiew, "NGO-Military Relations in Peace Operations"; Winslow, "Strange Bedfellows: NGOs and the Military." Winslow reviews the antagonistic relationship between military and humanitarian workers.

[63] Abiew, "NGO-Military Relations in Peace Operations," 28. Most of Abiew's article focuses on coordination issues between civilians (government and NGOs) and the military in humanitarian assistance operations. It also reviews tensions that are caused by military involvement, particularly for NGOs, and the disjuncture in goals between civilian and military agents.

[64] Abiew, "NGO-Military Relations in Peace Operations," 31.

65 Hinson, "U.S. Military Interaction with Humanitarian Assistance Organizations."

66 Earle, "Taking Stock," 43.

4

Accountability: A Critical Link in the Security-Development Nexus

Dustin N. Sharp

Implicit in the concept of a "security-development nexus" are broad notions of what constitute threats to security together with the necessary actors to address those threats. Consistent with this expansive "human security" paradigm, a diverse array of actors and institutions are now bringing their expertise to bear on sub-Saharan Africa's many security challenges, including key actors within the US government, both military and civilian. Despite this increasing sophistication, those working on security and development issues are often confronted with a paradox of sorts, which is that the traditional security sector itself—consisting of those actors and institutions with the central charge of providing defense and security—has too often instead become a persistent source of insecurity through acts of corruption, extortion, criminality, and various human rights abuses.[1] When such abuses are allowed to go unchecked over time, protectors become predators, operating in some instances with near total impunity.

Without accountability for corruption and human rights abuses in the traditional security sector, the rule of law is undermined, and the prospects for advancing both development and security in the long-term are diminished. In this sense, the problem of the accountability gap within the traditional security sector contributes to a negative feedback loop that makes addressing other issues of governance and insecurity, ranging from fraudulent elections and lack of access to justice, to the ability of the state to address inter-communal violence and competition over access to natural resources, all the more daunting. Attempts to address the security-development nexus must therefore include greater efforts to close this accountability gap in the traditional security sector. Far from being peripheral to the security-development nexus, issues of accountability and impunity for human rights abuses must be brought to the center of thinking and programming in areas of peace operations, development, and security and justice sector reform. In these efforts, giving greater prominence to the human security lens will also be important. Together, efforts to promote accountability and justice for human rights abuses constitute a critical link in the security-development nexus.

Human or Traditional Security?

The seeming consensus that a security-development nexus exists masks a multiplicity of contested narratives embedded in the notion of a nexus.[2] Possible narratives, which are not necessarily mutually exclusive, include: (1) nexus as traditional international security where economic development in poorer countries is thought to help protect wealthy countries from a series of twenty-first century threats like terrorism and drug trafficking; (2) nexus as regime security whereby the stability of a particular government is boosted by addressing potentially explosive economic deprivations; (3) nexus as a more holistic and people-centered approach to the full range of security issues and needs of individuals in which the satisfaction of economic needs through human development is integral. The third narrative best reflects the notion of human security as opposed to traditional and regime security.

In sub-Saharan Africa today, the chief security threats are not international wars, but a much broader array of internal threats to security that combine to produce conditions of insecurity and instability: poverty, inequality, environmental degradation, malaria and HIV/AIDS, criminality and drug trafficking, terrorism, and a youth-demographic and population explosion, among others.[3] The brunt of these threats is borne not by the state, but by ordinary individuals, even though in combination these factors may ultimately serve to undermine a particular regime's security and stability.

Considering the complexity and diversity of the security threats, it would be naïve to assume a military or traditional security solution would be sufficient to address them. Examples from the Niger Delta and elsewhere indicate that security problems rooted in bad governance, exclusion, and rights abuses require a comprehensive package of reforms and interventions.[4] In this context, addressing security issues—whether international, regime, or otherwise—must entail addressing the full range of security threats to individuals in the subregion by a variety of actors. To this end, the more holistic human security paradigm will best serve to account for the most prevalent factors of insecurity in the twenty-first century.

Human Security and Traditional Security Sector Actors

The human security lens helps us to understand the complexity of peacebuilding, expanding our notions of those actors, institutions, and issues needed to foster lasting security. The traditional security sector remains critical, however, both for its potential contributions as well as the ways in which it can serve to undermine human security. As the world has witnessed in recent decades, abuses perpetrated by security forces—both traditional and non-statutory—have taken a heavy human toll. From the brutal civil wars that spilled across porous borders in the Mano River region in the 1990s, to the killing fields of the eastern Democratic Republic of the Congo, foreign publics and policymakers today often associate sub-Saharan Africa, rightly or wrongly, with the human rights abuses that have become synonymous with some of the more notorious conflicts in the region.

The stunning brutality of these hotspots and the press attention they understandably draw serve to mask lower levels of persistent and widespread abuse and corruption meted out by member of defense and security forces in a number of other countries. Examples of these abuses in countries ranging from Guinea and Côte d'Ivoire to Nigeria and the Democratic Republic of the Congo have been amply documented in recent years by international human rights organizations.[5] In far too many cases, protectors have become predators as those entrusted to ensure security have themselves become a source of insecurity for much of the population.

What unites many of the abuses in question—from the most severe and explosive to the quotidian—is that in the vast majority of cases, violence perpetrated by security forces tends to go unaddressed and unpunished. This absence of accountability, in turn, leads to a further breakdown of the rule of law, and a climate of impunity and indiscipline in the ranks of traditional security sector actors and institutions. In all too many instances—Uganda and Ethiopia being two examples—the US government has appeared willing to overlook such impunity in the name of promoting its own military and security agenda.

The reasons for predatory behavior by traditional security sector actors are complex and include structural factors such as poor salaries and inadequate training. Compounding matters, in many cases security forces do not operate within an architecture of well-functioning checks and balances intended to foster a climate of accountability. At the same time, even with the proper institutional mechanisms in place, accountability depends in large measure on the existence of political will to pursue abusers, or to refrain from using security forces for repressive and illegal ends.[6] Courts and judges lack meaningful ways to enforce their rulings if not backed by the coercive power of the state. Where there is no political will to pursue justice for human rights abuses, and where security forces are complicit or themselves perpetrators, impunity sets in.

In some cases, the impunity unofficially granted to beat, extort, and steal can serve as a kind of compensation or encouragement to members of defense and security forces. One of the most crude examples of this was Sierra Leonean rebel leader Foday Sankoh's "Operation Pay Yourself" that encouraged troops to loot and pillage with impunity. The blind eye often turned to corruption by traditional security actors in many countries serves as a less extreme form of the same principle of patronage. Over time, rather than human security needs fostering momentum for regime change, impunity for corruption and human rights abuses has the potential to create an incentive to ensure regime security. At the same time, as illustrated in the case study on Guinea below, allowing impunity to take root is a dangerous policy as it can eventually move beyond the control of its creators, constituting a threat to the stability of the regime itself. In either case, the choice by a successor regime to address an entrenched culture of impunity is fraught with peril as attempts to further accountability can produce backlash and even endanger the new regime's survival—a dynamic amply discussed in the transitional justice literature.[7]

A paradigm shift from traditional to human security at the policy level could help to (re)conceptualize problems of accountability and impunity by traditional security sector actors in two ways. First, by taking a holistic and people-centered approach to security, focused on the needs of the individual and not just the state, the human security lens helps us to see abuses by security forces as among those dire security threats that must be addressed in order for overall security and larger governance issues to be advanced. In addressing these threats to individuals, state security will ultimately be strengthened as well, insofar as mechanisms and institutions that foster accountability are reinforced. Second, as discussed in greater detail below, a reorientation of traditional security forces to better enable them to address a wider range of human security issues, as opposed to just regime security, could itself help to improve the broader human rights picture by refocusing security actors on the proper beneficiaries of the security they are supposed to provide.[8]

Implications of Unchecked Impunity for Development and Security

Whatever our conception of the security-development nexus, lack of accountability within the security sector is a thorny problem that impedes progress with respect to both development and security. The principle of accountability—that a government will have to answer for its actions before its own people—underlies the most basic principles of democracy and good governance. While accountability begins at the ballot box, it does not end there. It must be constantly maintained through checks and balances, which in turn create a climate that helps to ensure that the next round of voting will be free and fair.

In other words, accountability is an ongoing and sustained process rather than an event. A well-functioning security sector is inseparable from democracy, good governance, and accountability. By contrast, "no sector is spared the ramifications and effects of corruption and impunity."[9] Corrupt judges, abusive police services, and impunity leading to lack of faith in the legal system all threaten the prospects for democratic governance generally, and the security sector in particular.[10]

While functioning accountability mechanisms are central to a healthy security sector and good governance more generally, accountability has also long been recognized as being key to development initiatives. For example, in the context of analyzing the paradoxical inverse relationship between natural resource abundance and economic development (the "resource curse"), it is widely understood that one of the contributing factors to authoritarianism, poor governance, corruption, and stagnant development is precisely that the ties between government and citizens—links of accountability—do not exist where the government does not have to rely on raising funds from its citizenry.[11]

Under these conditions, government actors become unmoored from the welfare of their people, and work to further only their own interests and the regime's survival. Human rights groups have long argued that impunity for human rights violations meted out by security forces plays a similar role, precisely by severing links of accountability and eroding trust in national systems of justice and security. Over time, the self-reinforcing dysfunctionality of unaccountable governments results in the breakdown of the social contract, which is replaced by an "impunity state." Addressing those violations is then key to rebuilding those links of accountability central to good governance and restoring the social contract.

Illustrating Unchecked Impunity: Case Study on Guinea

Beginning in the late 1990s, Guinea began a long slide into chaos as deteriorating economic conditions and the bleak mood of the country seemed to mirror the declining health of its ailing president, Lansana Conté. At the heart of this spectacular decline were Guinea's defense and security forces, which became increasingly notorious for human rights abuse, insubordination, mutiny, and criminality. While unchecked impunity brought Guinea to the brink, Guinea's new government must now balance precarious stability with the need to reestablish accountability within the armed forces.

President Lansana Conté, who ruled Guinea from the mid-1980s until his death in late 2008, came to power in a military coup after the death of Guinea's father of independence, Sékou Touré. Conté assumed power with a pledge to make the protection of human rights one of his primary objectives. Despite these pronouncements, the human rights record of the Conté regime in the 1990s was marked by frequent abuses and repression, including the arrest and detention of opposition leaders and supporters, routine torture of criminal suspects, and harassment of journalists.[12] Nearly all of these abuses were meted out by Guinea's defense and security forces: army, gendarmes, and police. Though there were instances of security forces being arrested and tried for threatening the regime's security, following a 1996 pay munity for example, there are virtually no recorded instances of a member of the security services being brought to account for abuses against the civilian population during this period.

Starting around 2005, economic conditions in Guinea began to deteriorate rapidly, with inflation making it increasingly difficult for many members of the population to meet basic needs. As popular frustration simmered, civil society began to take a stronger and more public role in pressing the Conté government for reforms. While officers remained loyal to Conté, conditions within the rank and file military were dire, with most soldiers barely subsisting on their military rice ration, along with profits from extortion of the civilian population. Guinea's officer corps was deeply divided along generational and ethnic lines, and some form of military coup led by young officers was widely expected in the event of President Conté's death.[13]

As the country continued its economic downward spiral, civil society groups, in particular the country's leading trade unions, organized a series of nationwide protests to call for better governance and improved economic conditions. There was initially hope that the army would remain "neutral" in the course of these peaceful protests. Unfortunately, in almost every instance of protest, civilians were brutally killed, starting with only a handful in various 2005 protests, but climbing to over a dozen in 2006, and as many as 129 in 2007.[14] In the course of the crackdowns, members of defense and security forces engaged in rampant shooting, beating, rape, and looting of the civilian population, driving deep into neighborhoods and areas not directly involved in the protests.[15] Despite the clear crescendo of abuses, in no instance was a member of these forces brought to account.

During this same period, members of security forces engaged in acts of outright criminality and lawlessness, exacerbating insecurity.[16] There were increasing reports of uniformed men engaged in acts of highway robbery and home invasion. This lawlessness extended to the highest levels of the military as members of the elite presidential guard, or "red berets," led by President Conté's son, Ousman Conté, worked with Latin American drug cartels to facilitate cocaine trafficking to Europe. At this time, members of the army engaged in a number of high profile pay mutinies—in 2005, 2006, 2007, and 2008—holding superiors hostage, and firing in the air, resulting in the deaths of civilians.[17] No Guinean regime has ever brought to account the members of the defense or security forces for these actions and abuses.

As anticipated, upon president Conté's death in late 2008, a group of young officers swiftly took over, led by Captain Moussa Dadis Camara, who had built influence and patronage as head of the army's fuel supply. Camara initially enjoyed popular support based in part on promises to "clean house" by reining in corruption and criminality. Anti-corruption measures took the form of public humiliation of senior officials engaged in the cocaine trade and other corrupt practices by featuring them on local television. Aside from these public exposures, however, Camara did little to discipline the army or bring to account those responsible for previous human rights abuses.

Popular unease with the junta's rule began to grow when it became clear that Camara intended to run for president despite initial promises to step down after an undisclosed period of time. Tensions reached their peak in September 2009 when members of the army and other security forces brutally crushed a peaceful opposition rally, killing at least 150 and shooting and severely injuring thousands more.[18] Especially shocking in this largely Muslim and conservative country were the number of rapes and gang rapes, estimated at over 100.

Camara denied any responsibility and publicly declared that he was being held "hostage" by the army and that he was powerless to bring any perpetrators to account.[19] His rise to power came to an end months later when he was shot by a close aide, possibly in a dispute over who would take the blame for the September 2009 massacre, and required long-term evacuation outside of the country for medical treatment. Civilian power was fully restored in October 2010 when long-time opposition leader Alpha Condé was elected as Guinea's president in elections generally deemed to be free and fair, the first in Guinea's history.

While there is great relief that a longer period of military rule was averted, to date, there has been little accountability for the massacres and abuses committed by traditional security forces in the final years of the decade, even if there have been some slivers of hope. Perhaps most significantly, judges have been appointed to investigate the country's 2007 and 2009 massacres of demonstrators, and have charged at least eight people, including several high ranking military officers.[20] While this is unprecedented in Guinea's history, it is important to note that the investigations have been plagued by security concerns for the judges and lack of material support years after their initial launch.[21] Thus far, investigations have been stymied by the refusal of security officials to respond to judicial summons; several suspects remain in high level government positions.

Despite the ongoing investigation and some progress in restoring a sense of badly needed discipline to the ranks, members of Guinean security forces continued to be implicated in incidents of excessive use of force in response to opposition demonstrations, together with acts of looting, extortion, and banditry. Meanwhile, the need for comprehensive security sector reform is acute—compounded by the informal recruiting that allowed Guinea's security forces to balloon from 10,000 in 2001 to as many as 45,000 in 2010—and currently inches along at a snail's pace.[22] Though some positive gains have been made, it remains unclear to what extent rigorous human rights vetting will feature.

In sum, the criminality, lawlessness, and human rights abuses of the last decade continued unchecked for so long that they have created a culture of indiscipline and impunity that is proving difficult if not precarious to uproot. This creates a danger for civilians as well as the regime itself, as reflected in a July 2011 attack by soldiers upon the presidential residence. What remains clear is that it will be difficult to make advances in the provision of human security and economic development in Guinea without restoration of a sense of accountability and the rule of law within the traditional security sector.

In analyzing patterns of impunity for the last several years in Guinea, one might ask whether the root of the problem lies at the level of reckless and undisciplined "rogue" soldiers, or with the political leaders who have been willing to use the nation's various security forces to violently suppress dissent. The case in Guinea illustrates that, after a period of time, such distinctions become very difficult to make. It appears clear that the most egregious abuses of the last decade have been orchestrated at the highest political levels and that the resulting impunity exists in part due to a lack of political will from those in power to implement measures of account-ability. At the same time, the case of Guinea suggests that once a culture of impunity has been allowed to take root, it can move beyond the control of its creators, constituting a threat to the stability of the regime itself, as well as an enormous threat to the human security of a country's ordinary citizens.

Impunity and Accountability in Reform Projects

Rule of Law Reform

Once the domain of lawyers and jurists, the rule of law is increasingly seen as relevant to peace operations, development, and security. An entire "rule of law industry" has been spawned in the last two decades. From a security perspective, the rule of law is viewed as essential to ensure transparency, accountability, and control of security forces.[23] From a development perspective, establishing the rule of law is often seen as a prerequisite for the emergence of stability and "positive peace."[24]

Despite a growing consensus as to the relevance of the rule of law, there is a lack of consensus as to both the destination (what the rule of law is) and the means of getting there.[25] Rule of law programs have often been criticized as "cookie cutter" and generally ineffective.[26] Historically, many rule of law programs have limited themselves to relatively shallow, quantifiable, technical, and "apolitical" interventions such as rewriting or reforming the laws on the books, providing trainings to judges, renovating courthouses, and delivering tools such as case management software.[27]

For key actors in the development sector such as the World Bank, the rule of law has often entailed a narrow focus on those institutions thought important for the operation of a free market, and little more.[28] In general, rule of law programs have had only an oblique focus on potentially politically contentious issues such as accountability for human rights violations within the defense and security forces. After over $1 billion spent during the past two decades to build the rule of law in countries transitioning to democracy, it is increasingly clear that while US officials might "know it when they see it," there is little consensus as to how to build the rule of law in its absence.[29]

In a seminal article examining the resurgence of interest in building the rule of law, Thomas Carothers criticizes the shallowness of traditional efforts. He then points to a category of rule of law programs and reforms which have received the least money and attention, yet which may nevertheless have the potential for profound impact: those programs that have the deeper goal of increasing government's compliance with the law and thus bridging the gap between the law on the books and the law in action.[30] In other words, programs that focus more directly on issues of accountability for corruption, human rights abuses, and other instances where government actors effectively stand "above the law."

According to Carothers, these reforms demand "activities that help bring pressure on the legal system from the citizenry and support whatever pockets of reform may exist within an otherwise self-interested ruling system," and powerful tools that "aid providers are only beginning to develop."[31] If traditional rule of law programs have been largely "top-down," providing training for judges, for example, this category of initiatives is more heavily oriented towards "bottom-up" reform. While these initiatives therefore hold strong potential to further reform efforts, such programs comprise a category that development and other external actors tend to shy away from because enacting them "requires a level of interventionism, political attention, and visibility that many donor governments and organizations cannot or do not wish to apply."[32] Thus, while there is recognition that efforts to close the accountability gap are central to building the rule of law, such reforms are difficult to achieve in practice, and receive the least amount of money and attention from traditional development assistance providers.

Particularly in the context of postconflict reconstruction, one might also point to various measures of transitional justice as one potential means of performing rule of law reform and restoring some sense of accountability.[33] Prosecutions, truth commissions, reparations, and vetting and dismissals of human rights abusers all have been important transitional justice tools in the wake of massive human rights abuses.[34]

The difficulty with the transitional justice paradigm, however, is that it tends to focus primarily on the "big fish" in cases of egregious and massive abuse, and often fails to capture the more persistent and lower levels of ongoing abuse by security forces.[35] In many other instances, prosecutions do not take place at all; transitional justice initiatives begin and end with a truth commission.[36] In addition, the tools of transitional justice are often only politically feasible in instances of regime change. Experience in countries like Guinea, Côte d'Ivoire, and Nigeria has shown that persistent and lower-level abuses may pose a serious threat to human security without necessarily rising to the level of abuses typically dealt with in the context of transitional justice. Finally, packages of transitional justice measures often reflect political bargains struck between the elite groups involved in the transition more than vigorous attempts to impart widespread justice and account-ability, and may not serve to break down the impunity state.

While important and possibly instructive, the policy community should therefore not look to transitional justice tools alone to close the accountability gap. Rather, greater efforts to incorporate a human security focus into broad-based rule of law reform programs must be made. Under this approach, the protection of civilians and the full spectrum of human rights would be established as the ends to be achieved through various rule of law reform projects rather than more abstract, technical, apolitical reform.[37] These efforts could potentially entail perceptions of increased "politicization" of rule of law projects as issues of accountability and human rights protections are addressed more directly. While caution is therefore called for, the alternative—continuing with inoffensive and "apolitical" reform projects—is unlikely to produce greater results than it has in previous decades. Finally, as discussed below, much of this work must focus on not just the supply side of the accountability equation, but also on generating demand for accountability among the citizenry.

Security Sector Reform

While recognition is steadily growing, the importance of accountability and the rule of law has historically been underestimated in postconflict reconstruction programs such as security sector reform.[38] Given the political openings provided by moments of transition, security sector reform programs might provide a useful framework for addressing larger issues of justice and accountability.[39] This framework could include broad police and judicial reforms, but would also specifically address issues of corruption and impunity for human rights abuses within defense and security institutions and the establishment of accountability and oversight mechanisms.[40] However, notwithstanding qualified successes in restructuring military forces as in Liberia, building accountable police and other security forces and constructing impartial judiciaries able to act without regard to the traditional impunity of powerful elites have proven extremely challenging.[41] Perhaps at least in part because of these enormous challenges, all too often "initiatives to entrench the rule of law, establish democratic oversight structures, and instill respect for international legal norms and standards—fundamental tenets of the security sector reform model—have been sidelined in deference to the train-and-equip component of the process."[42]

Despite the challenges, efforts to strengthen the rule of law by combating impunity could provide an important foundation upon which to (re)build security institutions.[43] Addressing issues of accountability and impunity in the security sector reform process could also become part of an effort to position security forces to respond more effectively to holistic contemporary threats to populations—not merely to regimes—thereby reorienting them around a human security paradigm. Reorienting defense and security forces along a human security axis might entail forms of military humanitarianism—that is deploying military expertise and skills for development—especially in civil engineering, agriculture, medicine, regional peace support operations, and other internal security challenges.[44]

In this vein, as discussed in the preceding case study on Guinea, some governments in the subregion are wrestling with how to manage an army that has swollen to unsustainable numbers. Abrupt large-scale cuts in troop levels could endanger regime stability, and could also wreak havoc on the human security of the population as out-of-work former soldiers engage in various forms of criminality to earn money.[45] Easing those soldiers into a development corps that would engage in various forms of military humanitarianism could be one way of reducing the size of the army while providing skills training and short- to medium-term employment for former soldiers.

Promoting Accountability in the Traditional Security Sector

The Role of the United States Government

The broader US foreign policy community must do more to promote accountability and justice for human rights abuses if long-term economic development and security are to be realized. On the military side, a strategy that emphasizes traditional assistance—encompassing joint military and naval exercises, military training, visits to the Pentagon by senior African military officers, etc.—will continue to contain only the effects of regional insecurity unless interventions begin to focus on a more comprehensive series of threats to individuals, as suggested by the human security paradigm.[46] While terrorism and drug trafficking are indeed serious threats to regional security, and the US efforts in this regard are welcome, there must also be renewed emphasis on some of the other broad threats to human security, including issues of accountability and impunity within the traditional security sector.

The civilian side of the US government—the Department of State, the Agency for International Development, and others—can and should serve as a stronger voice on justice and accountability issues. Their foreign assistance budgets should be reprogrammed as necessary to provide greater emphasis on the development of more robust local justice and accountability mechanisms. Much of this can be achieved by increasing support to local and international civil society organizations working on these issues, as discussed below. Both military and civilian sides of US government could better use their influence, including by placing conditions on continued training and assistance, to persuade their counterparts to take concrete steps to combat impunity within the traditional security sector. This persuasion must be done publicly, but should also be reiterated wherever possible in the course of private discussions and backdoor negotiations.

Ultimately, stronger efforts to promote accountability by the US government could further greater US policy aims in the subregion. While combating impunity is an end in and of itself, a serious and evenhanded commitment to issues of accountability and impunity in programming by the US government, both military and civilian sides, could help to quell existing fears regarding the role of US security doctrine vis-à-vis the continent. There currently exists "a growing apprehension within African civil society that the US-African security doctrine risks undermining fledgling democratization processes in favor of 'strong leaders' who can guarantee oil flows and clamp down on perceived extremists at the expense of human rights."[47] Measures that would help dispel this perception could prove to be a "win-win" for all concerned and, if applied evenly, would be a welcome departure from the historic willingness of the United States to support abusive autocrats where it was politically expedient.

The Role of Civil Society

Accountability is a public resource that cannot simply be provided by the government and external partners alone.[48] Rather, building a culture of accountability within governments generally and security forces in particular depends on active scrutiny by citizens and nongovernmental organizations (NGOs). While pressure and incentives from the top remain critical, pressure from the bottom is equally if not more important to long-term success in building accountability. Thus, even though direct efforts by the US government and other international partners will be essential, caution should be exercised as local ownership will always be key to the success of any rule of law and justice reform project. Moreover, the perception that accountability reforms are externally imposed could create a backlash and lead to accusations of hypocrisy given highly publicized US human rights abuse scandals in Iraq and Afghanistan, coupled with the general impunity associated with those situations.

Civil society, both international and local, can work to help build accountability in a variety of ways. Much of this work falls upon traditional human rights NGO personnel, who work to investigate and document abuses by security forces, publicize them, and then lobby governments and other actors for accountability and reform. In addition to "naming and shaming," such groups can also work on behalf of victims associations to utilize courts and other mechanisms of accountability to promote reform. The work of Human Rights Watch and a coalition of Chadian and Senegalese NGOs to bring the former president of Chad, Hissène Habré, to trial is one example of this approach.[49]

Beyond these traditional advocacy strategies, local civil society groups can also work to build the rule of law and a culture of accountability in more sustained and less dramatic ways by focusing not just on pressuring the government for accountability through the media and in the courts, but on creating greater demand within the citizenry for accountability as well. This is the logic underlying efforts such as the Extractive Industries Transparency Initiative, applied to governance of extractive resource sectors. Stephen Golub has argued that the failure of traditional rule of law programs can be accounted for in part based on their failure to see the limits of a top-down, supply-side approach. Golub advocates what he calls "the legal empowerment alternative," involving the provision of legal services to ordinary citizens who wish to challenge government abuses, failures, and arbitrariness.[50] If government is to be held accountable, this approach suggests, it will require a large citizen base with the tools to demand accountability. By contrast, the efforts of a handful of elite NGOs, either local or international, will never be sufficient.

Ultimately, it is going to be a citizen-led push for accountability and better governance that will be central to promoting the consolidation of security, development, and lasting peace, but the US government can serve as a useful partner in this regard. One of the key ways that US government actors can help is by offering greater support and training to local civil society actors pursuing the approaches described above. The efforts of groups working on the demand side of the accountability equation are an area where US government training and support would be especially useful.

Conclusion

If security and development are like a rope of interwoven strands, there are now many actors and institutions with an important role in pulling the rope forward, ranging from government and traditional security institutions to civil society and community groups. Though sometimes overlooked, accountability is an essential public good—one of the core strands in the rope—inextricably intertwined with both security and development. Building security depends on the presence of accountable, professional, and disciplined security forces.

When impunity takes root these same forces can do much to undermine security. Going forward, building human security requires that the United States and the international community bring issues of accountability and impunity for human rights abuses by security forces (including their own security forces) to the center of thinking and programming in areas of peace operations, development, and security and justice sector reform. Central to the success of these efforts will be "bottom-up" citizen-led initiatives to pressure local governments and security sector institutions and actors for accountability and reform.

To be sure, addressing issues of accountability within the traditional security sector in order to foster greater human security for all is but one of the many governance challenges and sources of instability with which African governments and their external partners are confronted today, as illustrated by the various chapters and case studies in this volume. Nevertheless, accountable security forces constitute a critical link in the complex feedback loop between governance, security, and development. Any policy that fails to acknowledge the centrality of this link will face severe challenges when it comes to reducing insecurity in sub-Saharan Africa today.

Notes

[1] The examples used in this chapter are largely drawn from West Africa. Nevertheless, the dynamics discussed herein are not unique to West Africa, but are also found in many other countries in sub-Saharan Africa.

[2] Stern and Öjendal, "Mapping the Security-Development Nexus," 8.

[3] Musah, *West Africa,* 3-6.

[4] Musah, *West Africa*, 12.

[5] For but a small sampling of human rights reporting documenting abuses by security forces in these countries, see, for example, Human Rights Watch, *Bloody Monday*; Human Rights Watch, *Dying for Change*; Human Rights Watch, *My Heart Is Cut;* Human Rights Watch, *Everyone's in on the Game;* Human Rights Watch, *Arbitrary Killings by Security Forces.*

[6] Ellis, "Combating Impunity," 141.

[7] See, for example, O'Donnell and C. Schmitter, "Transitions from Authoritarian Rule," 57-64.

[8] Ebo, "Security Sector Reform," 23.

[9] Ibid., 19.

[10] Ibid.

[11] Ross, "The Political Economy of the Resource Curse," 312; see also Karl, *The Paradox of Plenty*, 172.

[12] Human Rights Watch, *The Perverse Side of Things*, 5.

[13] International Crisis Group, *Stopping Guinea's Slide*, 7.

[14] Human Rights Watch, *The Perverse Side of Things*, 19; Human Rights Watch, *Dying for Change*, 54.

[15] Human Rights Watch, *Dying for Change*, 3-4.

[16] International Crisis Group, *Guinea: Reforming the Army*, 8-10.

[17] Ibid., 9-10.

[18] Human Rights Watch, *Bloody Monday*, 4.

[19] International Crisis Group, *Guinea: Military Rule Must End*, 3.

[20] Human Rights Watch, "Guinea: High-Level Charges."

[21] Ibid.

[22] International Crisis Group, *Guinea: Reforming the Army,* 2.

[23] Hurwitz and Studdard, *Rule of Law Programs in Peace Operations*, 1.

[24] Ibid. The term "negative peace" refers to the absence of direct violence. It stands in contrast with the broader concept of "positive peace," which includes the absence of both direct and indirect violence, including various forms of "structural violence" such as poverty, hunger, and other forms of social injustice. Galtung, "Violence, Peace, and Peace Research."

[25] Carothers, "The Problem of Knowledge," 15.

[26] Mani, "Exploring the Rule of Law," 35-39.

[27] Ibid.

[28] Rajagopal, "Invoking the Rule of Law," 1364.

[29] Carothers, "The Problem of Knowledge," 19.

[30] Carothers, "The Rule-of-Law Revival," 7-8.

[31] Ibid., 12.

[32] Ibid.

[33] For a review of potential tensions and complementarity between transitional justice and traditional rule of law assistance, see Herman, et. al., "Beyond Justice Versus Peace."

[34] UN Secretary-General, *The Rule of Law and Transitional Justice.*

[35] In Sierra Leone, for example, prosecutions focused only on those bearing the "greatest responsibility" for international crimes.

[36] Liberia is one such example where the only individual to be tried for crimes carried out during the civil war, former president Charles Taylor, is actually on trial for crimes committed in Sierra Leone under the auspices of the Special Court for Sierra Leone. For most Liberians, the national truth and reconciliation commission has been the only form of justice they have seen, and it has not led to strict accountability measures against any of the many former perpetrators serving in power.

[37] Mani, "Exploring the Rule of Law," 40.

[38] Schneider, "Placing Security and the Rule of Law on the Development Agenda," 14.

[39] Ebo, "Security Sector Reform," 22.

[40] O'Neill, *Police Reform in Post-Conflict Societies*, 9.

[41] Schneider, "Placing Security and the Rule of Law on the Development Agenda," 14.

[42] Sedra, "Security Sector Reform in Afghanistan," 109.

[43] Ibid., 105.

[44] Ebo, "Security Sector Reform," 23.

[45] This danger has been recently illustrated in Côte d'Ivoire, where former soldiers continue to be implicated in acts of criminality and banditry, leading to a generalized climate of insecurity in the region surrounding the central town of Bouaké. Human Rights Watch, "Côte d'Ivoire: Lethal Crime Wave."

[46] Musah, *West Africa*, 12.

[47] Ibid.

[48] Collier, "A Worldwide Pact for Security and Accountability," 11.

[49] Brody, "The Prosecution of Hissène Habré."

[50] Golub, "The Legal Empowerment Alternative," 161.

5

Security Sector Assistance in Africa, but Where is the Reform?

Andrea M. Walther-Puri

The attacks of September 11, 2001, brutally highlighted that the most persistent and potentially dangerous threats come from fragile states that offer violent extremist organizations a safe haven to exist, plan, and carry out attacks. Weak states lack effective and accountable security sectors that uphold the rule of law, enforce laws, and protect their own borders. An ill or non-functioning security sector provides opportunities that other actors can exploit. Consequently, multiple operational terrorist groups currently threaten the security and prosperity of not only Africans across the continent, but Europe and the US as well.[1] Accordingly, the 2002 *National Security Strategy* highlighted Afghanistan and Iraq as the focus for US security cooperation and assistance. Close behind, however, was attention to sub-Saharan Africa, as African countries make up 18 of the top 25 entries in the 2014 Failed States Index.[2]

For nearly three-quarters of a century, the US has provided large amounts of governance and security assistance in support of fragile states globally. The geographic distribution and timing of this assistance spiked during the height of the Cold War and during the post-9/11 Global War on Terror periods. As the threat posed by weak and failing states pose peaks again, so has pressure for the creation of a strategy to address the underlying factors that make states fragile. Security sector reform has been re-invigorated, as a method to address underlying factors of governance and insecurity.

Recent policy and approaches have adopted a myopic focus on the provision of security sector assistance to combat terrorism, however, instead of launching a comprehensive security sector reform policy that would focus on reforming states so that they are more stable and less vulnerable to being taken advantage of by terrorist groups. While the launch of the State Department's first Quadrennial Diplomatic and Development Review (QDDR) and the release of a presidential directive on security sector assistance (Presidential Policy Directive-23) have been encouraging steps forward, this chapter argues that they to be truly effective, they need to be complemented by an equitable prioritization of a broader security sector reform agenda that changes the way the US government (USG) is organized to interact and coordinate in this arena.

To advance this argument, this chapter examines the USG's current defense sector approach to weak states in North and West Africa, which ultimately has focused on tactical capacity building, rather than a larger reform of the security sector to ensure they are more capable of combating threats. While there are some relatively new programs that look promising as they focus on strengthening security sector institutions, they remain individual programs and do not comprise an overarching policy which also addresses governance and development. On a continent that has perhaps the worst and most recent history of military coups, poor governance, and extreme poverty, the continuation of this imbalance could likely lead to the creation of the very instability that we are focused on combating.

Background: US Strategic Interest in Africa and the Sahelian Threat Environment

Six key factors have worked to steadily shape and increase US interest in Africa in the past fifteen years: terrorist threats, interests in securing natural resources, changing patterns of global trade, the desire to contain armed conflicts and humanitarian crises, attempts to halt the spread of HIV/AIDS and other deadly diseases, and the objective of balancing the spread of Chinese influence on the continent. These combined factors have led to a conceptual shift and a new US strategic view of Africa.[3] Despite the presence of Osama bin Laden in Sudan and the attacks against the US embassies in East Africa in 1998, issues on the African continent have not been historically identified as strategic priorities for the US military. Shortly after the terrorist attacks of 9/11 this changed, however, when Susan Rice, assistant secretary of state for African affairs during the Clinton administration, testified that "Africa is unfortunately the world's soft underbelly for global terrorism."[4]

The Sahel region has and continues to experience many longstanding political, economic, and humanitarian vulnerabilities. It is comprised of countries that suffer from poor governance and weak democratic institutions, lack development and economic opportunities for their citizens, and have vulnerabilities that can easily be exploited by violent extremist and criminal organizations. During the decade after 9/11 the Sahel experienced three coups (Mauritania in August 2008, Niger in February 2010, and Mali in March 2012), chronic drought, two Tuareg rebellions (in 2007-2009 and in 2012), and multiple acts of terrorism.

The 2011 Arab Awakening created an enormous security vacuum in the Maghreb that had severe consequences for its Southern neighbors. The fall of longstanding authoritarian leaders and their police states in Tunisia, Egypt and Libya also meant that these regimes lost their ability to control and eradicate any potential violent extremist sentiments within their populations. Events in the Middle East and North Africa also flooded the Sahel with new sources of advanced arms, munitions, and experienced returning fighters. These events worsened the security situation and terrorist threat facing their Sahelian neighbors to the south.

In 2014, several terrorist groups were operating throughout the Sahel region. These included al Qaida in the Islamic Maghreb (AQIM), the Movement for Oneness and Jihad in West Africa (MUJAO, primarily Algeria), Ansar al-Dine (Mali and throughout the region), Ansaru and Boko Haram (Nigeria), Ansar al-Sharia (Tunisia), and the al-Mulathamun Battalion (Algeria).[5] They operate in an area that stretches from Mauritania through central and southern Algeria, into the southwestern territory of Libya, and extends southwards to include the northern halves of Chad, Mali, Niger and Nigeria.[6] Of these groups, al Qaeda in the Islamic Maghreb poses the largest threat to regional and US global interests, though the threat to US interests beyond the Sahel and Maghreb regions is limited.[7]

US Counterterrorism Response

Since 9/11, the US counterterrorism strategy in Africa has focused on the argument that threats "are likely to emanate from states that cannot adequately govern themselves or secure their own territory. In these situations, the effectiveness and credibility of the United States will only be as good as the effectiveness, credibility, and sustainability of its local partners."[8] US counterterrorism strategy is addressed through a wide spectrum of different initiatives. At one end, programs exist to address the root causes of terrorism, and at the other end, military operations may occur to destroy terrorist targets through military strikes. Shortly after 9/11, the US created the Trans-Sahara Counterterrorism Partnership (TSCTP), a program that coordinates activities by the Department of State (State), Department of Defense (DoD), and the US Agency for International Development (USAID) to address the underlying drivers of instability in the Sahel and Maghreb regions.[9]

The TSCTP is a regional approach that attempts to make countries less vulnerable to recruitment and radicalization, build partner capacity so nations are better able to detect and deter threats, and enhance regional coordination and cooperation efforts to combat terrorism.[10] With eleven partner nations, the TSCTP has a combined annual interagency budget of approximately $120 million.[11] The TSCTP is supposed to present an integrated development, governance, and security approach, enabling Sahelian nations to address longstanding drivers of extremism in the region, including poverty, political marginalization, and social alienation. The TSCTP focuses on building partner capacity and is made up of "targeted efforts to improve the collective capabilities and performance of the Ministries of Defense and their partners."[12]

US Security Sector Assistance

While the amount of US security assistance to Africa has increased steadily over the course of the past seven years, a cohesive security sector–wide approach does not exist. Different offices at State and the DoD, which are responsible for formulating security strategy, control different pots of money and have overlapping authorities to work with Ministries of Interior and Defense; there is no formal mechanism for the coordination of security sector reform. By not having a mandated formal coordination structure, each agency focuses on its own resources and goals vs. a larger integrated SSR effort. Furthermore, the DoD has continuously argued for (and received) additional authorities to tactically train-and-equip partner nation forces. This has led to both an increase in the authority of the DoD to control foreign assistance and the duplication of existing traditional State Department security cooperation programs.[13] What's more, DoD military train-and-equip funding significantly trumps State Department resources that focus on long-term change, two to one. The current US security assistance approach therefore prioritizes building short-term counterterrorism capacity and not institutional capacity building.

State Department Authorities and Resources

The Foreign Assistance Act of 1961 allocated leadership for foreign assistance to the State Department, including the design, administration and oversight of military assistance. This authority allows the State Department to decide who receives funding, what kind, and in what amount. The DoD then implements the funding through a suite of assistance accounts that work to professionalize, train, equip, and sustain partner nation militaries in an effort to build their overall security capacity to deter and defend against threats.

State oversees a variety of international military assistance programs that include the International Military Education and Training (IMET) program, which is focused on professionalization and designed to expose foreign military officers to US military schools, procedures, and the manner in which military organizations function under civilian control. Foreign Military Financing (FMF) allocates money for partner nation purchases of the US defense articles, services, and training through grants. Foreign Military Sales (FMS) provides guidance on what training and spare parts packages partner nations need to sustain equipment received through other US capacity building programs.

Finally, Peacekeeping Operations (PKO) is used to support "peacekeeping operations and other programs carried out in furtherance of the national security interests of the United States."[14] The spectrum of US international security assistance also includes criminal justice sector programs, the oversight and management of which lies with the State Department's Bureaus of Counterterrorism, Conflict Stabilization Operations, and International Narcotics and Law Enforcement in close coordination with the Bureau of Africa Affairs. This chapter focuses its analysis on military assistance.[15]

Sub-Saharan Africa receives only a small portion of funding for these programs, compared to other world regions. For example, the fiscal year (FY) 2015 State Department's Foreign Operations Account for International Security Assistance allocated only 3 percent of its funds ($239,116) to sub-Saharan Africa, excluding the Maghreb.[16] The largest account administered by State supports global foreign military financing (72 percent of international security assistance funds), and sub-Saharan Africa has received an average of only 0.27 percent of global FMF resources each year for the past six years (in FY15, only 0.19 percent).[17] Sub-Saharan Africa received a larger share of the peacekeeping and education and training funds: 36.3 percent of global funds for peacekeeping operations (PKO) and 14 percent of global funds for international military education and training. Table 5.1 shows the stark imbalance between sub-Saharan Africa and the rest of the world in terms of how much security assistance it receives from the United States and points to the fact that sub-Saharan Africa receives only a small portion of all military assistance.

Table 5.1: Security Assistance in Africa

Assistance Account	FY15 Dollars, in Thousands		
	Global Total	Africa	% Africa
IMET	$111,815	$15,690	14.0%
FMF	$5,647,645	$10,950	0.19%
PKO	$336,150	$122,100	36.30%
INCLE*	$1,117,911	$48,500	4.30%
NADR*	$605,400	$41,876	6.90%
TOTAL	$7,818,921	$239,116	3.00%

Source: US Department of State, FY 2015 Congressional Budget Justification, 152-186, 206-209. The figures for sub-Saharan Africa exclude Egypt, which is included in the Middle East accounts.

While the title Peacekeeping Operations assistance clearly describes its goal of supporting countries' participation in ongoing peacekeeping operations, in reality this category supports much more than peacekeeping. The PKO account mandate also seeks to "help diminish and resolve conflict; address counterterrorism threats; and reform military establishments into professional military forces with respect for the rule of law in the aftermath of conflict."[18] State is able to use PKO assistance in such a diverse way due to the way the authority is written in the National Defense Authorization Act of 1961: "The President is authorized to furnish assistance to friendly countries and international organizations, on such terms and conditions as he may determine, for peacekeeping operations *and other programs carried out in furtherance of the national security interests of the United States* [italics added]."[19]

The Department of State traditionally focuses this assistance on the most urgent situations where countries are emerging from conflict and are in urgent need of rebuilding their security sectors. In FY15 there was only approximately $313 million available; the majority of this assistance was allocated to Somalia (34 percent, to support the African Union mission in Somalia), South Sudan (11 percent), Mali (6 percent), the Central African Republic (3 percent), Democratic Republic of Congo (3 percent), and Liberia (1 percent). The rest of Africa receives support from the overall

Global Peace Operations Initiative funds (21 percent of the account), Africa Regional PKO funds (7 percent), and TSCTP funds (6 percent).[20]

State provides military assistance to support counterterrorism efforts in the Sahel/Maghreb region under this peacekeeping operations account, supporting the TSCTP. In addition to the 6 percent of global PKO assistance that TSCTP partner countries directly receive, they also gain a small portion PKO resources through allocations to the Africa Regional Account's Africa Maritime Security Initiative and the Africa Military Education Program.[21] Since 2009, TSCTP partner nations have received over $108 million in PKO assistance to enhance their military capacity to counter terrorism. The TSCTP has provided training and related equipment to develop capable border security and counterterrorism units, enhanced military intelligence capability, regional information sharing, logistics, and communications systems interoperability, and enhanced military infrastructure such as improving shooting ranges or building airplane hangars to house aviation ISR assets. While the above programs provide assistance to train and equip partner nation forces, to date, none of this assistance is focused at security governance institutions.

Defense Department Authorities and Resources

Title 10 of the United States Code outlines the role of armed forces in the US.[22] Therefore, DoD security assistance is commonly referred to as "Title 10 assistance," which enables the US military forces to train and equip foreign military forces in partner countries. Traditional Title 10 security assistance includes the Combating Terrorism Fellowship Program (CTFP), the Regional Centers for Security Studies (such as the African Center for Strategic Studies), Disaster Response (Humanitarian Assistance), Mine Action Programs, Drug Interdiction and Counter Drug Activities, and the transfers of Excess Defense Articles.

The goal of Title 10 assistance is to provide US Special Forces the opportunity to enhance their own training in different operational environments and foster communication and cultural exchanges bilaterally and regionally among militaries. It also serves to pass on and exchange skills between the US and partner nation forces. Newer post-9/11 authorities have been requested from and granted to the DoD by Congress through amendments to the National Defense Authorization Act (NDAA). The "12 series" programs discussed in Chapters 2 and 3 of this volume—1203, 1206, 1207, and others—focus specifically on building partner capacity.[23]

These programs have significantly augmented the DoD's traditional budget and expanded their authorities. In FY 2006, the National Defense Authorization Act allocated the Secretary of Defense with temporary global authority to train and equip foreign military forces for two specified purposes—counterterrorism and stability operations.[24] Originally, the intent of the 1206 program was to support ongoing operations and coalition support efforts in and towards Afghanistan and Iraq, but it has also been utilized in Africa: since 2009 the 1206 account has provided TSCTP countries with over $214 million.

The overlapping projects covered by these accounts shows the significant mixing of counterterrorism, stabilization and reconstruction, and security sector assistance programs. The multiplicity of accounts and administering agencies, when combined with all the different mandates delivers a situation in which there are few overarching goals, little high-level guidance to align the activities of all the actors, and therefore a program-specific approach. The individual programs rarely amalgamate into a coherent, multifaceted strategy in which all the pieces work together to build a greater outcome. It also means that there is significant loss of coordination between the State and Defense departments.

Why Do Such Coordination Challenges Exist?

Without an overarching mandate and structure directing a government-wide approach, and given the severe resource imbalances between the diplomatic, developmental and security agencies of the USG, monumental obstacles still remain for security sector synchronization and planning efforts. Without a clear interagency framework and approach, unique departmental planning processes, budgets, goals, and missions create a situation in which various programs become "siloized" and in which they compete for prioritization.

There has been some attempt to coordinate these processes since the creation of AFRICOM, as the command convenes annual continent-wide and bilateral planning conferences. These attempt to bring together federal, operational, and tactical US interagency security cooperation players to review policy and the security situation on the ground, and to plan for the year ahead. Because each federal department still operates according to a different, budget-driven planning cycle, these planning conferences are limited in their ability to actually coordinate programs and activities. Rather, they tend to serve as briefing and information sharing events, or opportunities for support and contracting agencies to put in bids to execute programs that have already been planned.

Additionally, as discussed in chapters two and three of this volume, diplomatic and development resources remain woefully out of balance both in staffing and funding from defense sector resources. For example, President Obama's FY 2015 *Foreign Operations Budget* for the State Department, USAID, and other foreign affairs agencies totaled $50.08

billion, a decrease of 3 percent over the FY 2014 total.[25] This allocation represented a mere 1.2 percent of the total US FY 2015 entire federal government's budget.[26] The amended FY 2015 budget request for the State Department's international security assistance consisted of 16.1 percent of its entire foreign operations budget.[27] In contrast, the Defense Department's FY15 base budget was $495.6 billion and the Overseas Contingency Operations budget (OCO) equaled $58.6 billion, brining DoD's total to $554.2 billion. Defense spending amounts to 14.2 percent of the overall federal budget.[28]

Thus, the agencies whose missions are to "shape and sustain a peaceful, prosperous, just, and democratic world and foster conditions for stability and progress for the benefit of the American people and people everywhere" receive one-tenth the funding of the military.[29] As learned in reconstruction experiences world-wide, statebuilding cannot be done on the cheap, which further underscores the ways in which these instruments of power are not given the resources to fulfill their mandates. With respect to security assistance and counterterrorism programs, it becomes impossible for the diplomacy, development and governance components to balance the efforts of their military counterparts.

The resource disparities manifest in staffing levels as well. In 2013, the US military had over 1.4 million uniformed active duty employees and over 718,000 civilian employees, while State had only 71,000 employees.[30] While AFRICOM, the geographic combatant command for Africa, has approximately 2,000 assigned personnel, the Africa Bureaus within the US State Department and USAID have a fraction of that total amount.[31] Furthermore, as a result of a lack of civilian capacity in partner departments involved in stabilization and reconstruction activities, on January 23, 2009, the DoD created the Civilian Expeditionary Workforce to compensate for the lack of capacity of its partner agencies.[32]

There are a number of recent warning signals that the imbalance amongst federal departments may be becoming more extreme. Each year since FY 2006, Congress has extended the mandate and authorities of the DoD's 1206 program. At the time of writing in September 2014, Congress was in the midst of deliberations to permanently grant these authorities to the DoD (rather than relocating them within the Department of State or USAID). Over the past nine years, the 1206 funding available has nearly doubled from $200 million in FY 2006 to $350 million in FY 2015.[33]

Furthermore, in the FY2014 defense authorization the 1206 authority was extended for three years through FY2017, and it extended the DoD's authority to train and equip for counterterrorism purposes not to just military but to all types of foreign security forces. In the past, the US military was prohibited from providing training to police and gendarmeries.

These changes were made to allow for a longer-term planning cycle in the defense department for how it utilizes 1206 funds, and to allow military actors to work with all the security agencies in a partner country. These are positive in intent, but they also mean that resources that could have been allocated to State and USAID will continue to be given to the DoD instead.

On May 26, 2014, while delivering the commencement address to West Point's graduating class, President Obama announced a "shift [in] our counterterrorism strategy" and asked Congress to approve a new $5 billion Counterterrorism Partnerships Fund with broad purposes and authority to help build partner counterterrorism capacity. Without providing much specific information, the administration asked Congress to provide new, largely unrestricted authority for a sizable amount of money that would not be subject to budget limitations and would undergo little congressional oversight. For months prior to the launching of this new initiative, the White House had indicated that it would continiue to pursue the whole-of-government approach articulated, for example, in the June 2011 National Strategy for Counterterrorism and at a speech at National Defense University in May 2013. But the new initiative focused on military action.

In 2008 former Secretary of Defense Robert Gates warned that "the United States military has become more involved in a range of activities that in the past were perceived to be the exclusive province of civilian agencies and organizations. This has led to ... what's seen as a creeping militarization of some aspects of foreign policy,"[34] in line with many of the concerns reviewed in Chapters 2, 3, and 10 of this book. Unfortunately, since 2008 this has is become more and more of a reality.

Consequences of an Imbalanced Approach to Security Sector Assistance

Choosing a security sector assistance approach that focuses on the supply side and prioritizes military over other assistance strategies has consequences for both the US and partner nations. Under this current trajectory, I argue that the US will not realize the impact it is trying to achieve. Billions of dollars will continue to be spent each year on security sector assistance, yet institutionally countries will not be better off. And the enhanced partner security capacity that the US attempts to build in terrorism-stricken regions to ensure that US boots on the ground are unnecessary will not be realized.[35]

The TSCTP is a congressionally earmarked program. It is supposed to embody the "three D" (defense, diplomacy/governance, development) framework through which the US counterterrorism strategy and policy is articulated and programmatically implemented throughout the region. It is a framework to ensure that holistic US government coordination exists and is maintained. Other counterterrorism and related security assistance programs exist, which are coordinated with, but are not officially under the budget of, the TSCTP. This exists because of legacy programmatic budget lines that are at times bilaterally captured, instead of falling under the TSCTP's regional budget. Given the fact that these specific types of programs ensure they are couched underneath the balanced "3D" nature of the partnership, and maintain close coordination and synchronization, they can co-exist in a mutually supportive manner.

However, as Figure 5.1 shows, the 1206 program provides double and sometimes triple the amount of security assistance to the region than the counterterrorrism programs. In this off-kilter scenario, resources clearly drive priorities. The significance of these additional military resources also significantly unbalances the development and governance programming that is decided upon based on earmarks under the TSCTP. Furthermore, under the current paradigm there seems to be no prospects for prioritization and clarification of effective interagency collaboration. While other supporting CT programs that are not officially funded by the TSCTP coordinate and operate under the framework of the partnership, 1206 programs do not work in concert with TSCTP planning processes.

Figure 5.1: 1206 and TSCTP Funding in Sub-Saharan Africa (FY09-14, millions of dollars)

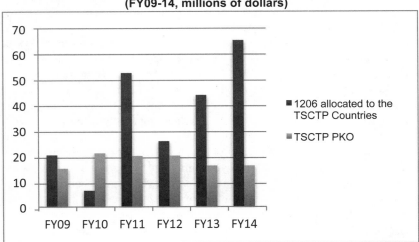

Source: Congressional Notifications of 1206 and PKO assistance, FY09-14.[36]

For the partner nations, a supply side approach creates dangerous incentives that focus on equipment furnished and tactical trainings provided, rather than encouraging partner nation interest and focus on broader transformation of the defense sector. The emphasis on creating new specialized counterterrorism units prioritizes them without reference to the country's larger defense planning process. Normally no steps are taken to ensure that a counterterrorism unit's creation is in line with the country's larger defense strategy (if it has one), or if the Ministry of Defense (and other Ministries such as Finance) are taking the necessary steps to incorporate these new units into the larger defense framework (recruitment, lodging, supply, and salaries).[37]

Finally, by focusing on these tactical level objectives, in certain countries, the amount of military resources the US provides actually creates an imbalance among the security structures in many countries. To date, there has been a major focus on operational effectiveness, particularly of intelligence services and elite units, which has been elevated above the development of security governance and oversight mechanisms.[38] When the majority of security assistance a country receives is for tactical programs, the country's priority becomes those tactical programs, rather than the development of strategic planning processes. Soon the entire defense structure becomes driven from this bottom-up approach, with an appreciable negative impact on the ability of these countries to develop their own coherent and cohesive approach to governing and managing their security sectors.

Senior US leadership has stated that security sector assistance efforts "must address the immediate security threat posed by violent extremists and transnational criminal networks, while at the same time building the institutional capacity needed to address the Sahel's political economic and humanitarian challenges." [39] Unfortunately, this has not been achieved in practice. This limited tactical approach inappropriately allows immediate counterterrorism objectives to be a near term lens through which kinetic capacities are prioritized over a longer term and broader, defense sector transformation. The problem is that training and equipping assistance alone does not create the professional institutions, government accountability and oversight, and appropriate civil-military structures and relationships that will ensure that partners can transform their defense sectors to be able to absorb and institutionalize the capacity the US (and other international partners) are able to provide them to effectively combat terrorism.

Mali provided the most blatant evidence for this: for elite units to carry out specialized counterterrorism functions they primarily need to feel an allegiance to and be supported by their governments. That means getting paid, being properly educated and promoted, and having functioning institutions that properly outfit, train, and resource them. Without this, coups are more likely to be staged by these elite unites trained and equipped by the United States, as occurred in Mali in 2012. African militaries need both operationally and institutionally effective organizations supporting them to ensure battlefield success. The US threatens to create a potentially destabilizing situation where it is building the capacity of armed forces that are stronger than the civilian-led governing institutions that are supposed to have jurisdiction over them.

How Can the US Do Better?

While there is significant cause for concern, there are encouraging initiatives and programs whose positive progress may have the potential to re-orient our national security strategy. These include educational initiatives to increase the strategic awareness of African military leaders; security cooperation programs that seek to develop partner country ministries of defense; and the Security Governance Initiative (SGI), launched in 2014. These represent a significant effort to develop capacity in partner countries and to move the DoD away from its focus on tactical training. They also begin to build interagency principles into program design, so that they provide an avenue for more effective coordination across the range of civilian and military assets. At their current funding levels, however, they may potentially burn out as their miniscule budgets stand no chance against the much more highly funded, tactically-focused programs.

The DoD manages five regional centers of excellence, including the Africa Center for Strategic Studies (ACSS). The ACSS plays a very important role in advancing SSR development as its mandate is to engage with African partner nations, institutions, and security sector actors through targeted meetings, roundtables, and other events that focus on security sector transformation.[40] Through these programs, ACSS instills principles of security sector governance, shares best practices, and builds relationships between African and American leaders, and between African leaders. ACSS also has developed and sustained a vibrant alumni community to help cement the capacities developed during workshops and similar events. A comprehensive program of seminars, symposia, conferences, research, and other academic programs enable ACSS to maintain active communication and dialogue on a targeted and important range of pressing, strategic and operational issues.

The Office of Security Cooperation within the Office of the Secretary of Defense develops and oversees the DoD's ministerial capacity building programs and develops and implements coalition policy. In 2009, this office created a Ministry of Defense Advisor (MODA) program and the Defense

Institution Reform Initiative (DIRI) program. The MODA program has been designed to forge long-term relationships that strengthen a partner state's defense ministry, and involves civilian to civilian, high-level education and training. The program began in Afghanistan in 2009, and was expanded to other countries in 2013. MODA is essentially a form of embedded technical assistance to improve governance capabilities in the security sector. It does this by sending senior DoD civilians to work directly with foreign counterparts in similar defense specialties in their own countries for a period of up to two years. Ultimately, the MODA program helps partners build core competencies that support effective and accountable defense ministries. MODA is also interagency, as it works with the OSD office of personnel readiness, the United States Institute for Peace, and the Center for Complex Operations.[41]

The DIRI program was designed to help assess the needs of the defense sectors, and from that assessment to recommend a mix of various USG programs that together would take a comprehensive approach to defense sector development. The assumption was that this would simplify both the interagency coordination process and help partner countries navigate the complex terrain of US security cooperation programs. The ultimate goal is to create a coordinated and integrated set of programs that utilizes multiple tools in the USG communities to help partner countries develop accountable, professional, and transparent defense establishments. DIRI is explicitly focused on assessment tied to capacity building programs, to help countries develop the capacity to can manage, sustain, and employ their forces. The challenge is that DIRI's global FY15 budget request was only $12.184m,[42] a level of funding that does not give it adequate resources to be truly effective. Only five countries in Africa have been a part of the DIRI program to date: Botswana, the Democratic Republic of Congo, Guinea, Libya (on hold for security reasons), and Liberia.[43]

At the first-ever Africa Leadership Summit, which gathered 52 African heads of state in Washington, DC in early August 2014, President Obama launched an impressive new effort, the Security Governance Initiative (SGI). The SGI is a $65 million dollar "comprehensive approach to improving security sector governance and capacity to address threats" initially in six pilot countries: Ghana, Kenya, Mali, Niger, Nigeria, and Tunisia. SGI promisingly prioritizes its focus on the systems, processes, and institutions that reinforce democratic security sector governance, and if this works, will more effectively enhance African security than programs that focus solely at the tactical level. The stated goals of the program are very encouraging, including a focus on working to ensure governments can meet the human security needs of their citizenry, improving the effectiveness and sustainability of other US security sector assistance efforts, and re-affirming positive behavior and gains made by countries in the area of security sector governance.[44] This is the kind of program that matches security and governance efforts, so that both of these drivers of insecurity can be addressed.

Recommendations

A change in policy in needed. A more cohesive and balanced security sector reform approach is sorely needed if any real change in the current security environment is of interest. Significant and fundamental challenges remain that can begin to be addressed in the following concrete ways:

> *Prioritize security sector reform over security sector assistance.* The lack of an official US SSR policy and framework concretely affects the US security strategy, program formulation and cohesiveness, and success on the ground. The US needs to re-formulate its security strategy from a CTPF-centric approach to an SGI-type one. A second Presidential Policy Directive should be issued that supersedes PPD-23 and re-orients US security goals to be tied to concrete security sector reform priorities and away from building partner capacity.

> *Build up a conceptual understanding of security sector reform, training opportunities, and a SSR practitioner corps.* A very small percentage of the individuals responsible for programming and monitoring security and governance assistance have an understanding of greater SSR concepts and how their programs fit therein. The lack of a comprehensive US approach to SSR has resulted in the lack of prioritization of SSR training for staff in comparison to other types of programs. More practitioners through-out the interagency system need to receive basic training to better understand the development-security nexus, SSR concepts, and best practices to better impact US SSR work. The US interagency system continues to work in very isolated missions; reporting systems and programs need to be structured in a more interoperable manner.

> *Create interagency frameworks to manage security sector reform across the interagency similar to the TSCTP approach.* Lack of structure and engagement mechanisms will ensure that programs continue to exist based on their own departmental stove-piped priorities. By articulating and insisting on interagency coordination mechanisms, shared priorities, co-located teams, and parallel budget cycles,

whole of government programs will become more of a reality. An interagency team should be established that works on security sector reform for Africa. Technical experts from various agencies should be seconded to the office to ensure a balanced and holistic approach to US SSR strategy is achieved.

Grow federal capacity to manage current security sector reform programs. Insufficient manpower exists within State and USAID to appropriately manage and monitor security sector reform and assistance programs so that they are as effective as possible. If State and USAID do not receive necessary increases in such resources, the DoD will continue to be given more responsibility for these programs, and former Secretary of Defense Robert Gates' concept of a "militarization of foreign policy" will continue and grow. SSR is particularly problematic for the US because its civilian and military resources are greatly imbalanced, and the different federal departments involved deal with daily challenges of funding means and mechanisms, authorities, and inabilities to dedicate long-term resources.[45] Manpower and resources need to be devoted so that these agencies can begin building such important capabilities and a balanced approach to issues at the security-development nexus can be achieved.

Facilitate synergies between security sector reform policy and programmatic implementation. SSR concepts and theories are constructed at headquarters but actual programs are planned and implemented at the country team, field level. Oftentimes issues such as limited funding and short timelines hinder effective implementation. More flexible programming for US SSR activities is a must. SSR programs need to be tailored to specific conditions on the ground and thus require a broad toolbox of programs, flexible funding streams, and the ability to be responsive to local concerns. This flexibility is only possible through better dialogue and oversight between policy designers in Washington and implementers of SSR programs in the field. Continual communication and feedback are needed for programs to be as effective as possible as well as for lessons learned to be captured and reflected in future policies and programs.

Increase understanding of stability-focused monitoring and evaluation tools. Performance metrics are required to correctly design, monitor, review, and evaluate SSR programs. In addition to considering quantitative data, these metrics should take into account citizens' perceptions. US government officials need to develop and invest in SSR-tailored management tools such as the Metrics Framework for Assessing Conflict Transformation and Stabilization if they want to move from ad hoc, quantitatively focused initiatives that have limited impact to enduring SSR outcomes.

Elevate civil-military concepts to approved doctrine. Because stability operations and SSR fall within the security-development nexus, doctrine is lacking that bridges civilian and military expertise and skills and prioritizes different types of defense sector reform engagements. The priority for enhanced civil-military operations and relations among African partner nations should be elevated in AFRICOM/DoD policy documents. A comprehensive US approach to SSR that also incorporates such language will help to institutionalize this goal at the strategic level, operational level, and tactical level. Doctrine, implementation guidelines, and specific programming tools need to be articulated and clarified.

Conclusion

For many years, the DoD had little interest in security assistance activities, as they were regarded neither as a military mission nor as an activity of more than marginal value to ensuring national security. DoD perspectives on training foreign military forces slowly began to change after 9/11. Defense officials now regard the defeat of terrorist groups in the countries where they train and prepare as essential to US national security. Foremost among the new security challenges in Africa has been the decentralization and regionalization of terrorist organizations, particularly in the Sahel. This has necessitated a reexamination of what "security" entails. While the old colonial ties between Britain, France, and Africa naturally meant that these two countries would play a pivotal role in developing security and security governance systems in Africa, the post-1998, and especially the post-9/11 environment has made it necessary for the United States to be part of this important process.

While becoming an active international player in Africa, the US has faced a two-fold challenge. First, the United States lacks historical ties to many African countries. Second, the US government lacks clarity about what it means by SSR. While it would seem that the establishment of AFRICOM was a logical response to the complexity of the US security challenge in Africa, the evidence suggests that while the intention to respond to this challenge exists conceptually, the articulation and implementation of a proper approach has lagged far behind. It is clear that the US government's interagency TSCTP is an interagency holistic approach to Africa, from which many best practices can be gleaned. However, the program has been undermined by the imbalance in availability of resources among the three key players in this process: State, USAID, and the DoD. The suggestions contained in this chapter are geared to recommend a more comprehensive approach to security sector reform, which meets both American and African needs.

Therefore, a security sector reform approach that strives to institutionalize a professional security sector that is effective, legitimate, apolitical, and accountable to the citizens it is sworn to protect, should be the cornerstone of the US's approach.[46] Such an approach would prove much more effective for helping reduce the insecurities facing most African states and citizens. Creating strong militaries without corresponding civilian institutions makes military coups more likely, which both threatens state sovereignty and serves to exacerbate the individual level insecurities plaguing many African citizens. Embedding more capable security forces within a transparent government that can restrain them from excess and which will utilize the forces responsibly will help to improve the individual level insecurities that many Africans live with daily.

Notes

Note: All opinions and analysis in this chapter are my own, and do not reflect official positions of the State Department or the US government.

[1] These include al-Shabaab, al-Qaeda in the Islamic Maghreb (AQIM), Boko Haram, and Ansar Bayt Al-Maqdis (ABM).

[2] Fund for Peace, "2014 Failed States Index,"

[3] Kansteiner III, "Rising U.S. Stakes in Africa," 2.

[4] Rice, "Africa and the War on Global Terrorism."

[5] State Department Bureau of Counterterrorism, "Foreign Terrorist Organizations."

[6] GAO, *Combating Terrorism: U.S. Efforts in Northwest Africa,* 5, includes a map that depicts the operating areas of these groups, current as of June 2014.

[7] Yamamoto, "The Growing Crisis in Africa's Sahel Region."

[8] Gates, "Helping Others Defend Themselves," 2.

[9] TSCTP was created following the Pan-Sahel Initiative (2002), and the Trans-Sahara Counterterrorism Initiative (TSCTI) (2003-2004), which focused

on military training and equipment provision for Chad, Mali, Mauritania, and Niger from 2002–2004.

[10] Benjamin, "Examining U.S. Counterterrorism Priorities."

[11] LeSage, "The Evolving Threat of al Qaeda in the Islamic Maghreb," 1.

[12] US Department of Defense, "QDR Execution Roadmap," para. 1.3.1.

[13] IMET is a State Department program, permanently authorized by the Foreign Assistance Act of 1961 that "promotes regional stability and defense capabilities through professional military training and education." The FY15 global IMET budget is $112 million (State Department *FY2015 Congressional Budget Justification*, 182). CTFP is a Defense Department security cooperation program permanently authorized by the National Defense Authorization Act of 2004 (10 USC 2249c) that "allows DoD to provide foreign military officers and government security officials with strategic and operational education to enhance partners' capacity to combat terrorism." The FY15 CTFP budget estimate is $34 million (Defense Security Cooperation Agency, *FY15 Budget Estimate, 7.)*

[14] Foreign Assistance Act of 1961.

[15] A description of all these programs by year can be found on the website of the State Department, "U.S. Foreign Military Training Programs," www. state.gov/t/pm/rls/rpt/fmtrpt (verified March 15, 2015).

[16] In this chapter I examine sub-Saharan Africa amounts; the Maghreb receives significantly more assistance than does sub-Saharan Africa.

[17] US Department of State, "Foreign Military Financing Account Summary."

[18] US Department of State, *FY 2015 Congressional Budget Justification*: Appendix II.

[19] 1961 National Defense Authorization Act, ch. 6, s551, 188. Emphasis added.

[20] US Department of State, *FY 2015 Congressional Budget Justification*, 179-181, 208. GPOI funds are global; approximately 75% of them are allocated to support peacekeeping training in Africa.

[21] Burkina Faso, Cameroon, Chad, Mali, Mauritania, Niger, Nigeria, and Senegal. While Mali is a TSCTP partner nation, it recently came off coup sanctions and is not included in the above TSCTP totals as it is receiving separate bilateral funding.

[22] 10 U.S.C. § 101, et seq.

[23] US Department of State, *Foreign Military Training*.

[24] Section 1206 of the FY2006 National Defense Authorization Act (NDAA), P.L. 109-163.

[25] Epstein, et al., *State, Foreign Operations, and Related Programs*.

[26] The White House, *Budget of the US Government, Fiscal Year 15*, 163.

[27] Epstein, et al., *State, Foreign Operations, and Related Programs*, 2.

[28] The White House, *Budget of the US Government, Fiscal Year 15*, 163.

[29] US Department of State, *FY 2015 Congressional Budget Justification*: Appendix I.

[30] The State Department directly employs 13,000 foreign service officers and 11,000 civil service officers (http://careers.state.gov/learn/what-we-do/mission, accessed March 15, 2015). In 2010, USAID directly employed approximately 9,900 personnel, with an additional 400 – 900 hired in short-term or contracted positions (GAO, *Foreign Assistance*, 8). As of September 1, 2014, over 1.4 million men and women were on active duty in the US military and there were 718,000 DoD civilian personnel. Another 1.1 million served in the National Guard and Reserve forces (US Department of Defense, "About the Department of Defense").

[31] US Africa Command, "About the Command" (2014). This staffing level includes military, US federal civilian employees, and US contractor employees.

[32] US Department of Defense, *DoD Decision Directive 1404.14*.

[33] National Defense Authorization Act for Fiscal Year 2006 (Public Law 109-163, STAT. 3457).

[34] Gates, "U.S. Global Leadership Campaign."

[35] Serafino, *Global Security Contingency Fund*, 11.

[36] See also Serafino (2014), *Security Assistance Reform*.

[37] I was part of the US Interagency Assessment to Mali (November 2013), where the EU Training Mission (EUTM) had a plan to add six new Malian Battalions to counter the threat in the north. When the team met with the Ministry of Finance, the senior Malian budget analyst was not aware of these plans, and there were no provisions in future budget years to account for these forces.

[38] Ball et al., *Security and Justice Sector Reform Programming in Africa*, 59.

[39] Yamamoto, "The Growing Crisis in Africa's Sahel Region."

[40] McFate, *Securing the Future*, 2.

[41] For additional information, see www.defense.gov/home/features/2011/0211_moda (accessed March 15, 2015).

[42] U.S. Department of Defense, *Fiscal Year 2015 Budget Estimates*, 17.

[43] U.S. Department of Defense, *Defense Institution Reform Initiative Factsheet*.

[44] The White House, "Factsheet: Security Governance Initiative."

[45] Andrews and Kirk, *Integrating 21ˢᵗ Century Development and Security Assistance*.

[46] The Organization for Economic Cooperation and Development (OECD), *Security System Reform and Governance*.

6

Civil-Military Operations in East Africa: Coordinated Approaches

Maureen Farrell and Jessica Lee

One of the ways in which the US military attempts to use development to promote security is through civil-military operations (CMO). These efforts bring uniformed personnel into close contact with civilian populations to advance larger strategic objectives such as shaping a country's strategic environment, promoting stability and development, building local capacity, and ultimately enabling countries to begin to recover from conflict. In East Africa, empirical research shows that CMO can be an enabling tool to further US government objectives when they are distinctly military in purpose and coordinated extensively with other American projects. This chapter seeks to elucidate how CMO are employed in East Africa, drawing on case studies from civil affairs teams in Kenya and Tanzania. The results show that CMO grounded in the military's strengths and well-coordinated with US Embassy colleagues resulted in advancements for broader US government aims.

According to the US Department of Defense's (DoD) Joint Publication on CMO, JP3-57, "civil-military operations (CMO) are a primary military instrument to synchronize military and nonmilitary instruments of national power, particularly in support of stability, counterinsurgency and other operations dealing with 'asymmetric' and 'irregular' threats."[1] In East Africa, the Combined Joint Task Force-Horn of Africa (CJTF-HOA) designs and implements CMO programs in an effort promote regional stability and to promote US security objectives in East Africa.

The CJTF-HOA maintains a command and control element at the headquarters in Djibouti, (at Camp Lemonier) while most projects are carried out by groups of military members located within the various countries. These smaller groups are most often composed of Civil Affairs Teams and/or Seabee detachments (Naval engineers), based in outlying areas. Each group is authorized to conduct projects in a specific area of the country, and the teams vary in size from almost 80 people in Lamu, Kenya, to independent Civil Affairs Teams of 5 to 8 people living in hotels or rented apartments in Uganda.

Most of the civil affairs and humanitarian assistance projects undertaken by the CJTF-HOA are funded through the humanitarian and civic assistance programs that were reviewed in chapter three of this volume. The CJTF-HOA draws primarily on three of these funding streams for major project: the Humanitarian Assistance Other (HAO), Humanitarian and Civic Assistance (HCA), and Overseas Humanitarian Disaster and Civic Assistance (OHDACA) programs. All these projects are carried out by the Civil Affairs Teams attached to the CJTF-HOA, the Seabees at the camp, or through local and international contractors. In late 2008, the newly-established Maritime Civil Affairs Groups began to operate alongside the US Army civil affairs soldiers.

Military doctrine defines CMO as:

> The activities of a commander that establish, maintain, influence, or exploit relations between military forces, governmental and nongovernmental civilian organizations and authorities, and the civilian populace in a friendly, neutral, or hostile operational area in order to facilitate military operations, to consolidate and achieve operational US objectives. Civil-military operations may include performance by military forces of activities and functions normally the responsibility of the local, regional, or national government. These activities may occur prior to, during, or subsequent to other military actions.[2]

Through these humanitarian assistance programs, the DoD hopes to utilize military assets to shape a country's strategic environment, to help avert political and humanitarian crises, to promote democratic development and regional stability, to build local capacity, and to enable countries to begin to recover from conflicts. All CMO projects must address some or all of these goals, and there are strict limits on the types of projects that could be undertaken, who should execute them, and the objectives (most often, security focused). For example, the HCA program is first and foremost designed to train US military members through the practical exercise of humanitarian assistance provision; the secondary focus is to strengthen local communities through these programs.

In a classic counterinsurgency strategy, the camp also uses civic assistance projects to promote development and goodwill as a way to combat terrorism. CJTF-HOA activities are conducted on a project-basis within each country, and regardless of their funding source, all the humanitarian and civic assistance projects fall within three broad categories: water, schools, and health clinics. There are also civic action projects to deliver medical, dental, or veterinary care in short-duration events, and increasingly, projects in theater security cooperation or military-military assistance and engagements. They fall within the ambit of CMO, and as such are one tool in a range of methods to combat terrorism and strengthen local societies.

Unofficially, these projects are supposed to provide access for the US military should they need to engage in more aggressive activities in the region, and to open up areas for US influence more broadly. CJTF-HOA itself does not expect its actions alone to create these ends, but it generally sees itself as contributing to an overall US government effort.

As several authors in this volume have pointed out, at AFRICOM's creation defense was broadly construed in human security terms. Further, as Shannon Beebe has argued, it is critically important to frame security in Africa *in particular* within a human security paradigm. The most fundamental security issues in Africa are non-kinetic, and their effects are often realized on a local or personal level.[3] The DoD's role in building "security to lay the framework for long term development"—which it does through human security projects like school rehabilitations, well digging, clinic construction, and other CMO—reflects a broader understanding within the military about the importance of human security elements to US national security.

To the outsider, the HCA projects of the Civil Affairs Teams seem to be developmentally focused because of their involvement in the communities and their goals to "strengthen" local societies. It is exactly this aspect of the projects that sparked a debate about the appropriateness and effectiveness of military actors engaging in them. To the military, these projects can be included in a counter-insurgency strategy or be used to help stabilize an area and reduce insecurity.

Framing the Research

In light of the debates about the effectiveness of CMO in achieving the US government development and security objectives globally, we conducted a series of field studies in 2010 to explore the community-level effects of civil affairs projects in Kenya and Tanzania.[4] Why study CMO in East Africa? First, East Africa proved to be the region of Africa that has most directly presented the US with direct security threats. Initially embodied in the bombings of US embassies in Kenya and Tanzania in 1998, this security challenge was enlarged by the growth of Al Shabaab and other terrorist groups in the region over the past two decades. The 2011 *National Strategy for Counterterrorism* lists East Africa as one of the United States' priority areas.[5] Second, this region is also extremely vulnerable to domestic crises, and many African countries and citizens face deep insecurities in the region.

Third, US security programs in the region have experimented with a range of interagency approaches and developmental approaches to enhancing security. First born as the East Africa Regional Strategic Initiative, the now-named Partnership for Regional East Africa Counter-terrorism (PREACT) is the US government's interagency response to addressing the terrorism threat in East and the Horn of Africa. The guiding strategy for PREACT, written by the Department of State (DoS) Bureau of African Affairs, harnesses the strengths of and scopes the counterterrorism capacity building activities for the Departments of Defense, Justice, Homeland Security, and Treasury, as well as USAID, in in East Africa. PREACT is the East African parallel to the Trans-Sahara Counter Terrorism Partnership in the west. Through PREACT, the US government promotes and operationalizes a coordinated approach to its counterterrorism training, equipping, mentoring, and engagements in the region. The CJTF-HOA operates separately from the PREACT framework, but its activities contribute to the overall PREACT goals.

During the time of our study, CMO in East Africa included, but were not limited to, what we refer to as human security projects, such as well digging, school and clinic refurbishment, and community engagement with schools.[6] External observers have attributed development outcomes to these types of CMO such as improved access to clean water, sustainable advancements in education, and improved health care. Rather than these developmental outcomes, however, the stated objectives of CJTF-HOA and those implementing CMO have focused on security-focused goals: facilitating improved relationships between local military forces and their host communities, and providing services in areas where other US government agencies could not due to insecurity.

The immediate results of our research provided lessons learned and recommendations to those who plan, train, evaluate, design messages for, and conduct CMO. More broadly, though, we drew the conclusion that CMO were most effective in achieving their security-focused goals in the East African context when carried out in cooperation and close coordination with other US government agencies and with local counterparts. Absent US government interagency cooperation and close cooperation with key stakeholders on the ground, the CMO studied in this analysis generated vague outcomes.

This analysis is grounded in nine months of field research, beginning in February and concluding in August 2010, in North Eastern (Garissa) and Rift Valley Provinces in Kenya, as well as coastal Tanzania (Tanga).[7] We offer this analysis of the community-level effects of CMO in East Africa to contribute evidence-based research to the larger dialogue in academic and policy circles about the "militarization of development," as well as to the debates about the relative utility and impact of CMO.[8] The CMO community personnel are continually adapting their approaches based on leadership directives and the dynamic environments in which they work, and research such as this contributes to the refinement of these strategies.

Policy Guidance on Interagency Coordination

This research is framed within existing bodies of literature on several topics, including policy guidance on interagency coordination; an exploration of the diplomacy, development, and defense (or "3D") concept; and analyses of human security projects in East Africa supported by the US military. Advancing US foreign policy through interagency and nongovernmental collaboration is a topic of growing importance in policy circles and inside the development community.[9] The Presidential Policy Directive (PPD) on Security Sector Assistance, PPD 23, seeks to foster US government policy coherence and interagency collaboration, on the logic that

> transparency and coordination across the United States Government are needed to integrate security sector assistance into broader strat-egies, synchronize agency efforts, reduce redundancies, minimize assistance-delivery timelines, ensure considerations of the full range of policy and operational equities, improve data collection, measure effectiveness, enhance and sustain the United States Government's security sector assistance knowledge and skills, and identify gaps.[10]

Thus, there has been strong political momentum behind US government interagency coordination, which is also highly encouraged among the leaderships of US Embassies in East Africa and CJTF-HOA.

Similarly, there is and has been resounding support for the idea that US national security and general foreign policy objectives are best pursued through interagency approaches, as discussed in a prominent 2007 *Foreign Affairs* article written by three former US Agency for International Development (USAID) administrators.[11] In acknowledgment of this, the nongovernmental organization (NGO) InterAction, an umbrella organization representing dozens of smaller NGOs, signed a seminal memorandum of understanding with the DoD in July 2007 outlining the roles and expectations for civil-military cooperation, which has framed CMO for many years.[12]

Acceptance of the importance of interagency cooperation does not automatically translate into smooth coordination and effective programs, however. As articulated by the former Commander of US Army Africa, Major General William Garrett, "Perhaps the greatest challenge to creating positive conditions in Africa is synchronizing US defense efforts with diplomatic and development efforts."[13] In many cases, synchronization problems are rooted in differences in institutional cultures. The diplomatic and development communities have distinct cultures; but among disparate US government agencies and organizations, the DoD has a particularly unique way of analyzing problems, making decisions, and communicating.

Such differences in institutional cultures manifest in many ways, ranging from the simple use of language (e.g., "schedule" versus "battle rhythm"), to the application of complex problem solving strategies. Interviews carried out over the course of this research clearly revealed some of these dissimilarities between the ways agencies behave, analyze, interact, and communicate. These differences are particularly evident in interagency relationships. Former Secretary of State Hillary Clinton described the 3Ds - diplomacy, development, and defense - as the "three pillars of American Foreign Policy."[14] The third "D" in the 3D approach to US government policy, the DoD plays an important role but one that is clearly secondary to DoS as the lead agency, and in most cases, tertiary to USAID on the African continent.

The US Military's Work in East Africa and the Horn of Africa

The CJTF-HOA operates under a mission statement that emphasizes partnership and interagency cooperation. Military-to-military training in Africa is not carried out in a vacuum, independent of other US government efforts, but in concert with them. As the CJTF-HOA describes its mission,

> The Combined Joint Task Force – Horn of Africa, in partnership with our joint, interagency, intergovernmental, and multinational teammates, conducts theater security cooperation activities to enable regional actors to neutralize violent extremist organizations and enables regional access and freedom of movement within East Africa in order to protect and defend United States interests. [To] plan, prepare, and on order execute crisis response within East Africa in order to protect and defend United States military, diplomatic, and civilian personnel, facilities, and interests.[15]

This focus is in line with Major General Garrett, who recommend "an enterprise approach" to improving capacity building on the continent. Together with other senior Army officers, Garret has advocated multi-sectoral efforts directed toward security sector strengthening "tied to political benchmarks."[16]

Thus, while military-to-military training may seems like an area for exclusive DoD involvement, we argue that the military's success in implementing CMO is contingent on its linkages to other arms of the US government, most prominently the DoS and the policy-making bodies of the government. Specifically, CMO require close coordination with all of the 3D partners and NGOs. Consequently, CMO receive a great amount of attention from other government agencies and external observers of the military, making analyses of their effects that much more important.[17]

Case Studies: Assessing the Sociocultural Effects

The following case studies offer a foundation upon which to analyze how CMO affect development and security in East Africa, particularly illuminating issues related to collaboration across US government agencies.

Tanga, Tanzania

We carried out a series of semi-structured group interviews with 84 community members in Tanga to gain a better understanding of the development and security effects of CMO at the local level. We explored issues such as: (1) how CMO have influenced Tanga residents' views of the US government; (2) how CMO projects and activities are received by locals; and (3) what the Maritime Civil Affairs Team (MCAT) could do differently to better support US Embassy Country team and CJTF-HOA goals for Tanzania.[18]

Field observation and interview data confirmed that the MCAT only maintained relationships with select leaders in the community, thereby limiting their access to the people of Tanga. Correspondingly, interviews revealed that few people outside of formal leadership structures were aware that the US military (or US government generally) supported certain projects. For instance, interview participants frequently attributed the well digging and school refurbishment projects to other donor nations, such as Japan or Sweden. Part of the challenge for the MCAT members in this context was that a US Embassy policy prohibited them from wearing their US Navy uniforms in Tanga; the uniform could have been a branding tool that might have enhanced the visibility of the projects their team sponsored.

At the conclusion of our research, we were left with questions about the intended outcomes of CMO in Tanga, as the cumulative community-level effects of successive CMO initiatives on development and security were fuzzy. Field research findings indicated that the MCAT operated in isolation of other USAID projects in and around Tanga. Moreover, the MCAT's projects were disconnected to the larger objectives that the US Embassy hoped to advance in the region, which focused on infrastructure development and trade enhancements between this region of Tanzania and neighboring Kenya's key port of Mombasa. Questions about the intended outcomes of CMO became clearer in future studies, where the military's efforts were more closely synchronized with interagency partners.

Garissa, Kenya

For the second case study, a mixed civilian and military research team led by one of the authors, composed of civil affairs (CA) soldiers from CJTF-HOA and elements from the Kenya Army, conducted joint technical and qualitative assessments of well projects completed between 2006 and 2008 through a joint effort of US Navy Seabees and the Kenya Army's Engineering Battalion in North Eastern Province. Based on interviews with 139 participants in seven villages in Garissa and Lagdera Districts, the assessment team gathered information about the function of each well (i.e., was it producing water, and was the equipment technically sound), and uncovered a wealth of material regarding local views on the process the joint US and Kenyan military teams pursued in digging the wells.

In visiting a diversity of locations - including attempted wells where there was no water in the ground, wells that produced clean drinking water, wells that produced non-potable water, wells that had run dry, and wells that were not functioning - the assessment team learned a great deal about the effects of these joint US and Kenyan CMO projects on water security locally, as well as local populations' views toward military forces.[19] Given that only two of the well sites visited in all seven villages produced clean drinking water and that many others were not functioning or were producing non-potable water, water security was not greatly enhanced by this two-year engineering effort in Garissa. However, in terms of enhancing relationships between US and Kenyan forces, as well as between the local population and the Kenya Army, these well projects generated tangible and important outcomes.

Specifically, the research revealed that there were several aspects of this series of well projects that should be replicated, most prominently the successful coordination - in this case with Kenyan Defense Forces, District Water Commissioners, and local stakeholders on digging sites. At all research sites, community members confirmed that the joint team of engineers coordinated closely with the Kenyan District Water Commissioners on the drill location sites, allowing little room for disputes over where to apply the engineering capabilities in each village. Additionally, while the research population previously had little interaction with the US military, interview participants in Delolo village, for example, reported that the presence of the Kenyan military allowed the villagers to trust the US service members.

Thus, the intended outcome of providing greater water security (which some might define as a development objective) to Garissa and Lagdera Districts was not achieved given the small number of well sites producing potable water. However, the research demonstrated that this series of well projects produced a broader security outcome of building an important partnership between US and Kenyan engineers, and in building a foundation of trust between the local populace and US forces operating in a key area close to the Kenya-Somalia border.[20]

Rift Valley Province, Kenya

Much like in Garissa, coordination was a key component for CA teams supporting school reconstruction in the Rift Valley, focused on the town of Eldoret. In the aftermath of Kenya's December 2007 to January 2008 post-election violence, this area faced significant trauma and instability. The CA team's school rehabilitation projects from 2008-2010 in Kenya's Rift Valley Province illustrate the application of CMO in an environment where people had concerns for their personal security and a lack of confidence in their government to adequately respond to the crisis.

Based on 71 interviews with 135 participants looking at 14 schools in the Rift Valley, we identified two key findings related to the central theme of coordination. First, in addition to working closely with DoS in identifying the projects, CA teams coordinated with the local government, NGOs, international organizations, and civic groups working in the area. Second, local community members welcomed the US military's support for school rehabilitation and found the CA team members to be a trusted presence in the community, particularly at a time when USAID implementing partners and other donors could not operate in the Rift Valley due to security concerns. In this case, CA teams provided a unique service and assisted in the restoration of security. They were universally recognized as providing significant contributions in a sensitive situation.

CMO Contributions to Development and Security in East Africa

Overall, we found that military engagements, particularly CMO, can have positive outcomes both for security and development, but only when undertaken in close concert with civilian agencies like State and USAID and with local counterparts. Without interagency cooperation, the outcomes of these programs for improving security were vague at best. The level of interagency cooperation for US government programming in East Africa varied by country, and coordination efforts between the DoD, DoS, and USAID were heavily dependent on more ephemeral issues like the personalities managing these relationships. This is an area in which more robust mandates from CJTF-HOA leadership that streamline and make more uniform the ways that civil affairs teams operate, and which require interagency collaboration, could improve outcomes.

Such requirements were put in place once AFRICOM assumed full control over the CJTF-HOA, in late 2008. Before then, coordination was ad-hoc and personality-dependent. For example, CA teams work under Chief of Mission authority in every country where they operate in East Africa. That is, their activities are conducted under the purview of the US ambassador and with the concurrence of interagency partners from the DoS and USAID who are members of the US government Country team.[21] This means that, by the rules, CA teams only work with the permission of the ambassador. In some cases, the relationship between the DoD and its partners is mutually reinforcing, advancing both the military's and the ambassador's objectives. In other cases, the relationship can be quite tense, with turf battles and seemingly never ending discussions about roles and responsibilities. Ambassadors could also put in place coordination require-ments, which, while effective, would not solve the lack of a uniformly cooperative engagement strategy.

The examples of interagency coordination demonstrated in Tanga, Garissa, and the Rift Valley illustrate that CMO are most effective in advancing their security-focused objectives when the military works with DoS and USAID as partners—that is, when the military is viewed as a "force multiplier" in carrying out US policy, rather than the military driving the engagement. The reasons that this was not the standard procedure in our cases has do to with civilian capacity. The attendant shortfalls in interagency coordination decreased the effectiveness of the CMO in reaching either US or African security objectives: they led to problems with strategic communications efforts, missed opportunities for synergy with other US government programs, and difficulty identifying key local populations with which to partner on CMO.

Documented problems with military-supported projects and purported mistakes in the realm of CMO in East Africa and the Horn of Africa might have served as a motivating factor for Country teams to attempt to minimize the possible negative effects of CMO projects and engagements.[22] Some of these issues included the selection of CMO project sites with inadequate coordination across US government agencies, a lack of attention to the sustainability and long-term local ownership of military-supported activities, and a general pattern of insufficient cultural awareness for East Africa. We saw evidence of this, to varying degrees, in both Kenya and Tanzania, where the embassy Country teams restrained CMO by restricting the geographic areas where they operated and the kinds of projects they undertook. Framing interactions in a manner that seeks to limit the effect of CMO—rather than capitalize on the military's strengths—wastes resources, however. When Country teams limited the military's contribution, they set a negative tone for the cultivation of cross-agency relationships instead of welcoming the military and their associated projects as implementation tools in a coordinated US government strategy.

In Kenya, for example, the Embassy State and USAID staff placed great attention on defining and policing strict "lanes" for the activities of each US government agency. They placed much less emphasis on collaboration across the multiple agencies working in the country. While this did achieve the desired effect of making all aware of the others' programs, it did not mean that the spirit was collaborative. Military actors would propose or nominate projects before a meeting of Country team representatives to gain the approval of DoS and USAID colleagues, not to seek their input and collaboration in program design. This was underscored by the nature of the dialog; the responses of other agency partners to these requests were framed in a manner to keep the military in its "lane" and mitigate the potential risk factor of a US military mistake.

Complementing the Other Ds

When the CMO were employed in support of and in coordination with other embassy programs, they had better results and delivered more concrete and observable improvements for African populations and US foreign policy objectives. Based on field research and interviews, we observed a mutually reinforcing working relationship between the US government Country team in Tanzania and the MCAT's work on the island of Pemba. In this case, all parties in the 3D relationship worked to capitalize on the strengths of each respective agency in order to best advance US foreign policy goals. For example, in 2010, CMO on Pemba were strategically selected with the close coordination of the Country team in order to complement other US government-funded efforts on the island. Specifically, we witnessed open dialogue about how and where to apply the military's resources so that CMO could expand the effect of a US Embassy initiative or another USAID project. Collaboration between interagency partners of this nature, multiplying the impact of the US government efforts in Tanzania, is somewhat unique and seems to be a productive application of the military's resources.

IS CMO the Right Tool?

Questions emerge in such settings about the military purpose behind CMO projects. One might also ask how an incinerator fits in the larger US government policy led by the US Embassy. Oftentimes, there is a security-based reason for the military to initiate such projects, but the military purpose for pursuing them may be secondary to other US government reasons. As an illustration, in Kenya's Rift Valley, the US ambassador requested the assistance of CA teams in reconstructing schools as part of the US government's efforts to mitigate violence in the aftermath of the 2007-2008 post-election clashes. There were varied discussions among the 3D partners about whether the use of a CA team was the right fit for this project. Ultimately, CJTF-HOA's decision to dedicate resources to meet this request drew criticism from other partners in the interagency process, who questioned why the military should build schools, projects that seem at first glance more appropriate for the development community to undertake.

However, in this case, we found that the presence of a CA team sent an important message about the US government's interest in ensuring a quick return to stability and security in an area that had experienced severe trauma with the post-election violence. It was also where Kenya needed the most help at the time, which would not only send a signal, but would deliver a concrete result that corresponded with a direct need of the Kenyans. Along these lines, it could also be postulated that having representatives of the US Army in the region, working alongside the Kenya Army also promoted security during a time when tensions were still high (even though the US servicepeople were unarmed and not there in a security enforcement role). The US military's involvement in human security projects like school rehabilitation, well digging, and clinic construction can easily be criticized for looking like "development projects" that should fall under the purview of USAID and development organizations. As the case studies evaluated for this chapter reveal, the reality is in fact much more nuanced, necessitating closer coordination efforts between multiple US government agencies.

Sub-Saharan Africans are familiar with international development and aid activities. Nonmilitary groups and organizations with extensive experience with these kinds of interventions have a greater portion of their funds designated for project implementation, and are often more active and more visible in the community than the military. So when a small CMO project - incinerator construction - remained incomplete after several years in Kenya, certain frustrations no doubt emerged in the host community over the slow pace of progress. In this particular example of the incinerator construction, the military's project had become hamstrung in local politics and patronage networks. Not having had extensive experience working in this specific community, the military was unfamiliar with approaches to streamline negotiations with local partners for the construction and repairs in a timely fashion. Had military personnel reached out to the USAID implementing partner working in that same area for targeted advice on this subject, they might have received advice on how to successfully navigate business relationships in the community.

Other examples in Kenya and Tanzania include wells that do not produce water or only produce undrinkable water; or cases where a building (a school or clinic) was constructed with US military support, but the host nation's government failed in its commitment to furnish the structure with staff or equipment. Therefore, when the relationship between the military and its counterparts at DoS and USAID is uncoordinated, CMO is less likely to lead to substantive outcomes like enhancing relationships between uniformed personnel and their civilian hosts.

Notably, the relationships between the military and other US government agencies in Kenya have evolved in new directions, particularly since 2010. CJTF-HOA created the position of Unified Action Advisor in February 2010, a senior civilian post, to coordinate the interagency relationships. Additionally, later that year, the deputy chief of mission (DCM) in Nairobi assumed greater leadership in guiding the relationship between the US Embassy and the military. As chair of the monthly 3D coordination meetings at the US Embassy, the DCM articulated his hope to capitalize on the resources and capacities of the different US government agencies, including not only the 3Ds, but also the Department of Agriculture, Center for Disease Control, Peace Corps, and others. In the same vein, the staff at CJTF-HOA attempted to reiterate the specifics of the distinctly military purpose of CMO—thereby distinguishing CMO projects from development interventions—and deliberately identified and shared with interagency partners where and how their capabilities nested within the US Embassy's broader bilateral policy objectives. These efforts have introduced different and more collaborative working dynamics into the 3D process in Nairobi.[23]

CMO have had a long history in East Africa, and one can find a broad range of examples in terms of their effectiveness in advancing shared US government development and security goals. As illuminated through these case studies, a critical point in the success or failure of CMO hinges on the coordination between the 3Ds. Project problems can sometimes come about through no fault of any US government agency. In the end, people on the receiving end of a project that has been delayed, poorly executed, or not completed due to a lack of follow-through by other partners often perceive a generalized failure to deliver on behalf of the US government. This perception becomes a shared problem across the US government, as in the case of Tanga, where villagers blamed "the Americans" for certain problems with projects, not specifically pinpointing the work of the military's CMO. Thus, there will always be hurdles to overcome regarding inter-agency coordination efforts, particularly related to the history of CMO in East Africa, as our research shows.[24]

Conclusion

These research findings are meant to inform members of the interagency community, as well as military decision makers, planners, evaluators, trainers, and implementers, and scholars who think and write about US military activities in Africa. This work is also intended to contribute to the broader community of knowledge about CMO in East Africa and the Horn of Africa, the evaluation of associated projects and engagements, and the sociocultural contributions of such CMO to the implementation of the US government's foreign policy. Fundamentally, we argue not only that coordinated programming across the US government will contribute to greater effectiveness, but also that this coordination should not be ad hoc. Interagency coordination is a work in progress. Relations between the various US agencies working in a given country are dynamic, shaped by the personalities occupying certain positions and the legacy of previous activities and programming initiatives. If not put within a structured framework, personalities and personal relationships will determine the quality and direction of these interactions, and that could undermine their effectiveness.

There are multiple examples where several US government agencies working in a given area have developed complementary program initiatives, but it is also not difficult to cite illustrations of a lack of coordination with unsatisfactory outcomes. For example, in the Rift Valley the close coordination between the military and DoS with multiple stakeholders (including NGOs, local leadership, and religious organizations) facilitated a more holistic response to the trauma of post-election violence, and interagency collaboration helped to steer the application of US military capabilities within defined security and stability parameters. In other settings, where there were limited communications and coordination between CA teams and USAID, such as in the previously cited example of the wells in Tanga, projects did not meet their maximum potential.[25]

The US military has strengths in many areas and can serve as a valuable tool in the promotion of US government foreign policy goals. The temptation remains for interagency partners to limit the reach of military elements in order to mitigate possibly negative effects of their activities. Such an approach is inefficient, though, and current political thinking is clearly leaning in the direction of closer collaboration across government agencies. A more productive approach is for 3D partners to seek areas for the application of military capabilities, rather than restricting their activities, in order to utilize the military as a tool to expand the reach of US government foreign policy implementation. Thus, collaboration among agencies is critical and remains an important area where sizable personnel resources are merited.

Our conclusions are limited to the data from case studies in Tanga, Garissa, and the Rift Valley. There is a paucity of data on related issues since the collection of these data. However, issues illuminated through this research can have implications for the implementation of CMO elsewhere in sub-Saharan Africa. The resulting data from these case studies clearly illustrate that diverse local environments and political particularities specific to the respective US government agency objectives reveal a complex picture. Interagency coordination, while complicated and possibly laborious to execute, is critical in ensuring that US government resources as a whole are most effectively applied in pursuit of foreign policy goals. The military can be an important partner in advancing these goals through activities that are distinctly military in purpose and planned in a collaborative fashion with other US government agencies.

Call for Further Research

Additional research is required to develop more nuanced understandings of some of the complexities related to assessing the impact of CMO and how they contribute to security and development. Currently there are no long-term studies of CMO in East Africa. Without periodic rigorous studies, one cannot make claims about the impact of CMO in specific locations. In light of such knowledge gaps, we call for further study, and for collaboration between the military and sociocultural experts to carry out such research. Resulting analyses can provide important insights into larger questions about CMO on issues pertaining to: the effectiveness of 3D coordination, qualitative assessments, CMO planning, and the contribution of the US military to the promotion of US security and development objectives in the region. Through longitudinal coordinated research efforts, sociocultural information can add substantial value in assessing the long-term effects of CMO. In the initial planning stages, understanding the cultural landscape helps everyone to work smarter and more effectively in advancing a coordinated government approach.

Notes

Note: The views expressed in this chapter are our own and do not represent official positions of the United States government. Jessica Piombo contributed to the introductory section of the chapter.

[1] Chairman Joint Chiefs of Staff, *Civil-Military Operations*, viil.

[2] Ibid, GL-6.

[3] Beebe, "Solutions Not Yet Sought."

[4] At the time, the authors were civilian researchers contracted by AFRICOM and worked as a Sociocultural Analysis Team.

[5] The White House, "U.S. National Strategy for Counterterrorism," 14.

[6] See section "The U.S. Military's Work in East Africa and the Horn of Africa" for further discussion of human security.

[7] Detailed descriptions of the qualitative research methods can been found in the individual reports associated with each project. All findings were submitted to AFRICOM and CJTF-HOA in the form of assessment reports.

[8] For a sample of the discussion see Bradbury and Kleinman, *Winning Hearts and Minds?*; Piombo, "Civil-Military Relations in the Horn of Africa;" House Committee on Oversight, *AFRICOM's Rationales, Roles and Progress*; and Keenan, "U.S. Militarization in Africa."

[9] Gates, Landon Lecture; Pincus, "Pentagon Recommends."

[10] The White House, "Fact Sheet: U.S. Security Sector Assistance Policy."

[11] Atwood, et. al., "Arrested Development."

[12] U.S. Institute of Peace, *Guidelines for Relations*.

[13] Garrett, et. al., "Forward in Africa," 25.

[14] Clinton, "Remarks with Reporters."

[15] Combined Joint Task Force-Horn of Africa, www.hoa.africom.mil/about-the-command (accessed July 20, 2014).

[16] Garrett, et al., "Forward in Africa," 25.

[17] See Bradbury and Kleinman, *Winning Hearts and Minds?* and GAO, DoD Needs to Determine the Future.

[18] The Tanga research was conducted in an area where projects had been jointly conducted by CJTF-HOA's CJ34, the functional specialty group, and civil affairs (CA) teams. Both U.S. Army CA teams and U.S. Navy Maritime Civil Affairs Teams (MCATs) have operated in Tanga on behalf of CJTF-HOA. This research focused on the cumulative efforts of all civil-military efforts, not singling out either U.S. Army or Navy initiatives. Consequently, all references in this chapter to CA henceforth are not specific to either the army or navy.

[19] The technical assessment revealed that a large number of the engineers' attempts between 2006 and 2008 to strike water were unsuccessful, resulting in no wells. The assessment team uncovered that the Kenyan district water commissioners had directed the military engineers to areas where they previously had difficulty striking water, assuming that military technology was superior to that of the local government.

[20] Notably, the resulting report from this study highlighted several features which might be adjusted for future well drilling initiatives in Kenya's North Eastern Province. These included: finding ways to invite the local population into the construction processes, despite security issues and the technical nature of the work; casting an information net much more broadly in the community to explain what the Americans were doing with the Kenya Army with these well projects; encouraging a greater focus on community relations; and considering implementing a fee structure for physical projects to support future maintenance needs.

[21] A Country team is an interagency working group chaired by a senior DoS official. Country teams in East Africa generally hold monthly coordination meetings at US embassies.

[22] See Bradbury and Kleinman, *Winning Hearts and Minds?* and Government Accountability Office, *DoD Needs to Determine the Future.*

[23] This is not to say that interagency processes in Kenya work seamlessly or without the extraordinary efforts of individuals in all agencies to collaborate across disparate institutional operating preferences and patterns.

[24] See Lee and Farrell, "A Study of U.S. Civil Affairs in East Africa."

[25] The authors are unable to comment on the relationship between CA teams (both U.S. Army and Navy) and USAID in Tanzania both prior to and following the conclusion of fieldwork. However, during the research period in February 2010, there was limited communication between the MCAT and USAID officials in Dar es Salaam.

7

Maritime Security: The Africa Partnership Station in Ghana

Alison Rimsky Vernon and Margaux Hoar

Many, if not all, coastal African nations face a number of maritime security threats, including oil insecurity, piracy, the threat of environmental disasters, trafficking, and illegal fishing, yet until recently, few countries have paid attention to these threats and made efforts to address them. Around the same time African regimes began to take an interest in their maritime security, the US Navy launched the Africa Partnership Station (APS). APS is a strategic initiative aimed at enhancing maritime safety and security through building partner capacity, conducted along the east and west coasts of Africa. The overarching objective of APS is to enhance maritime security in these regions by helping partner nations increase their capacities and capabilities to secure their own territorial waters. In this chapter, we explore the US Navy's APS activities and their impact on African maritime security concerns for the time period between 2007 and 2010.[1] APS activities have continued since that time, and at the end of the chapter we briefly address how our findings apply to more recent APS deployments.[2]

Following APS deployments in 2007/2008, and 2009, we sought to understand what impact APS had had in the countries it visited, specifically whether APS activities had had an effect on maritime security. The research involved interviews with African, US, and European participants in APS; African military and government leaders; and recipients of APS humanitarian and community activities. We also examined formal documentation on APS activities, media reports, and indications of behavioral changes in the countries APS visited.

Overall, we found mixed results regarding improvements in maritime security. There seemed to be few sustained improvements in capacity and skills of the included navies and sailors. APS *was* successful in increasing collaboration and communication between US and partner nation forces *and* among the African nation forces themselves—and we found that this collaboration and coordination could help mitigate some of the hindrances to APS's strategic success. When we interviewed sailors from the nations with which APS had operated, nearly all of the respondents expressed their gratitude for the invaluable training they received from American and European trainers. When asked if they had used their newly acquired skills, however, most responded that they had not. Moreover, our own analysis has indicated that most of the partner nations had not subsequently conducted operations or activities aimed at increasing maritime security. In other words, the activities performed by the US military in APS missions between 2007 and 2009 were successful at winning the hearts and minds of African maritime forces and training them in new skills, but the missions did not reach their strategic goals of increasing the active engagement of African maritime forces in securing their littoral domains.

In this chapter, we examine why APS was tactically and operationally successful, yet, to date, has been unable to fulfill its overarching objective of enabling partner nations to secure their own territorial waters. We use Ghana as a case study, exploring its specific maritime security issues and the extent to which APS appeared to affect them, as well as how impact could be improved. By delving in-depth into one country that has received APS visits for each of the years we examined (2007-2009), we can narrow down the possible reasons that APS succeeded on some fronts, but not on others, and explore whether US Navy efforts on APS make sense to continue, given their potential to impact maritime security. While it would require more research to generalize these results across the region, we believe that this analysis is an important first step in understanding how security sector development can succeed on some levels, but not on others.

Maritime Threats in Ghana

African governments have traditionally paid little attention to maritime threats because of greater land-based stability concerns, a tradition of former colonial powers providing maritime security assistance, and weak maritime forces. Beginning in the mid-2000s, African leaders began to pay more attention because of concerted international focus on piracy off the Horn of Africa, the convening of regional- and continent-wide maritime conferences, and increased US focus on both the West and East coasts of the continent. This new emphasis on maritime security in Africa has focused on three main threats: piracy, illicit trafficking, and energy theft. The relative importance of these threats varies by region and country, as does their perceived importance to the United States and African nations.

As a coastal nation, Ghana experiences a number of maritime threats that impact its overall security. The three main maritime issues threatening Ghana during the 2007-2010 period were energy insecurity; narco-trafficking; and illegal, unreported, and unregulated (IUU) fishing, the last a maritime threat not deemed critical to the United States. We examine each of these threats in turn.[3] Specifically, we focus on the significance of the threat in absolute terms, as well as how US and Ghanaian officials evaluated the threat's significance. We note the discordance among these three perspectives and what that means for the ability of the United States to achieve its strategic goals.[4]

Energy Insecurity

Energy security can be compromised through a variety of means. Theft of the oil itself can be accomplished through bunkering, illegal vessel loading, and vessel hijacking. Energy security can also be undermined by the creation of safety hazards (to either individuals or the environment) that then create public backlash against energy oil and gas extraction or political reluctance to pursue such extraction. In Ghana, energy security concerns relate to the country's new oil sector. In 2007, a successful drilling campaign by relatively small oil companies yielded Ghana's first large-scale, commercially viable oil field. Drilling officially began at the Jubilee field, operated by the British company Tullow Oil, in December 2010. In 2013, the Jubilee Field produced 29,296,466 barrels of oil, worth an estimated $3.3 billion.[5] Energy security is high priority to Ghanaian civilian and military leaders, as well as to American officials interested in diversifying the country's oil suppliers.

In interviews we conducted in Ghana, military and civilian leaders cited the threat to their energy security as one of the most critical maritime threats facing Ghana. Although the type of energy security threat which the leaders cited as most critical-oil theft (bunkering, hijacking, revenue theft, etc.) or oil disaster (fishing-caused oil disasters, environmental disasters, etc.) varied, almost all leaders worried a great deal about the future of their energy security. At the time of our 2010 interviews, oil production had not yet begun and thus, threats had not yet materialized; however, Ghanaian political and military leaders already were worrying about the future threat.

They believed there was a strong link between oil insecurity and piracy, stating that the "pipeline could become a target for pirates."[6]

Military officials were much more worried, however, about the possibility of oil disasters and the involvement of artisanal fishermen in such an event.[7] They were not concerned with how the oil would affect the fishing industry, but how the fishermen might threaten oil exploitation. As one military leader stated, "We worry a lot about the security risk the fishermen pose to the rigs when they get close. We really worry about collisions with the rig." Officials' concerns were exacerbated by their fear that they had little capability to respond to any energy security threat event. One military official commented, "We do not have equipment to respond to accidents and … in the case of oil spillage, we have no resources to respond or even prevent this event." As another government official explained, "We need more training on how to contain spills and we must have more ships."

Oil production in the Gulf of Guinea, and in Ghana specifically, is a fairly important strategic concern for the United States. Driven in part by President Bush's call to reduce dependence on Mideast oil by 25 percent and in part by the declining production of oil in the Nigerian Delta region—due mostly to oil theft—the United States has prioritized keeping open alternative sources of African oil. This is part of a larger US strategy since the United States has sought to increase its economic relations with sub-Saharan Africa. In 2000, the US signed a comprehensive US trade and investment policy for Africa: the African Growth and Opportunity Act (AGOA; Title I, P.L. 106-200).[8] Natural resources, particularly energy resources, dominate the products imported from Africa under AGOA. Africa supplied the United States with 16 percent of its imported oil in 2013.[9]

Trafficking

In 2007-2009, cocaine trafficking appeared likely to be the greatest maritime trafficking threat in Ghana. Ghana has been identified as one of the primary transshipment points for South American cocaine, particularly from the ports at Tema, Sekondi, and Takoradi.[10] Along with the narco-state of Guinea-Bissau, Ghana is one of two hubs for West African narco-trafficking.[11] Between 2003 and 2008, the United Nations Office on Drug and Crime (UNODC) reported that 2,418 kilograms of cocaine and 61,958 kilograms of marijuana had been seized in Ghana.

Although trafficking appears to have declined somewhat since 2007, in 2011 UNODOC assessed that the region was vulnerable to resurgence.[12] At the time of the UN's study, most of the cocaine and trafficking profits remained in the hands of South American drug lords; as a result, the direct negative effects on Ghana as a transit nation were small. In the UN's assessment, however, there was only a small likelihood that trafficking would continue to have little adverse effect on the country. Ghanaian law enforcement efforts had focused primarily on stemming the exit of cocaine via commercial air. As a result, it appeared possible that Ghanaians facilitating cocaine transit—who are commonly paid by their Colombian counterparts in cocaine—would seek local markets to sell their commission. This could subsequently fuel domestic drug consumption and the negative societal effects that follow, this in a country already hampered by health and poverty concerns.

The illicit networks required to sustain narco-trafficking also depend on, and reinforce, corruption at all levels. As Dustin Sharp argued in his chapter in this volume, entrenched corruption creates a culture of impunity, which then affects multiple other sectors. Deep corruption is detrimental to Ghana's societal foundations and potential for economic growth. Alongside economic degradation, the illicit trade has implications for stability as well. In the 2011 report, the UN warned that the high profits cocaine traffickers were earning had helped them to generate the resources to challenge any of the region's law enforcement agencies.[13]

US and Ghanaian officials had highly divergent views of the threat of narco-trafficking. From the US perspective, narco-trafficking was the most critical threat facing Ghana *compared to all other threats,* not just maritime ones. In fact, reducing narco-trafficking has been a priority for several US ambassadors to Ghana. US officials emphasize drug trafficking because it has a direct effect on the United States in two important ways: (1) it allows South American cartels to remain strong and active, even as other transit routes in the Caribbean Basin are being shut down; and (2) while cocaine is currently directly shipped to Europe, this same cocaine could conceivably be shipped onward to the United States. Thus, US officials have prioritized drug trafficking as a key threat in Ghana. In our interviews, we found that it is the threat they most often cited when asked to identify the maritime threat most critical to address.

Interestingly, almost all of the US Embassy's efforts toward countering narco-trafficking during 2007-2010 were focused on stopping the transit of drugs (both cocaine and heroin) *out* of Ghana; very little effort was put into preventing the transit of drugs *into* Ghana. For instance, an enormous amount of US and European resources and activity focused on increasing security at the Accra airport. US Africa Command (AFRICOM) provided funds to Ghana for the purchase of a body scanner and construction of a secure storage facility for confiscated drugs. According to US officials in Ghana, there had not been a similar effort focused on maritime entry points.

Although the United States provides available intelligence to Ghanaian forces on narco-traffickers entering Ghanaian waters or ports, the US government had not provided resources to help interdict the cocaine entering Ghana. US officials acknowledged that cocaine had and will continue to have a negative impact in Ghana. The growth of Latin American cartels in Ghana may eventually lead to the formation of native organized crime syndicates; the transit and local sale of cocaine has caused a rise in drug use.[14] US officials, however, did not appear to view these implications as a threat to the United States, and, therefore, they were not greatly concerned about the trafficking of cocaine into Ghana.

Conversely, Ghanaian officials did not appear to see narco-trafficking as a critical threat in any respect; if they mentioned it at all, it was ranked low in importance. In his article about criminal networks, Kwesi Aning noted that there was a "perception by Ghanaian leaders that organized criminal networks [such as those supporting narco-trafficking] pose far less security risk in a subregion engulfed in civil war."[15] In part, this perception may be due to a lack of awareness of the potential long-term ramifications of drug trafficking. Ghana had experienced few of the potential ramifications of drug trafficking on a large scale. While there had been some rise in crime, it had not been significant. Similarly, while the number of Ghanaian addicts had grown, the overall level of addiction was not on a scale to cause national concern. Furthermore, Ghanaian officials claimed that money-laundering, corruption, or other illegal activities associated with drug trafficking were not occurring at a significant level.

Illegal, Unreported, and Unregulated Fishing

IUU fishing can threaten fisheries-based economies and livelihoods, and therefore food security, economic security, and community security.[16] Of the three maritime security challenges discussed, it is the one that affects the most Ghanaians on a daily basis. US and Ghanaian officials perceive the importance of this threat very differently. It is listed as the second-most important maritime challenge by Ghanaian officials. To those at the US embassy, IUU is recognized as an important economic threat, but not a security threat that the US should or would care about. This reflects a narrow view of what the US should prioritize (threatening the livelihoods of Ghanaians can lead to other adverse effects, discussed below), and a marked divergence in how the US and Ghanaians view the same problems.

According to the Fisheries Centre at the University of British Colombia, Ghana relied heavily on fish as a source of "food, employment, and revenue."[17] In fact, per capita fish consumption in Ghana represented 60 percent, or nearly 30 kilograms per year, of the average Ghanaian's diet-one of the highest amounts in all of Africa.[18] Moreover, nearly 290,000 tons of fish per year were caught in Ghanaian waters, predominantly by small, local businesses.[19] In Ghana, the fisheries subsector accounted for approximately five percent of its agricultural gross domestic product (GDP) and, given development of appropriate tax codes, had the potential to yield "substantial tax revenues" for the state.[20] Thus, IUU fishing was highly likely to contribute to direct economic losses for Ghana (which could in turn have repercussions for the budgets of the Fisheries Commission or the navy).[21]

Most of Ghana's fisheries are located within a very narrow continental shelf; this means that Ghana is one of the two regional nations most likely to have "the most heavily overfished, and depleted, marine fish resource base."[22] IUU fishing includes activities such as unlicensed fishing/poaching, fishing with illegal gear, exceeding established quotas for fish or fishing outside of defined seasons, and misreporting or failing to report catch data.

For the period we examined, there was evidence that IUU fishing occurred regularly and in volume in Ghanaian waters. According to the Fisheries Centre:

> Compliance with laws and regulations are virtually non-existent and the government has failed to persuade fishermen in both artisanal and industrial sectors to comply with mesh size and zoning regulations. The Directorate of Fisheries has been unable to prevent illegal operation of trawlers in the In-shore Exclusion Zone ... [and] fishing with lights, illegal since 2002, is widespread.[23]

Unsustainable illegal fishing practices, combined with more than 100 legal industrial trawlers registered under the Ghanaian flag and an increasing number of fishing canoes, were putting more pressure on already depleted fishing stocks. According to Ghana's Marine Fisheries Research Division, in 2006 there were 11,200 fishing canoes; by 2010, this number had increased to nearly 20,000.[24] According to Ghanaian officials, with the exception of tuna, by 2010 most fishing stocks had completely disappeared.

IUU fishing has the potential to have direct and indirect negative effects on Ghana. For instance, artisanal fishermen, faced with the absence of non-tuna fish stocks and unable to reach blue-water tuna stocks, might have to seek alternative sources of income, up to and including narco-trafficking or IUU fishing itself. IUU fishing can also indirectly hurt Ghana's economy by reducing incomes from port activity and from fisheries-associated businesses, such as processing and packing; these individuals may also find themselves jobless and seeking alternative income. As Ghana's oil industry matures, these unemployed could also become involved in oil theft.

Moreover, the social impacts of IUU fishing could undermine food security for those communities whose major sustenance comes from fishing, and, in turn, increase the potential for conflict as artisanal fishermen compete (with each other and with commercial fishing vessels) for catch. The food security issue could extend beyond the fishing community: because of IUU fishing, Ghanaians import large quantities of fish. From 1992 to 2009, fish imports (excluding tuna) increased 438 percent.[25] These imports are contingent on Ghanaians' ability to pay for them; at a lower GDP, it is conceivable that Ghanaians might be unable to feed themselves through either fishing or imports. This could create a crisis in food security that itself could threaten social and political stability.

IUU fishing might also have a surprising indirect impact on Ghanaian politics. The coastal communities where artisanal fishermen reside sit outside of the ethnic divide on which Ghana's two major political parties are based, making them an important swing vote. Significantly, in Ghana's 2008 democratic presidential election, where the margin of victory was extremely narrow, voters along the coast were important to John Atta Mills' victory. Disgruntled, unemployed fishermen thus have the potential to sway the existing political balance in Ghana; this may be an additional reason that Ghanaian officials prioritize IUU fishing as a threat. Finally, unsustainable overfishing can do major damage to marine species and ecosystems, and certain types of illegal fishing techniques can directly damage the marine environment.[26]

As with narco-trafficking, US and Ghanaian officials perceived and prioritized IUU fishing differently. Officials from both countries acknowledged that IUU fishing was a serious problem for Ghana, but its relative importance to each country differed a great deal. US officials were clear that IUU fishing was a problem for Ghana. As one official stated: "Fish stocks are over-exploited. Trawlers are a big threat and food security is a potential problem." Our interviewees also noted that the Ghanaian maritime forces and organizations were relatively powerless to stop it: "There are not enough assets, fuel costs are high, and rules are not enforced." However, IUU fishing in Ghana was not perceived to be a threat that the United States should be concerned about, at least when compared to other threats.

During our interviews in summer 2010, officials in Ghana, conversely, strongly emphasized the significance of the IUU fishing threat. They consistently ranked it as one of the two most important maritime threats facing Ghana. They worried not only about immediate effects, such as depleted fishing stocks and less fish protein for the average Ghanaian diet, but also about secondary effects, such as unemployed fishermen who are forced to find other, possibly illegal, sources of income.

The Africa Partnership Station

APS consists of multiple US Navy peacetime activities: from maritime patrol aircraft detachment fly-ins, to large-deck port visits in littoral African nations. The US Navy's stated objective at the time it initiated APS was to improve maritime safety and security in the regions that it visited. Implicit in this objective was the notion that the improved safety and security would be both long-lasting and maintained by the participating African nations themselves. Thus, APS would serve to contribute to what the US Navy has called a "global maritime partnership," in which global cooperative security can be achieved by collective efforts of the world's maritime forces and commercial entities.[27]

If it achieved its objectives, APS would help African navies and coast guards contribute in a substantive way to preventing and combating maritime threats, thus alleviating the burden on US forces to do so. In the early years, APS focused on the West and Central African regions, although the initiative now includes engagement activities with East African countries as well. The main APS activity each year has been a multi-month deployment of an amphibious or other ship to several partner nations, during which US Naval forces, Marine forces and civilians would engage in cooperative exercises, training programs, and maritime security awareness programs with their African counterparts.

The Inaugural Deployment: 2007/2008

The inaugural APS deployment of USS *Fort McHenry* took place from November 2007 to April 2008. It visited countries from Senegal to Gabon in a rotation that allowed several countries to be visited twice. The APS staff was multinational, comprising U.S, European, and African officers. This first major APS deployment sought to achieve maritime safety and security objectives primarily by training the partner nations' maritime security forces (where they existed) in the skills and procedures necessary for them to perform day-to-day security activities. Training included courses, demonstrations, and practical application in patrol craft navigation; engine repair; and visit, board, search, and seizure procedures.

In addition, APS held media events and tours in which mission leadership and spokespersons extolled the virtues of maritime safety and security. Representatives from local, regional, and international media (print, radio, and television) attended these events. APS engagement activities also included community relations events. Sailors painted schools and played soccer games with local teams. Members of a naval construction detachment undertook several construction projects, including a military-civilian clinic in Ghana. Project Handclasp—a US Navy-affiliated program that transports donations by communities in the US to overseas destinations—brought humanitarian supplies to local clinics and health ministries. These components added a public relations and outreach aspect to the event, meant in part to raise awareness about maritime safety and security, and in part to improve the perception of the USA. APS staff leadership also conducted office calls and held receptions with influential host nation individuals (particularly those in the maritime forces and defense ministries) in order to foster awareness of the mission and to interact with host nation leadership both onboard the ship and ashore.

The 2009 APS Deployment

The 2009 APS deployment of the amphibious ship USS *Nashville* was the second major deployment under the APS initiative. The USS *Nashville's* deployment to West and Central Africa occurred from January to May 2009. The APS staff was again international, comprising officers from 21 different countries: nine European nations, Brazil, and ten African nations. African counterparts were both participants in and deliverers of APS engagement activities. Engagement activities were conducted during port visits of approximately two weeks in Senegal, Ghana, Nigeria, Cameroon, and Gabon. Brief stops were also made in São Tomé and Liberia, although these countries were not the focus of APS engagement. During port visits, APS sailors participated in a wide variety of activities, including:

- Training courses for more than 1,750 maritime professionals and stakeholders;
- Maintenance and construction assistance, such as Naval Construction Battalion (SEABEE) construction of a pier in Limbe, Cameroon;
- Office calls, ship tours, and receptions with military and civilian leaders;
- Community relations and outreach events, such as medical and dental outreach, engineering outreach, band performances and sporting events with local teams/groups;
- Provision of humanitarian supplies through Project Handclasp; and
- Delivery of 1206-funded patrol boats.[28]

In addition to in-port activities, USS *Nashville* also conducted an embarked trainee program, through which 65 personnel from 12 African countries lived onboard the ship, shadowing APS sailors and attending workshops. Throughout the deployment, significant efforts were made to garner local and international media attention on APS efforts and aims.

The objectives of this APS mission changed from the previous 2007/2008 goals of enhanced maritime safety and security in the Gulf of Guinea. For the 2009 deployment, the US Navy revised the desired outcome to a reduction in the maritime threats, specifically piracy, threats to energy security, and trafficking. The reason behind the change was the need to connect APS mission objectives to US strategic interests. In the region, these three threats were the ones of most importance to US foreign policy. As we have shown, though, this did not mean that these were the same threats that partner nations in the region would identify as the most pressing.

The Impact of APS

APS missions were incredibly well received by the nations they visited, and there were many requests for future return visits. This feedback was provided directly to APS staff and sailors, as well as to CNA analysts who interviewed African participants several weeks after the visit for both deployments.[29] We discovered surprisingly similar findings when we analyzed both of the APS missions between 2007 and 2009. Following each mission, we found the same attitudes among specific audiences (military and government leaders, and trainees) about the same things. Therefore, in our discussions of what worked and what did not, we discuss these missions together.

African sailors were appreciative of the training they had received and the opportunity to interact with their US, European, and other African counterparts. Moreover, the alacrity of their responses demonstrated a clear motivation and eagerness to demonstrate their newly acquired skills and use them to contribute to their nations' maritime security. Because the same feedback was given to APS-affiliated personnel (in anonymous surveys) and to impartial interviewers, we assessed these expressed positive feelings toward the missions to be genuine.

Unfortunately, in many cases this motivation to use new skills did not translate into actual behavioral change. Although sailors now had the requisite skills, they often were missing crucial functional patrol craft, fuel, or other equipment/supplies necessary to perform security tasks. Without the requisite resources, there was no way that they could channel their motivation into achieving maritime safety and security objectives.

Moreover, outside of those directly touched by APS missions, citizens and leaders of the participating African nations were virtually unaware of the visits or of their messages. APS is designed to have an impact on the capabilities of African militaries, but it is also just as much an effort to "win hearts and minds" and positively influence public attitudes towards the USA. It did not meet these goals. When interviewed by CNA analysts in summer 2010, members of the Ghanaian Parliament indicated that they had never heard of APS—and this was after the program's flagship had visited their country twice. The purpose of APS was opaque even to Senegalese employees of a logistics company directly involved in facilitating APS activities: although they facilitated supply deliveries during the USS *Fort McHenry* port visit and interacted directly with the ship's crew, they were completely unaware of the purpose of its visit.

The general public's and government officials' lack of awareness can largely be explained by the narrow aperture through which APS engaged partner nations during these two missions. Although staff members conducted office calls, most were held with high-ranking military, not government, officials. Similarly, distinguished visitor receptions were seldom attended by the highest-level government leaders (who sometimes were not invited), and messages regarding maritime safety and security often were lost in the excitement of the party. Although media days and press conferences were widely attended by reporters, it was not clear that the media coverage of APS activities either reached or influenced decision-makers. Obviously, APS had no chance of influencing the motivations or behaviors of individuals who were unaware of its existence or of its purpose.

This is important, because African naval officers frequently complain that their governments do not prioritize the maritime domain and that as a result they do not have the resources to conduct their missions. The main APS objective, to improve the maritime safety and security in African coastal nations, therefore cannot be achieved unless it gains traction at a national policy level in each country. Thus, the failure to affect national leadership was a serious hindrance to the achievement of the APS goal. This is a concrete area where, had APS planners engaged more thoroughly with embassy counterparts, they could have included a diplomatic engagement element to the program. In these years, however, the APS staff in Naples did not secure enough participation from embassy staff to add this diplomacy element to the program.

Overall, during its first two missions, APS was successful in achieving its tactical goal of training partner-nation maritime forces and in paving the way for future engagement with these nations. However, its strategic success was limited: it failed to assist nations in building maritime safety and security in any substantive way, due to both its failure to engage government officials (a key target actor population) and its failure to recognize that trained and motivated maritime forces alone, without tangible resources, are insufficient to achieve maritime security. In the next section, we use Ghana as a case study to explore whether APS's lack of success in achieving its strategic goals can be improved in future engagements and to understand whether the impact warrants the US Navy's efforts.

What Is the Value of APS and Should Efforts Continue?

Improving the Strategic Impact of APS

For many years, Ghanaian political interest in the maritime environment was negligible. Public officials focused their attention and government resources on land-based concerns, such as border security or ethnic divides. As a result, Ghana's maritime forces had limited capability to secure the maritime environment. Our 2010 interviews showed that there was limited awareness within the political community about the importance of the maritime environment to Ghana's economic security. This lack of awareness poses a serious roadblock to maritime security since the government is the ultimate source of most mitigation actions. The first step that APS might take to overcome this constraint is to increase and target engagement with the key stakeholders in the region. Our interviews showed that many of the important personnel who could have critical input into decisions about the resources devoted to maritime security knew very little about APS in particular or maritime security in general. An increased amount of US Navy and/or US government interactions with the appropriate personnel is needed to raise awareness. However, it is just as critical to think about the content of those engagements: what is the message that key US leaders can stress that will influence Ghanaian leaders to give more resources and attention to their maritime forces with the goal of securing their own territorial waters?

The Message: Finding the Overlap Between US and Ghanaian Interests

Since its inception, APS had focused on enhancing safety and security in the maritime realm by assisting partner nations to improve their own capacities and capabilities. According to US Navy communications and APS literature, this is important because a secure maritime realm will help to address critical threats for the United States: piracy, trafficking, and energy security. However, communicating the maritime threats that concern the United States did not necessarily motivate Ghanaian leaders to address maritime safety and security. As we have described, the US concerns did not necessarily align with those of Ghana.

First, piracy at the time was not a critical threat to Ghana, neither empirically nor perceptually, although it was a key threat to US interests.

Second, trafficking was empirically a real threat to Ghana and was critically important to US leaders, but it was not perceived as a threat by Ghanaian elites. Third, the most critical maritime threat to Ghana, empirically and perceptually, was IUU fishing and the accompanying detriment to food security; however, this threat was not part of the APS message to partner nation maritime forces or governments.

It is not surprising that the Ghanaian government had not provided resources to Ghana's forces to protect the maritime realm as a result of US conversations and APS activities. Via APS, the United States failed to adequately engage Ghanaian government leaders and did not deliver a message that convinced the Ghanaians to take their scarce resources and put them toward maritime security.

This is the rub: aligning Ghanaian and US interests need not be difficult. The actions it would take to mitigate IUU fishing, for example, are almost, if not completely, the same actions that would mitigate most other maritime threats, including trafficking, harm to energy security, and piracy. Regular patrols to deter and/or interdict illegal activity could help mitigate all of these threats. Therefore, APS could engage the Ghanaian government by re-crafting its message to include those maritime concerns that are the most important to the Ghanaians, and still keep its focus on its own national interests and the reduction of certain threats. In other words, US interests could be better served by APS and other endeavors if those efforts included a much greater component of diplomacy and strategic communications.

Of note, although the US interests did not at the time include IUU fishing, we argue that perhaps they should have. The skilled and available labor supply offered by unemployed fishermen as a result of IUU fishing could further amplify the maritime threats that are already a concern to both Ghanaian and US officials. APS could have addressed IUU fishing, helping to cultivate recovering fishing stocks and, thus, posssibly preventing some of the fishermen from engaging in illegal activities that are of direct interest to both Ghana and the United States.

Resourcing Maritime Safety and Security
Like almost all West African maritime forces, the Ghanaian Navy is severely underfunded. While there is very little data available on Ghanaian armed forces budgets, we know from interviewee reports and first-hand observation that, at least at the time, the Ghanaian Navy suffered from insufficient equipment and personnel. The Ghanaian Navy and other maritime organizations in Ghana did not have the necessary materiel and personnel resources to engage in mitigating behaviors. This is largely because (1) Ghana does not have many resources in general, and (2) like

most African countries, it faces many more pressing needs than it has revenues to address.

This makes for difficult "guns versus butter" choices for government officials (and, really, "butter versus butter" decisions too); in this context securing the maritime environment was not a top priority. As one respondent explained, "Ghana does not have the resources—it is not a choice about how they are allocated." This leaves the maritime forces without enough funds to buy equipment, train, or adequately execute missions. One interviewee stated, "We need more ships and aircraft patrols; we need platforms and spare parts." Without a bigger budget, there is little hope that Ghana will be able to secure its own maritime environment without sustained outside help.

Another reason that the maritime forces lack necessary resources is corruption in both the Ghanaian government and military. In short, it is the reason that the limited funding that *is* allocated to the navy is frequently not used to purchase the equipment for which it was earmarked. As one interviewee remarked, "Corruption is huge, especially in the legal and military realm. President Mills is anti-corruption, but he stands alone." Corruption also provides disincentives to secure the maritime environment, as individuals in the government or military may actually profit from maritime threats. One official stated, "Oil has hurt the Ghanaian Navy and compromised their integrity;" while another argued that "drugs are a corrupting factor in politics. Proceeds go into political campaigns and democracy is undermined." Ghanaian sailors and naval officers are reportedly highly susceptible to narco-traffickers' bribes, given the very low wages they receive.[30] Companies engaging in IUU fishing also purportedly bribe the Fisheries Commission and the navy in order to conduct their illicit activities undisturbed in Ghanaian waters.[31]

We believe this is critical to understanding what APS, the US Navy, and the US government can and cannot influence. US officials can engage Ghana's government more to raise awareness around these issues and can craft their messages to represent mutual interests on both sides. If it is merely a question of how to allocate existing resources, then APS might have some influence on those decisions. APS cannot address systematic corruption; if the United States is to influence this dynamic it will have to come from other government programs, those run by civilian agencies. Even those may not be able to do much about the lack of resources or the amount of corruption that exists, but they will have more chance to do so than military actors. If there are not enough resources, or if those resources are drained by corruption, then the impact from APS on Ghana's maritime security concerns will continue to be limited.

Understanding which type of constraint exists in each country and to what degree is a critical step to take before engagement even happens. This is where military planners need to reach out to civilian and/or nongovernmental counterparts who are embedded within the country. If a country is too poor or too corrupt, the barriers might be too high for APS to have any hope of improving the country's maritime safety and security. If, however, limited resources might be partially diverted or reprioritized toward improving maritime safety and security, motivating the right audiences with the right themes could lead the way toward APS strategic success.

APS as a Resource Multiplier

Over several years of analysis, we have come to understand that APS has the greatest influence when it facilitates the development and strengthening of regional relationships between African militaries and their governments. Regional communication and interaction are critical for mitigating all types of maritime threats, particularly when the resources and capabilities of individual nations are limited. Traditionally, African maritime forces have not had strong relationships with one another. This is due in part to long-standing rivalries between countries, as well as to the fact that many of these navies lack the resources to coordinate logistically. This lack of regional communication and coordination has opened the maritime realm in West and East Africa to criminal operations. Multiple short sovereign coastlines and limited maritime security force coordination mean that criminals can simply cross the maritime border from one country to the next to evade enforcers.

Significantly, the umbrella of APS activities—mostly training, but also conferences, planning meetings, etc.—allowed maritime personnel from countries across West and East Africa to interact, often for the first time. Moreover, since APS deployments occurred annually, some personnel were able to engage in iterated interactions, which helped to establish and then cement professional relationships that have grown with each APS rotation. While the US military cannot engage in sustained development activities like USAID, it can arrange programs to deliver several rounds of shorter engagements that over their course generate more comprehensive capacity and relationship building outcomes. These relationships, in turn, can lead to increased regional communication and coordination regarding maritime threats. Since there are few channels for official communication between navies, APS helped to develop informal channels between people who knew each other from interacting during APS activities.

We have heard, first-hand, stories about navy personnel contacting former APS classmates during hot pursuit of criminals, even when no formal communications between partner-country forces existed. We have seen similar relationship building among the various agencies in Ghana. For example, prior to the APS, it was uncommon for the Ghanaian Navy and Department of Fisheries to work together; during the 2009 APS deployment, the Fisheries Commission *for the first time ever* provided a list of licensed fishing boats to the Ghanaian Navy to aid in apprehension of unlicensed fishermen. Time and time again, participants in APS, as well as civilian and military officials, commented that without APS there would not be the amount of regional (or national) cooperation existed following APS visits. This impact of APS bears out in our analysis of behaviors as well. Actions by Ghana associated with regional and inter-national cooperation appeared to be correlated directly with APS engage-ment in the country.

Besides more effective enforcement, the relationships facilitated by APS might lead to a broader understanding of the regional maritime threat environment, and consequently more accurate threat assessments for each country and a deeper understanding of appropriate regional responses. These are concrete improvements to maritime security in West Africa that can be traced to this particular program. Thus, these relationships and recognition of the importance of a regional approach to securing East and West African waters have been the most critical contribution from APS.

As we have discussed, African maritime forces often lack resources. However, if the forces could communicate, coordinate, and cooperate, they would be more effective, and the waters in the region might be much safer, even if there is not an increase in resources. Again, this argues that the strongest contribution that APS can make to mitigate maritime threats in Ghana is in the arena of relationship building. APS provides a forum for relationships to grow between national maritime forces, between country agencies, and between international partners. Moreover, if APS could use this same forum to allow relationships to grow with key government resource stakeholders and US Navy/US government leadership, then it would come much closer to being able to realize its overarching objectives in countries that have the characteristics to allow for a growth in maritime security.

APS Post-2010

The US Navy has continued APS deployments since the period we analyzed. In 2011, the APS was still divided into two deployments: APS East and West. The West still focused on the "hub" concepts and several US ships were involved, though European partners, specifically Belgium, also contributed assets. APS also started to include nascent multinational exercises, notably, Cutlass Express, that were, at least initially, a proof-of-concept attempt to have African navies work together.

The 2012 APS deployment involved three US ships that were deployed in both West and East Africa over the course of the year and involved the traditional maritime training. It also added a component of medical outreach, providing medical care to local communities during port visits (these are called medical civic action programs).[32] In 2013, APS was expanded to include not only individual deployments, but also multinational exercises, which had become an important part of raising the capabilities and capacities of partner nation navies. Specifically, the 2013 APS involved Cutlass Express, Obangame Express, and Saharan Express. Additionally, because there were no US assets that were part of the APS umbrella that year, partner nations (such as the Netherlands and France) contributed ships for individual country visits.

As time has passed, the objectives of APS have also evolved to include a focus on maritime security that benefits the country directly. DoD materials state that "APS is inspired by the belief that effective maritime safety and security will contribute to economic prosperity and security on land."[33] The emphasis on specified threats remains the same: piracy, trafficking, and energy theft.

Recent strategic communications and activities also reflect that the Navy may be adopting some of the recommendations we provided for making APS a more effective initiative. For instance, the US Navy's Sixth Fleet APS website now discusses the importance of shared vision and goals to achieve security in Africa.[34] Moreover, during the USNS *Spearhead's* APS deployment in 2014, US and Ghanaian service members partnered to interdict and fine small fishing boats illegally operating in Ghana's territorial waters.[35] These both are promising developments that we assess are likely to improve APS's ability to impact Ghanaian, and African, maritime security concerns, and argue for continued and sustained US Navy engagement in the region.

Notes

[1] APS deployments we discuss were conducted 2007-2009; however, some of our interviews were conducted, and other data gathered, in 2010.

[2] The findings we discuss in this chapter are based on a number of CNA studies conducted for the US Navy by the authors and numerous other CNA analysts.

[3] Because our analysis was focused on 2007-2009 deployments, our interest was on maritime threats to Ghana during this same time period. For updated information on maritime threats to Ghana, see Lowe, "Protecting Hydrocarbon Wealth."

[4] We assessed each threat in terms of both its objective impact—using data, mostly from international organizations such as the World Bank, the United Nations, and the International Maritime Bureau—and its perceived impact according to US and Ghanaian officials, which we gathered through interviews conducted in the summer of 2010. Combining objective and per-ceived threat impacts provided a comprehensive picture of these threats as they pertained to Ghana and to the United States. The juxtaposition of Ghanaian and US interests vis-à-vis these maritime threats provided context for how the US Navy and US government might play a role in threat mitigation.

[5] Marais and Gismatullin, "Tullow Delays," and Xan Rice, "Deficit Fears Cast Shadow."

[6] We should note that Ghanaian leaders appeared to define piracy broadly, to include armed robberies and other theft activities occurring on oil rigs or aboard oil tankers. As of this writing, oil theft has still not proved to be a major problem for Ghana.

[7] Our interviews were conducted a few weeks after the 2010 oil spill in the Gulf of Mexico, so concern about environmental issues may have been un-characteristically high.

[8] Ploch, *Africa Command: U.S. Strategic Interests* (2007).

[9] U.S. Energy Information Administration, "How Dependent Are We on Foreign Oil?"

[10] US Department of State, *International Narcotics Control Strategy*.

[11] United Nations Office on Drugs and Crime, *Drug Trafficking as a Security Threat in West Africa*.

[12] United Nations Office on Drugs and Crime, *World Drug Report 2011*.

[13] Ibid.

[14] Indeed, in 2011 the Narcotics Control Board of Ghana reported that the abuse of cocaine, heroin, and cannabis had witnessed an average annual increase of 65 percent each year between 2003 and 2010. "Ghana Drug Abuse Cases up 61 Percent," *Ghana Business News*.

[15] Aning, "Are There Emerging West African Criminal Networks?"

[16] The authors are grateful to Veronica DeAllende for her assistance on this section of the chapter.

[17] Pramod, "Sources of Information."

[18] The first statistic was provided during authors' interviews with US Embassy personnel, summer 2010; the second by an Internal World Bank document provided through informal correspondence.

[19] Ibid.

[20] World Bank, *Report on Fisheries Sub-Sector Capacity*, 2.

[21] Reflecting that, Ghana recently signed on as a partner with the World Wildlife Foundation, the UN Food and Agriculture Organization, and the International Seafood Sustainability Foundation to focus on identifying IUU fishing and improving sustainability, especially with regards to their tuna supplies. "Joint Global Efforts to stop IUU Fishing," MercoPress.

[22] Pramod et al., "Sources of Information;" Internal World Bank document provided through informal correspondence. The other country is Senegal.

[23] Pramod et al, "Sources of Information," 85.

[24] Data was provided by the Ghana Ministry of Food and Agriculture, Marine Fisheries Division.

[25] These are our own calculations based on the data provided by the Ghana Ministry of Food and Agriculture, Marine Fisheries Division.

[26] Ibid.

[27] Global maritime partnership is a term coined by Adm. Mike Mullen, former chief of naval operations, when describing his concept of a thousand-ship navy.

[28] For an explanation of "1206 funds," please see Chapters 3 and 5 in this volume.

[29] Throughout this chapter, we have reproduced quotations from our interviews with participants in APS programs. Due to human subjects protection and CNA embargoes on releasing individually identified data, we have not identified our interviewees or the specific dates of the interviews.

[30] There are unsubstantiated reports that when the Ghanaian Navy was given an intelligence tip about a ship that contained cocaine, it seized the ship and brought it into port, where no drugs were found by Ghanaian or US authorities when they were allowed on the ship a few hours after it was in port. There was apparently some evidence that drugs were on the ship, but they were removed before outside authorities were allowed on.

[31] This was suggested to us multiple times in various interviews.

[32] Commander, US Naval Forces Europe, "Africa Partnership Station 2012 Begins."

[33] "About Africa Partnership Station," Commander, US Naval Forces Africa.

[34] Ibid.

[35] Lederer, "Being There Matters."

8

Civil Society and the US Africa Command

Teresa Crawford and Trina Zwicker

Early on, the US Africa Command's leaders decided that the organization should have a strategy through which it would reach out to nongovernmental organizations (NGOs). AFRICOM's leaders had heard the messages that the complex security challenges in Africa would not respond to solely military instruments, and that coordinating with governmental civilian and nongovernmental agencies would help the command successfully address the multiple drivers of insecurity in Africa. Thus, the idea of "public-private partnerships" captured the imagination of several influential leaders in AFRICOM.

To attempt this engagement in a coordinated manner, AFRICOM developed an NGO interaction strategy housed within the Outreach Directorate (a directorate that was dedicated to engaging with nontraditional partners like academia and think tanks, businesses, and nongovernmental organizations). Reaching out to NGOs in such a general way proved challenging, as there was no roadmap or official guidance to help promote interactions with NGOs. Furthermore, while many NGOs had become accustomed to working with military actors on concrete programs with limited timeframes, many others were hesitant to enter into vague, general relationships with the command when it attempted to create cooperation not driven by a specific engagement. This experience reveals the complexity of attempting to integrate ongoing efforts with nongovernmental communities, exacerbated by the suspicion with which many NGOS regarded AFRICOM.

In this chapter we examine this early attempt by AFRICOM to develop a strategy for interactions with nongovernmental organizations. We review the lessons learned and discuss subsequent questions for future AFRICOM interactions with NGOs. Within this context, we describe the current thinking around public-private partnerships and address why civil society and the NGOs that make up part of civil society are an important group to partner with to achieve national security goals. We also give some examples of the challenges and opportunities that have arisen from those relationships and discuss why designing a long-term strategy is a key step for AFRICOM to take.

Civil society is comprised of the associations and structures through which citizens organize themselves. It includes both informal and formal associations and groups. CIVICUS, a global network of civil society organizations, defines civil society as "the arena, outside of the family, the state, and the market where people associate to advance common interests."[1] Often called the "third sector," civil society serves as a counterpoint to government and business. It can mobilize for good and bring about positive changes in a society. It can also mobilize for ill and organize to bring down a democratically elected government, or support the aspirations of armed groups, as the charitable arm of Hezbollah does in Lebanon.

In an era of decreasing financial resources, leveraging partnerships has been identified by the United States government, in particular the agencies that implement foreign assistance programs, as a key to success. Africa Command was asked to decrease its budget in fiscal year 2013 by 6 percent.[2] The Department of Defense over all "estimates a 20 percent drop in the overall defense budget" by 2021. As the US government's budget tightens, it will become increasingly important for the public and private sectors to work together. How does the DoD view its relationships with NGOs?

Often the military uses the phrase "force multipliers," signaling a mindset that NGOs extend the reach and impact of military programs. If the DoD, and in particular AFRICOM, sees these partnerships as merely force multipliers, then what sorts of partnerships are possible? The term "partnership" connotes equality, mutual benefit, and a spirit of give and take. In contrast, thinking of (and treating) NGOs like force multipliers means conceiving of them as subordinates, subject to the will of the command, and not of equal authority. On a fundamental level NGOs are conscious of this divergence, and most are not comfortable with being considered force multipliers.

AFRICOM's Current Partnerships

When AFRICOM was established it sought to develop a variety of partnerships to further its goals. AFRICOM saw these partnerships as mechanisms to help it to gain legitimacy, information, and access; and to help the command address new and emerging threats and complex challenges. AFRICOM has built partnerships with other US government agencies, European governments and allied militaries, and African militaries and their civilian leaderships. Beyond these partnerships, it continues to conduct outreach to a diverse group of new stakeholders: academics, civic organizations, community and religious leaders, and journalists in Africa, Europe, and the United States. A majority of AFRICOM's service component commands also engage with civil society to aid them in achieving their goals.[3]

The United States military has a long history of interacting with civil society organizations both at home and abroad. The United Service Organizations (USO), founded in 1941 to support US troops and their families, is a private nonprofit organization with a strong relationship to the military. Armed forces stationed at military bases in the United States and in other countries often engage both personally and professionally with civil society organizations. These soldiers invariably become involved in the communities surrounding their posts. The relationships are often on an individual rather than a corporate basis.

Since the early 1990s, when Operation Provide Comfort served the Kurdish population displaced in Northern Iraq during the first Gulf War, the United States military has become more involved in peacekeeping and humanitarian assistance missions. These engagements have brought them into close contact, parallel operations, and occasional cooperation with international relief organizations, both intergovernmental and nongovernmental. Continuing this trend, the US military has become increasingly involved in aid delivery and civilian reconstruction efforts as part of the counterinsurgency campaigns in Afghanistan and Iraq and disaster relief efforts in countries like Indonesia, Pakistan, and Haiti.[4] These civilian-military interactions rapidly have broadened to include not only interactions with international and intergovernmental organizations, such as the United Nations, but also with charities and aid organizations. The military has engaged with NGOs on policy issues, joint training exercises, efforts to collaboratively provide basic provisional services to distressed populations, and, in rare instances, joint planning.

After working with civic organizations on an intermittent, program-dependent basis for a few years, in 2010 AFRICOM identified a need to develop a coherent approach to working with civil society, and NGOs in particular, in order to help guide the command's interaction with local populations. Staff believed that a more comprehensive approach would inform both the public information work of the command as well as the substantive and security cooperation work in which AFRICOM engages.

Given the complex environment in which AFRICOM was formed and operates, developing such an approach was no easy task.[5] As a result, the command created a "Public-Private Partnerships" branch within the Outreach Directorate. Its mission was to provide strategy and support for AFRICOM's engagement with civil society and businesses. The initiative was short lived: after two years this special emphasis was no longer deemed necessary, and in January 2012 this separate branch was reorganized and no longer exists.

The examples of civil-military interaction in this chapter, as well as the issues and questions for discussion, were developed as part of a stakeholder analysis completed by the authors at AFRICOM and in Washington, D.C., from February through August of 2010. We updated these initial interviews with a second round of interviews conducted in December 2011. We do not provide an exhaustive account of all the interactions AFRICOM's staff and offices have had with civil society organizations, but our study is illustrative of a broad range of interactions that staff have had since AFRICOM was formed. Interactions between AFRICOM and NGOs fall into the following categories:

- Strategic engagement
- Humanitarian projects
- Exercises and planning
- Tactical program implementation
- Information/outreach

Strategic Engagement

When the command was first established, strategic engagement focused on providing AFRICOM's senior leaders with information and expertise on issues that are relevant to the command's work on the continent. Dialogue with key leaders and NGOs has helped the leadership to shape the actions they take in support of US foreign policy interests. Examples have included workshops and conferences convened by groups such as the Atlantic Council, Africa Center for Strategic Studies, US Institute of Peace, and InterAction. AFRICOM's first commander, General William (Kip) Ward, convened a Senior Leaders Advisory Group (SLAG), which included prominent academics and policy makers on Africa. The leaders of the component commands also engage at a strategic level with associations such as the Corporate Council on Africa and Atlantic Council.

On strategic issues, AFRICOM usually engages with US- or European-based NGOs and think tanks. This interaction came about as part of a wider interaction with other US government partners and international organizations. In December 2011, representatives of the International Committee of the Red Cross (ICRC) visited the senior leadership at AFRICOM. Overtures to the ICRC were made in 2008 and 2011, and ICRC representatives made two trips to AFRICOM with the intent of establishing more open lines of communication.[6]

AFRICOM has interacted with these agencies mostly through joint participation in meetings organized by third parties, rather than in direct working relationships. The component commands often interact with NGOs on a more regular basis, but AFRICOM rarely enters into a contractual relationship with these groups or provides them with funding. These organizations have generally not engaged in joint planning with AFRICOM, though individuals at the command may form personal and professional relationships on which they capitalize when doing research and planning. Some of these same NGOs may be involved in projects that relate to other forms of engagement.

Outside of the routine military intelligence collection activities, it is unclear whose responsibility it is to identify, foster, and grow relationships at the command level. The only official guidance for engagement with civil society is the body of ethics rules that have been put in place to prevent conflicts of interest. As a result, the absence of a strategy, along with fear and misunderstanding related to the ethics rules, has led to the under-development of these types of relationships.

Humanitarian Projects

A second type of interaction occurs when developing and implementing humanitarian projects in specific countries. Here AFRICOM engages in more direct interaction with NGOs, though most often the US Agency for Internatinoal Development (USAID) serves as an intermediary between the military and NGOs. Military staff deployed in countries develop humanitarian project proposals for review and processing by the Humanitarian and Health Activities (HHA) branch staff at AFRICOM (usually in conjunction with US Embassy country teams, and, as ap-propriate, the service-specific component commands).

As they develop these project concepts, the military works with the host nation governments, local ministries, local NGOs, and international organizations to ensure a coordinated effort that avoids duplication. The country team submits project nominations to AFRICOM's headquarters in Stuttgart for policy review and to ensure that theater security cooperation objectives and overall US government objectives will be achieved through the implementation of the project. HHA staff review projects to ensure that AFRICOM's objectives are being met and to provide program oversight, including project funding, contract coordination, contractor payment, construction coordination (if required), and assurance of a project's long-term sustainability. The country teams are primarily responsible for coordinating with and vetting partner organizations involved in project implementation.

AFRICOM's J5 or Strategy, Plans, and Programs (SPP) Directorate neither directs country team members to work with specific NGOs nor directs how they work with NGOs in the implementation of projects. Since NGOs are embedded in their countries and have developed long-term relationships with local actors, AFRICOM encourages project planners to engage in dialogue with them. The goal of doing this is to provide the projects with more local knowledge and to give them a longer-term time horizon that will facilitate long-term project maintenance and sustainment.

AFRICOM's country teams primarily rely on USAID and Department of State (DoS) country team members to locate appropriate local groups and establish relationships with these NGOs. These civilian organizations are usually local, community-based organizations on the continent or international NGOs with operations in a particular country or region or with a focus on a specific topic. Interaction with these types of organizations can happen at the suggestion of three entities: (1) the Office of Security Cooperation (OSC) or Defense Attaché Office (DAO), (2) a Civil Affairs (CA) team, or (3) an individual who is undertaking a specific project that requires NGO involvement. All CA teams are required to vet their humanitarian assistance activities through the OSC/DAO.

These programs are implemented in cooperation with the country's government, and AFRICOM cannot turn over materials or structures to NGOs. The country must own the land, and NGOs can operate a facility and/or use materials only if the local government allows them to do so. Ultimately, local actors must be able to ensure the sustainability of the project. In some cases, AFRICOM might rehabilitate structures or provide excess equipment to the government, which are then managed and used by NGOs.

As an example of how this works, in postrevolution Tunisia there was a need for improved health services, but the country lacked local capacity. People with disabilities were one of the vulnerable groups hardest hit by the lack of services. The US Embassy's country team identified an HHA project that could benefit from AFRICOM's support: rehabilitation of a center that provides medical, social, and educational assistance for patients living with muscular dystrophy and counseling for their family members. The Tunisian government partnered with the Association des Myopathes de Tunisie, a local organization, to run this project. This is one of seven HHA projects in Tunisia that cost a total of $3,000,000.[7]

Exercises and Planning: Theater Security Cooperation Programs

A third type of interaction occurs during the development of exercises and the planning process for Theater Security Cooperation Plans. As described above, NGOs are rarely engaged in any of AFRICOM's planning processes. They are also not routinely involved in exercises or in the development of theater strategies. AFRICOM conducts two command-level exercises each year where plans, policies, and coordination are tested. AFRICOM also conducts engagement exercises in Africa. In 2012, the command conducted 19 engagement exercises; in 2014, there were 15 exercises. Subordinate commands lead these exercises, and the direct beneficiaries are US military personnel who learn from training with host nation militaries.

To date, there has not been a training goal or objective that specifically targets NGOs in these exercises, yet their planners routinely identify NGOs as stakeholders that should be included (if they are active in a particular country and on a particular issue). In some cases, interagency and NGO representatives may be identified as key players in a training exercise, and a majority of the time contractors are paid to play the role of NGOs in exercises. One exception was Natural Fire 10, a multinational exercise held with the Ugandan People's Force in Uganda in 2009. In this exercise, NGOs participated in a tabletop exercise before the field exercise and were briefed by members of the US Embassy country team and AFRICOM representatives. This type of engagement has not been a regular occurrence, and in this example, NGOs were not engaged in the planning for the exercise, neither as part of the initial assessment nor in the development of the tabletop exercise.

In addition to exercises, AFRICOM is involved in several US government–led continent-wide initiatives, including PEPFAR and the Global Malaria Initiative. Another humanitarian program, the Pandemic Response Program (PRP), provides a positive example of how AFRICOM and USAID have collaborated closely with international organizations, NGOs, and host nation partners to address a challenge. The aim of the PRP is to enhance the capacity of militaries in Asia and Africa to support their civilian-led pandemic and/or disaster programs. Originally conceived as a program to aid regional militaries, it has evolved into a comprehensive program that works with both the military and civilian leadership.

In this instance, both local and international NGOs were engaged, as well as the extensive networks of the World Health Organization and the United Nations Office for the Coordination of Humanitarian Affairs. The PRP collaboration continues. In February 2012, AFRICOM organized Ghana's National Government Pandemic Disaster Response Tabletop Exercise. Approximately 120 civilian and military representatives from five

African nations, the United States, and international aid organizations participated. The exercise was hosted by the government of Ghana, organized by AFRICOM, supported by the Center for Disaster and Humanitarian Assistance Medicine, and funded by USAID.[8]

Tactical Program Implementation

A fourth type of interaction relates to field-level program implementation. The DoD, in particular AFRICOM's component commands, have a number of programs that involve working with other US government agencies, US-based NGOs, local NGOs, academic institutions, and international organizations. Among the component commands, Naval Forces Africa (NAVAF) has the most structured and developed relationship with civil society organizations. As Alison Vernon and Margaux Hoar discussed in Chapter 7, NAVAF runs the Africa Partnership Station (APS), and it is through this program that NAVAF most directly interacts with civil society.

Ghana is a great example of how APS engages with civil society and helps to bridge civil societies and governments. In Ghana, APS has worked with the civilian government, the Ghanaian Navy, the World Wildlife Fund, local fishing cooperatives, and coastal communities to improve their ability to monitor fishing grounds using remote sensing technologies. APS personnel have worked with two NGOs in the Western Region of Ghana: Hen Mpoana (Our Coast) and Friends of the Nation. Both are local environmental and fisheries NGOs: Our Coast is sponsored by USAID and run by the University of Rhode Island. APS conducted a joint fisheries enforcement program between the Ghanaian Navy, Ghana Fisheries, and Friends of the Nation in April 2010. The primary recipients of APS training and materials are partner militaries, but NGO representatives are allowed to participate. When NGOs are involved, AFRICOM may provide funds to them under a contract and offer them training and materials. A new program, Africa Partnership Flight (APF), coordinated by Air Forces Africa and modeled after APS, launched with an event in Ghana in the winter of 2012.[9]

US Special Operations Africa also runs training programs similar to those of APS and APF. In September 2010, the Special Operations command trained Charlie Company of the newly designated 391st Commando Battalion of the Democratic Republic of Congo (DRC). This program sought to build a model professional military unit with members who adhere to international human rights standards. Years of war and insecurity in the DRC, during which members of the various armed forces committed human rights abuses, have deeply damaged civilian-military relations.

The NGO Search for Common Ground (SFCG) has worked with USAID and AFRICOM in the DRC to support their ongoing Security Sector Reform programs. Funded by the US government and several European governments, SFCG has worked in collaboration with the Congolese armed forces to reinforce their respect of human rights, enhance their conflict resolution skills, and improve military-civilian relations. SFCG has trained in-force educators to carry out awareness-raising activities in the areas of human rights and conflict transformation. The organization has also used media and outreach tools (e.g., radio programs, comic books, participatory theater, mobile cinema), as well as sports, culture, and joint civilian-military activities to improve relations and promote peaceful cohesion between the two groups. SFCG has also worked with the Police Nationale Congolaise on similar issues.

In this instance, working with a local organization, through the auspices of USAID, enabled military actors to more effectively engage in a sensitive topic. The DoD lacked the local knowledge to craft an appropriate training program for the Congolese battalion, but SFCG possessed the requisite information, local contacts, and local knowledge to successfully design and implement the program. While human rights training for the Congolese military has enjoyed only partial success, the reasons for that lay in the larger issues discussed by Andrea Talentino and Dustin Sharp in their contributions to this volume. It is almost impossible to create an effective human rights training program when the military forces are embedded in systems where civilian institutions and capacities are lacking, when they are not paid regularly, and when they find themselves in a situation where a deeply embedded culture of impunity undermines all the training that the US military and its associates can provide.

Information/Outreach

A final type of interaction relates to information operations and outreach. Military Information Support (MISO) teams from Special Operations Command Africa (SOCAF) work with the US Embassy's country teams as part of Operation Objective Voice (OOV). Objective Voice is an AFRICOM program focused on countering violent extremism in Africa. Its efforts are guided by the Department of State's Africa Bureau and by the chiefs of mission and country teams. There have been active Objective Voice programs in eight countries in Africa. In Ethiopia, OOV supports a community radio program with three radio stations. For this project, the embassy's Public Affairs Office selected the sites and the target participants; AFRICOM provided the technical assistance and training to set up the stations.

AFRICOM's Public Information Office is tasked to inform journalists from the United States and throughout Africa about the work of Africa Command. In July 2010, a group of journalists from the DRC visited AFRICOM's headquarters in Stuttgart, Germany, to learn more about AFRICOM and to discuss issues related to the work of the US military in the DRC. This meeting was part of AFRICOM's Public Information Partnership (PIP) initiative, an outreach effort designed to provide in-depth information on the command's programs and activities in Africa. The DRC group consisted of four editors of prominent media organizations. Joining the group was the president of a human rights NGO based in Kisangani, the location of an ongoing US train-and-equip mission. During the week-long orientation, the group received in-depth briefings on the command, its programs, and ways it engages with the DRC military as well as other African militaries.

Engagement with academia and the think-tank community constitutes another form of interaction with nongovernmental entities. Early in AFRICOM's operation, the Academic Outreach team organized a series of academic symposia to engage with think tanks and academic NGOs on issues of interest to AFRICOM. Team members conducted meetings in the United States, Germany, and Africa on topics including security sector reform, transnational threats, building civil-military democratic relationships, and regional peace and security issues.

Many of these activities have been implemented in collaboration with the Africa Center for Strategic Studies (ACSS). ACSS is one of several hemispheric studies center which was set up specifically to support scholarship, training, research for the regional combatant commands. While ACSS is a Department of Defense institution, it is able to facilitate relationships with nongovernmental organizations and individuals, especially academics. In 2010–2012, the Senegalese Ministry of Armed Forces undertook a gender mainstreaming program that brought together the Senegalese Armed Forces with AFRICOM, ACSS, and both local and international NGOs. In this program the ministry undertook efforts to improve the status of women within the armed forces of Senegal. Working with and through a multi-stakeholder platform established by Partners Senegal, a subsidiary organization of Partners for Democratic Change, the group analyzed current policies, practices, and budgets and also compared the status of women in their country with that in other countries in Africa and with best practices from around the world. In 2011, ACSS and Partners Senegal co-hosted several workshops in Dakar, and AFRICOM provided partial funding, technical expertise, and speakers who could contribute to the reform efforts.

Military–Civil Society Engagement Considerations

For each type of engagement there are at least three important questions to consider: (1) what type of engagement with NGO partners is desired and most critical for the achievement of AFRICOM's goals; (2) what authorities exist to engage in partnerships, and what funding exists to pay for the participation of the civilians who participate; and (3) how well coordinated and strategic is the engagement with NGOs? AFRICOM staff struggle to answer these questions, as there is no overarching strategy for engaging with NGOs, no clearly articulated analysis of the benefits from engaging with NGOs, and few skilled and experienced staff who can navigate the challenging aspects of working with NGOs as partners.

Advancing the Mission of AFRICOM with NGO Engagement

By definition, civil society acts independently from governments and is not an instrument of a government's foreign policy. However, to the extent that civil society works to promote the broader human security agenda— education, health care, economic development, environmental protection, human rights, and conflict resolution—as well as the establishment of democratic institutions and civil society, their objectives are aligned with AFRICOM's mission and US government interests. Although AFRICOM and the US government do not have command authority over any part of civil society, they can engage civil society actors, such as NGOs, as partners in achieving US foreign policy interests and improving the lives of Africans. Civil society can fill operational gaps where the US government or DoD might not have the expertise or jurisdiction to act. NGOs also have extensive involvement in local communities, local contacts, and experience that provide them with unique insights not available to the US government or military about local and regional affairs and civilian attitudes.

Conversely, situations may arise where it is determined that the US national interest requires that US military forces support NGOs during a humanitarian, natural, or environmental disaster. Working with "nontraditional partners" is not a new concept. In 1997, General John Shalikashvili, chairman of the Joint Chiefs of Staff from 1993 to 1997, asked,

> What's the relationship between a just-arrived military force and the NGOs and PVOs [private volunteer organizations] that might have been working in a crisis torn area all along? What we have is a partnership. If you are successful, they are successful; and, if they are successful, you are successful. We need each other.[10]

While missions to support NGOs are normally for a short-term purpose due to extraordinary events, it has long been recognized that these interactions are more likely to be successful if the relationships with organizations are already formed. Such missions usually involve logistics, communications, and security support. Having knowledge of and relationships with civil society help the military to remember the crucial point in such missions: the role of the armed forces should be to enable, not perform, NGO tasks.

Strategic Issues: Policy, Planning, and Funding Structures

If it has long been known that maintaining enduring relationships with NGOs leads to more effective integration of efforts during crisis situations, why are these enduring relationships relatively rare or not part of standard operating procedures? During our interviews, an oft-quoted reason why AFRICOM does not engage more with NGOs and other civil society organizations in exercises and planning was a lack of appropriate authorization to allow payment of expenses related to participation. Without that authority, AFRICOM could not sponsor NGOs to participate in planning sessions, exercises, and trainings. Given the resource constraints under which most NGOs operate, this constituted a significant hurdle that prevented increased collaboration between the military and NGO communities.

This simply was (and is) not true, however. The DoD received the authority to pay for NGO expenses in 2011, when US Code 1050a, *African Cooperation: Payment of Personnel Expenses*, went into effect. This code granted AFRICOM the ability to work with and pay for NGO services and activities. The code states: "The Secretary of Defense or the Secretary of a military department may pay the travel, subsistence, and special compensation of officers and students of African countries and other expenses that the Secretary considers necessary for African cooperation."[11] This provision removed one of the primary constraints on NGO participation in military activities, especially multi-day events and/or those taking place in remote locations.

This is an area in which AFRICOM could have taken initiative and developed strategy and procedures to encourage its staff to take advantage of this authority. Interviewees aware of this law cited the lack of direction from Office of the Secretary of Defense as the reason they felt constrained from acting under its authority. Without such overarching strategy, AFRICOM staff members have been limited in their ability to determine not only which NGOs are appropriate to talk to, but also what kind of activities they can undertake with NGOs and how to fund those activities. A lack of clarity on partnership is a core challenge to advancing relationships with civil society.

AFRICOM's leadership has repeatedly stated that engaging with people in nontraditional military activities is a priority. In 2010, then-Commander General Ward argued that "Security cooperation is more than just activities, programs, and expenditures. It's about people and relationships."[12] This was echoed by his successor, former Commander General Carter Ham, who stated, "the nontraditional military activities of the command are just as important as the military side. In fact, you could probably make a pretty good argument, because those contribute significantly to the underlying causes of instability across the continent, perhaps those, in the long term are more important."[13] These public speeches notwithstanding, AFRICOM does not yet have a robust and well-developed set of relationships with civilian leaders and NGOs. Instead, the command has a variety of ad hoc relationships with individual organizations that are largely dependent upon personal relationships, expertise, and contacts.

When Admiral James Stavridis and Evelyn Farkas examined twenty-first century public-private partnerships, they found that institutionalization and strategic planning is critically important to embedding and routinizing these relationships.

> Sometimes, projects are pursued because they are easy to execute, but not necessarily because the public-private collaboration will bring significant results aimed at addressing priority issues. Lack of institutionalization - models, guidelines, dedicated staff, and training - also results in resources committed to "one-off" or ad hoc projects when the same amount of effort could result in a strategic long-term sustainable program.[14]

Ironically, US government ethics rules were designed to limit the one-off events based on personal relationships because of the potential for conflicts of interest. Without an over-arching strategy, all that is left for the subordinate commands is to engage with the USAID-approved organizations they happen to meet while operating in their area of responsibility.

While it has been an often-stated aim of AFRICOM to advance partnership and coordination with other government agencies, the folding of the Public-Private Partnership Branch into another J9 branch in 2012 gave the appearance that partnership was not a high priority. There is less of an emphasis on partnership and, therefore, unclear direction on the priority of working with NGOs. As a result, those working at the AFRICOM headquarters often disregard NGOs, rarely consider how to engage with NGOs, and are unsure as to why they should or how they could legally engage with NGOs. In one interview a Civil Affairs officer, one of the very people one would assume would have an interest in engaging NGOs, said "NGOs are just like contractors. They are only looking for money so I don't talk to them." As a result of attitudes such as this, NGO interaction happens in a limited and ad hoc manner.

Without a strategy for engaging civil society, AFRICOM is unable to more deeply or broadly engage with organizations that could provide valuable insights, ensure greater effectiveness of programming goals, and help meet command objectives. The command is left relying on the personal and professional connections of staff. When links to civil society rely on personal connections, they also tend to be temporary, lasting only as long as that particular serviceperson is stationed at the organization. The diversity of NGOs with which the command interacts is also limited when it relies on personal connections. Rather than seeking out a diverse set of NGOs with a broad range of specialties and capabilities that are complementary to AFRICOM objectives, the command becomes linked with a relatively random set of organizations based on personal networks. When this happens, there can be operational consequences: the NGOs involved with the command's work may not be the most relevant organizations or ideal partners to handle particular projects and initiatives.

For example, to date, AFRICOM has had a great interest in Somalia, yet getting information from this part of the world is difficult. The few people with firsthand knowledge are those working in Somalia for international organizations such as the UN agencies or humanitarian NGOs. If the command had existing relationships with the staff of these organizations (i.e., if some of these actors had participated in exercises or other forums and there was a strategy to support these interactions), it could open an ongoing stream of relevant information from which AFRICOM could benefit.

One of the most important lessons learned from the post-earthquake operations in Haiti is that pre-established relationships and information sharing is essential for effective and rapid implementation of humanitarian efforts. These relationships could prove critical when/if the United States decides to intervene in failed or failing states. During our interview assessments in Stuttgart, AFRICOM staff regularly noted that NGOs are reluctant to speak and share information with them. However, those interagency staff and uniformed staff who had personal and professional relationships with international organizations and NGO personnel had no problem calling them, sending them an email, or meeting in person with them to discuss issues of shared interest. These same NGOs also had no problem meeting and talking with the military at events organized by third parties such as United States Institute of Peace and ACSS.

Operational Issues

AFRICOM's legal office has suggested developing a legal policy for working with NGOs. Yet, we argue, it is not clear if a legal department–driven policy is what is most required. A review of the appropriate authorities and relevant government policies that apply to interactions with NGOs could be useful, and this is what the legal department can provide.

Other operational interactions come in the form of financial support. When first formed, AFRICOM was limited in its ability to provide financial support to civilians. Yet, as just noted, AFRICOM has had the ability to pay for the participation of African civilians in training events, exercises, and conferences since January 2011. Civilians should not be the main recipients of training or the main focus of the command's work, but some participation as trainees or trainers would strengthen the ability of AFRICOM's programs to be truly effective in bridging the multiple communities that are important for improving African security. Other than the standard ethical restraints, there are no legal prohibitions against engaging with civil society organizations. AFRICOM is empowered to engage with civil society as one of the many stakeholders vital to the success of its mission.

AFRICOM personnel perceive limits on their ability to hire an NGO to do work that the command has identified or to fund an NGO's work that helps the command achieve its objectives. But there are no restrictions on hiring an NGO except those that govern all government procurement processes. NGOs selected through competitive processes, including Partners for Democratic Change and International Relief and Development, implement DoD-funded programs in Yemen. A gray area exists where an NGO has an existing program that could help the command achieve its objectives. It is unclear how funds could be allocated to support their existing activities.

One problem inhibiting increased collaboration in the form of joint activities is that AFRICOM headquarters staff do not have the contracting authority to enter into a grant or cooperative agreement with an NGO to support preexisting NGO programs; such contracting is primarily done at the component command level. This creates operational hurdles, but these can be overcome with creative approaches—collaboration is possible, but requires some maneuvering to accomplish. In the example of the Senegalese gender-mainstreaming program discussed previously, the Senegalese military initiated the program, and AFRICOM helped by providing funds to the Africa Center for Strategic Studies (ACSS). ACSS, in turn, created the partnership with the NGOs, set up the working relationship in Senegal, and created the forums in which AFRICOM, the Senegalese military, and the NGOs interacted. It was not a direct relationship between the command and the NGOs. Through ACSS, AFRICOM brought in US military resources to share best practices and experience. Without a workaround such as bringing in ACSS, the command would have been unable to pursue this program.

From the perspective of AFRICOM's Security Cooperation Program Manager, NGO interactions seem to be going well in the areas of humanitarian assistance, disaster response, and partnership programs pursued by the component commands.[15] The more challenging interactions with NGOs occur in the realm of strategy development, planning issues, task forces and counterterrorism, and civil affairs projects. Improving relations with NGOs across the board will aid AFRICOM and allow it to achieve the objectives outlined in President Obama's Presidential Policy Directive on Security Sector Assistance.[16] For example, if the Strategy, Plans, and Programs/J5 Directorate Regional Engagement Division teams tried to harmonize their command- and component-initiated programs with NGOs in their area when developing their regional strategies, it could make AFRICOM more efficient and effective.

Learning How to Work with NGOs

One challenge facing military personnel who may work with NGOs is their lack of knowledge and understanding of the value that NGOs could add to the military's work. This lack of knowledge translates into missed opportunities to engage with vital stakeholders and organizations that could help ensure greater success for the DoD's programs. With the possible exception of NAVAF, the members of AFRICOM and the subordinate commands have relatively little experience or expertise in working with NGOs. Those who do have some experience have often gained it in Iraq or Afghanistan, where working with NGOs is very different, both legally and culturally, from what it is in Africa.

While the placement of USAID staff at AFRICOM has improved coordination and communication, there is still an urgent need for members of the command who work with NGOs to share information and experiences and to help educate their colleagues on the benefits, opportunities, and challenges of working with NGOs. The senior development advisor from USAID who is embedded in the staff at AFRICOM could play a larger role in developing strategy related to engaging with NGOs and identifying appropriate training opportunities.

AFRICOM staff has some experience working with US and international NGOs. Nevertheless, most staff members have limited experience working with African civil society. This is slowly changing, however, as AFRICOM has matured and worked to develop more robust links. A few African organizations have attended conferences where AFRICOM was represented, such as the ACSS-organized conference on anti-corruption in Ghana and the AFRICOM-organized conferences on maritime safety and security. US and African academic institutions have participated in AFRICOM-organized academic partnership events, and these events have developed into one of the more robust relationships between AFRICOM and civilian academic and think tank organizations. Finally, the Maritime Partnership program has provided a successful model of training and collaboration as it has paired NAVAF sailors with local organizations for remote sensing and coastal monitoring projects. This program in particular has shown potential for expansion to other components and could be harmonized with other AFRICOM programs in a given country or on a specific topic.

One terrific example of partnering with an NGO exists at Southern Command (SOUTHCOM). Through the Southern Command Human Rights Initiative, SOUTHCOM partners with and funds an NGO in Costa Rica that serves as its subject matter expert and implementing partner. The events that SOUTHCOM organizes in its area of responsibility are facilitated by this partner NGO. This arrangement gives SOUTHCOM the opportunity to incorporate the assistance of NGO experts who facilitate the conversation among SOUTHCOM, civil society, and regional governments. Created in the early 1990s, this organization has been effective in broadening the dialogue on international human rights law and is held up as the gold standard for command/NGO collaboration.

Conclusion

From our interviews we come to a number of conclusions about the relationship between AFRICOM and civil society. There are many opportunities for greater partnership, and a more routine and robust interaction between civil society and military actors would greatly enhance the DoD's ability to respond to African security issues in a more adaptive manner. AFRICOM, being based in Germany, lacks the knowledge of African contexts that it needs to be able to develop plans and programs that take local specificities into account. Working with NGO communities at the country team level would help the command to develop programs and training that will have greater impact. Making these relationships more routine and institutionalized would avoid the ad-hoc and haphazard incorporation that currently exists, and would help the command and associated staff to reach out to a broader set of civic communities. Since many NGOs are hesitant to work closely with the US military (really, with any military), the interagency partners within AFRICOM and embassy staffs could and should serve as crucial intermediaries in these relationships.

There are a number of limiting factors that need to be addressed if these relationships are to truly become partnerships, and if they are to flourish. First and foremost, there is no strategy at AFRICOM for civil society engagement, partnership, and outreach. Without such a strategy, potential partners and valuable sources of useful information are lost, and partnerships are less effective. Civil society is a potentially untapped asset that could help the command and the US government to achieve their goals in Africa. Different offices and staff engage with representatives of civil society in an ad hoc manner depending upon their own personal or professional relationships and experience. Sometimes this engagement transfers when the staff person leaves but not always. Having a strategy and outreach guidelines would help to regularize these relationships.

Second, the knowledge about how to effectively interact with civic actors is patchy and limits the attempts made by headquarters staff to reach out and incorporate the nongovernmental communities. Thus, the quality and effectiveness of civil society engagement vary widely across the command and it supporting organizations. While component commands have the most experience and interaction with civil society, they are not the only organizations with experience working with civil society or an interest in engaging in these relationships. The understanding at the command level notwithstanding, AFRICOM does in fact have sufficient legal authority to engage with civil society, including the ability to fund participation in conferences and exercises, entering into contracts for the implementation of programs, and working in partnership with other US government agencies to provide financial support. However, this authority is not widely advertised or understood, making it a third factor limiting the development of robust relationships between the communities.

Despite these limitations, AFRICOM has been able to interact with a diverse group of NGOs at a variety of levels and on a diverse set of issues. We have argued throughout this chapter that developing a strategy for engaging civil society, which should include a clear statement of what the benefits and challenges are to working with NGOs, would enhance, deepen, and routinize these relationships. This, in turn, would enable AFRICOM and its defense partners to develop training and other programs that more accurately reflect real conditions on the ground in which they operate—thus bringing about more effective results both for American foreign policy and African security outcomes.

Notes

Note: The views expressed in this chapter are strictly our own and do not represent those of Partners for Democratic Change or the US governmnet.

[1] CIVICUS, "CIVICUS Civil Society Index."

[2] Statement made by General Ham at a January 2012 meeting in Stuttgart, Germany attended by author Trina Zwicker. In fiscal year 2012, the command headquarters executed an operating budget of $276 million ($274 million in fiscal year 2010, $286 million in fiscal year 2011). The 6 percent decrease represented a fiscal year 2013 budget of $259 million, $25 million less than spent in 2011. This was before sequestration cuts triggered in July 2013 decreased the budget even further. Budget figures are reported in "About the Command," www.africom/mil (accessed August 2, 2013; no longer available online).

[3] The component commands supporting AFRICOM are: Naval Forces, Africa (NAVAF), US Army Africa (USARAF), Marine Corps Forces, Africa (MARFORAF), US Air Forces, Africa (AFAFRICA), and Special Operations Africa (SOCAFRICA).

[4] Wheeler and Harmer, eds., *Resetting the Rules of Engagement.*

[5] Putman, "Addressing African Questions."

[6] Personal knowledge based on author Trina Zwicker's position at AFRICOM.

[7] Carmichael, "AFRICOM Supports Tunis Assistance Center."

[8] Owsley, "Pandemic Disaster Response."

[9] For more on APF, see Torres, "Africa Partnership Flight," and Brzozowske, "Week One of Africa Partnership Flight."

[10] Joint Warfighting Center, *Joint Task Force (JTF) Commander's Handbook,* 11-12.

[11] *Armed Forces,* U.S. Code. Title 10 (2011), § 1050a.

[12] Ward, "Opening Remarks."

[13] Ham, "AFRICOM Perspectives."

[14] Stavridis and Farkas, "The 21st Century Force Multiplier."

[15] Authors' interviews with AFRICOM headquarters and component command staff, 2010-2012.

[16] The White House, "Fact Sheet: U.S. Security Sector Assistance Policy."

9

Toward More Effective Development Assistance

Clarence J. Bouchat

In a world of globalization, Africa is of rising importance to the international community for the opportunities it presents and threats it poses. Africans and the world community need peace and prosperity in Africa to attain mutual security and humanitarian aspirations, and to incorporate Africa into the world's economy. These efforts serve the needs of Africans while also fulfilling the interests of foreign states in Africa. Foreign military assistance can support these goals by encouraging stability and security through economic development and good governance. Such support can be provided through an external security role and to a lesser extent in internal law and order. These are traditional military missions that are well understood and internationally recognized.

The military's role in the equally important requirement for economic development and better governance has precedents from humanitarian relief to stability operations, but a military forces' involvement in these endeavors is more likely to be controversial or misunderstood. This chapter considers a continuum of actions to better organize and administer assistance to show what has been done in the past and what could be done in order to better define the role of the US military in security, governance, and economic development.

Stability and Security

Many causes are debated for the chronic problems Africans endure, from social to geographic, imperialist, ethnic, or religious. Although Africans' problems are complex and diverse, they face two fundamental challenges within their control: establishing good political governance and sustainable economic development. Internal and regional security and stability enable the formation of proper governance and development, but good governance and economic improvement also contribute to stability and security.[1]

As this book's introductory chapters discuss, there is a feedback loop between governance, security, and development. Security and stability are important as the foundation upon which to build; without them nothing of duration can follow. Political governance and economic development are the structures upon which other problems will be solved.[2] These security aspects are relatively well understood, but their economic and political sides are less well known. Because they are crucial, in this chapter I survey economic and political ties to security and stability before analyzing ways that foreign military forces can contribute to all these domains.

Security and Stability as Foundations

Security and stability are precursors to solving problems in a country because they form a necessary foundation.[3] A secure and stable environment requires internal rule of law, order, and justice, while secure and stable conditions lay the foundation to sustain the good governance and economic development that make a state viable.[4] A US Army Combined Arms Center commander called actions to support governance "pre-emptive stability operations" that attempt to promote security and stability before, and not after, violence starts.[5] The foundational need for stability and security is recognized by Africans; leaders of the Economic Community of West African States (ECOWAS) realized that a "combination of poverty and bad governance is no doubt a great part of the causes of the conflicts in West Africa. Accordingly, there can be no economic advancement without a peaceful, stable and secure environment."[6] These are basic principles upon which Africans and those who wish to assist them can agree.

Stability and security contribute to human and economic development by establishing the conditions under which they can flourish, but security and stability also depend upon such development in a symbiotic way.[7] The entire premise behind the US Agency for International Development's (USAID's) philosophy on economic growth in postconflict countries is that "the fundamentals of economic growth increase the likelihood of successfully preventing a return to conflict."[8] Unfortunately, in 2008 the US

Department of Defense's (DoD's) *The Joint Operating Environment* forecasted that over the next 20 years it will be Africans who mainly constitute the bottom billion of poverty world-wide, resulting in violence within and between states.[9] Political access and change are necessary to allow the readjustment and balance often required to avert violence in fragile states.[10]

Such co-dependence among the essential conditions of stability, security, development, and governance makes improving the situation found in Africa challenging. During former President George Bush's last trip through Africa in 2008, he visited five countries to showcase that advances are possible.[11] President Barak Obama's 2013 trip to South Africa, Senegal, and Tanzania further highlighted the rapid improvements that many countries have been making in recent years. With proper international assistance in these areas, Africa's contributions to the world and the continent's own well-being should improve.

US Military Roles in Stability and Security

For military forces to assist in improving human development, an understanding of their role is in order. The US military has the ability to not only establish security and stability on foreign soil, but to promote better governance and economic development while doing so. In Iraq and Afghanistan, US forces attempted similar goals through stability operations, defined in Joint Publication (JP) 3-07 as:

> various military missions, tasks, and activities conducted outside the United States in coordination with other instruments of national power to maintain or reestablish a safe and secure environment, provide essential government services, emergency infrastructure reconstruction, and humanitarian relief.[12]

Thomas Barnett, an expert on global conflict forecasting, believes that the US military will intervene more in "gap and seam states" in places like Africa to ensure worldwide stability and security, which "requires the Army to engage not only military and insurgent forces, but to concentrate on economic, cultural, and sociopolitical structures and issues."[13] The US military is able to assist in establishing security and stability with economic and political advances to devastated or impoverished places.

Stability operations usually fall to military forces in the aftermath of conflict because the humanitarian need is immediate and their skills and resources readily available. These are often unwanted and unintended missions, but US forces nonetheless have managed political and economic reconstruction during operations ranging from Mexico in 1847 to Afghanistan in 2012.[14] US Army doctrine states that stability operations may occur before hostilities, and thus may prevent conflict and the need for armed intervention by addressing the causes of potential hostilities.[15] Stability operations are an important way for military forces to foster security through economic and political development, though to be effective these operations require military members to understand the underlying economic and political problems with which military organizations such as US Africa Command (AFRICOM) may assist.

Another method for attaining security and stability is peacebuilding. This is a more ambitious strategy that establishes long-term stability in weak states. The United States defines peacebuilding as: "Stability actions, predominately diplomatic and economic, that strengthen and rebuild governmental infrastructure and institutions in order to avoid a relapse into conflict."[16] The ends for US stability operations offered in Army Doctrine Reference Publication (ADRP) 3-07, *Stability*, are to achieve a "safe and secure environment, established rule of law, social well-being, stable governance, and a sustainable economy."[17]

Despite the seeming parallels between peacebuilding and stability operations, important differences exist in US doctrine. Stability operations are a lead mission for the military, while other parts of government, international organizations, and nongovernmental organizations take responsibility in peacebuilding. The focus and time horizon differ also, with stability operations specifically using near-term phrases like "essential," "emergency," and "relief," while peacebuilding touts broader goals and longer time frames as implied in the phrase "rebuild governmental infrastructure and institutions."[18] Military forces may help in rebuilding countries in need through stability operations and peacebuilding. The more complex role of peacebuilding operations is often avoided by armed forces, which prefer that civilian organizations dedicated to such long-term undertakings perform them.

The past use of aid has proven that external help alone will not solve Africa's problems. From 1948 to 2008, African states absorbed a net total of over $1 trillion in foreign development aid (adding $50 billion annually since)—with disappointing returns that confirm that current efforts to improve the situation are insufficient.[19] Corruption, instability, and underdeveloped infrastructure and human resources have discouraged most international business investment. As a result, 70 percent of gross capital formation in Africa stems from donor country hand-outs. Less than 15 percent flows from foreign investment, and most of that goes to the extractive industries, which rarely lead to broad-based growth.[20]

This remains a chronic problem with the amount of official development aid received by sub-Saharan countries roughly the same, relative to all
international aid, between 1995 and 2009 (although climbing in real terms
from $20 billion to $42 billion).[21] Africans have grown reliant on outside
aid, and may now be trapped in the paradox of needing aid to grow more
self-reliant. Outside help to Africa is still needed, but not of the type given
in the past. However it is delivered, aid to Africans should be given so as to
build Africans' economic and governing capacity while reducing their need
for such aid.

Current US Military Involvement in Sub-Saharan Africa

Security and stability are prerequisites for improvements in Africa, therefore
attaining them should be the first step for policy-makers. Barnett believes
that economic and political improvements depend upon the elimination of
conflict, and that military forces are an important way to achieve peace. In
this vein, he asserts that security is the United States' "most influential
public-sector export."[22] Where conditions have deteriorated beyond the
ability of local governments to provide a stable and secure environment,
foreign military forces could restore these necessary conditions.[23]

Sometimes coercive military actions are needed to counter political and
criminal threats and violence; international forces tried such actions in
Somalia in the 1990s, and face such choices again against Boko Haram in
Nigeria and other insurgent and terrorist organizations elsewhere in Africa.
Under other circumstances, a military force may act as a deterrent and not
be required to directly intervene.[24] Between these two options, the US
Army's stability doctrine suggests that military forces can transform conflict
by reducing the potential for conflict while enhancing political and
economic developments through partnership with local officials.[25] Pursuant
to ADRP 3-07, US ground forces are responsible for establishing security
and stability when military force is needed to meet US government interests,
but their role is often insufficient to promote local economic and
governmental development.

Peacetime Military Engagement Activities

Conflict resolution through "hard power" may be what most military forces
do best. However, the military may also deliver security and stability
through less lethal "soft power" methods, such as the DoD's peacetime
military engagement. Such engagement comes from AFRICOM and other
combatant commands' theater security cooperation programs, "which share
many of the same broad goals as stability operations ... to build partner

capacity, strengthen legitimate governance, maintain rule of law, [and] foster economic growth."[26] This is what AFRICOM's first commander, General William Ward, called "'active security'—defined as a 'persistent and sustained level of effort focused on security assistance programs that prevent conflict in order to foster dialogue and development.'"[27] He referred to the best known of many types of security cooperation, security assistance, which supplies defense-related articles, training, and services to another country.[28] Security assistance is just one of several defense programs supplied by the US military through US ambassadors to shore up similar values and mutual interests, however.[29] Such ongoing activities include professionalization assistance, humanitarian assistance, and the broader "nation assistance."

Since combined education, training, and exercises are highly visible and well established within the US military, they should constitute part of any solution involving assistance. An example in education is the DoD's African Center for Strategic Studies, which offers seminars for senior African leaders to provide understanding about military forces operating under democratic institutions. In the training realm, one particularly successful US program that instills discipline and basic military skills in African forces, while also directly contributing to continent-wide peace and stability, is the Africa Contingency Operations Training Assistance (ACOTA). ACOTA seeks to strengthen African states' peacekeeping and humanitarian response capabilities to resolve Africa's problems internally.[30] Since 1997, the program has trained and equipped over 250,000 African troops in 257 contingency units from 25 participating countries, and "provides the lion's share of operational experience for a growing proportion of African professional military leaders at every level."[31] Education, training, and exercises are traditional military missions that directly strengthen stability and security in African states.

Humanitarian and Civic Assistance

Although both stability operations and theater security engagement give US military forces a role in addressing development, professionalization activities do not adequately confront the underlying problems of economic development and good governance. Another form of military activity that addresses development problems better is humanitarian and civic assistance (HCA). This assistance benefits the local populace as secondary activities of planned military operations or exercises. HCA addresses basic human needs like health care and infrastructure construction for societies where US forces are operating.[32] During a training exercise in Ghana and Togo, for example, US sailors treated thousands with critically needed medical care. Such actions benefit the population with services they otherwise would not have received, improve the operational readiness of the military participants, and help US government members to gain contacts, cultural understanding, and good will.[33]

Programs like HCA help impoverished citizens with the basic health care and economic support in which Africa is deficient, but they do not significantly contribute to systemic economic development on the level that Africans need. AFRICOM's budget for HCA activity is very small, which severely limits its impact on development.[34] The tie between HCA programs and development problems in Africa is obvious, and might relieve distress. Such programs are transitory and only the ad-hoc by-products of military operations, however, and thus they lack perseverance or capacity building. They continue to be valuable add-ons, but do not address the root cause of problems in Africa.

Nation Assistance Activities

Each part of a theater security engagement may contribute in part or indirectly to economic development or good governance; by contrast, nation assistance operations allow military forces to address these issues more broadly. Nation assistance supports another country with "sustainable development and growth ... to promote long-term regional stability" under the direction of the Department of State (DoS). Nation assistance is an overarching category of US theater security engagement that includes sub-categories like HCA and security assistance, but emphasizes long-term development, which is not an explicit characteristic of other activities.[35]

Nation assistance operations may be conducted independently of operations or exercises, or in conjunction with other US government agencies, international governmental organizations (IGOs), nongovern-mental organizations (NGOs), and host nation authorities.[36] For instance, security sector reform (SSR) can improve organizations by "organizing new institutions and units from the ministerial level to the smallest maneuver unit."[37] An example of SSR is how the United States and the United Kingdom coordinated to reestablish professional and accountable ministries of defense and armed forces, respectively, in Liberia and Sierra Leone following devastating and interlocking civil wars in western Africa. Nation assistance in its grandest scale approaches the types and levels of economic and governance assistance needed for security and stability in African countries, and is the closest that US military forces may come under current practices to addressing African needs. Despite the very beneficial nature of nation assistance, the US military has shied away from such long-term missions, at least in Africa.

Peacetime Military Engagement Improvements and Criticisms

Proven useful as a stand-alone program or as part of larger interagency efforts, military theater engagement does have room for improvement and limits to what it can accomplish. Assuming that improved security and stability in Africa are priorities for theater engagement projects, one low cost improvement is better cooperation among donor countries to reduce administration and overhead costs. Donor countries also could increase a program's impact by broadening the capacity of locals through coordinated programs and increasing its duration for more lasting effects.[38]

Theater engagements could be improved by efforts to support regional cooperation initiatives, such as the African Standby Force, the African Union's response force for crises.[39] In the State Department's ACOTA program, US personnel consult with and participate in peacekeeping with subregional organizations, such as ECOWAS and the Southern African Development Community (SADC), thereby reinforcing the multinational nature of these operations.[40] Regional initiatives also better serve foreign-local collaboration because more expertise and resources remain in Africa, which increases capacity and persistence since neighboring countries can aid each other after donor support is gone.

Military engagement in Africa usually meets the foreign sponsor's interests, which is why these programs continue even when donor government budgets are lean. In professionalizing local forces and helping them contribute to stability, theater engagement activities also benefit host nations through the education, training, and exercising of armed forces. However, these security assistance programs only tangentially address the root causes of economic and political problems. Although better at addressing these core issues, HCA and the wider nation assistance programs remain limited in aiding development because they focus on military-related applications.

Given this, current AFRICOM military-security programs lack the depth, breadth, and persistence needed to address Africa's security and stability problems.[41] Foreign military engagement is limited in its effects because of general concerns that military involvement in economic and governing affairs sets the wrong example, and employing local forces in these ways gives them too much power, conflicts with civil organizations, and diverts them from their core military missions.[42] Thus, despite the fact that theater security cooperation programs support security and stability in foreign countries, in part through improving their economic and governing bases, they fall short of their mark. AFRICOM's theater security cooperation program is of minor assistance to combating Africa's real problems.[43] In any strategy used to support stability and security in Africa, this program will be a necessary part, but it is insufficient to achieve a significant lasting impact on its own.

Should the Military Lead?

If much of Africa is in dire need of assistance in establishing security and stability, would it make sense to change the current insufficient approaches for ones that hold more promise? For the past 65 years, the US military has been involved in reestablishing security and stability directly in foreign countries, and in improving their long-term economic well-being and political governance. By doctrine, stability operations and nation assistance may occur before a conflict, so a stronger peacetime military role in Africa is possible.[44] Such a military option could "help develop indigenous capacity for security, essential services, a viable market economy, rule of law, [and] democratic institutions."[45] With planning skills, manpower, resources, and appropriate expertise coordinating the whole of the US government, military forces could lead a concerted effort to significantly improve peace within Africa and set it on a course to prosperity.

Although US law specifically gives the lead to the DoS under these circumstances, in this section I explore the military's leading other government agencies as an option, although one requiring legal and policy changes. I examines why and how the military could take the lead, and the problems that detract from this approach. This is a reasonable option if the reader accepts that the ways military forces are preventing violence and instability are changing, and thus the military's role in security missions is also changing.[46]

Why a Military Lead

A military lead for the US government's efforts to improve Africa's security and its economic and political well-being is not farfetched. A military lead has practical advantages and strong advocates; to some degree, the military's role is already shifting through AFRICOM. Following World War II, the US military had a leading role in countering the greatest threats of the day: communism's economic and political challenges to stabilizing Europe and Asia. Later during the Vietnam War, the US military had an increasingly important role in the US government's peace and prosperity programs through a civil-military "single-manager concept" over "sociopolitical reforms, economic stimuli, and military assistance."[47] Giving the US military a similar role in Africa against today's leading threats, the economic and political ills that spawn instability and terrorism, would follow these precedents. When AFRICOM was proposed, its initial stated purpose was to bring "peace and security to Africa by promoting health, education, democracy, and economic growth"—seemingly a peacebuilding program.[48]

Supporters of an expanding military role believe "that defeat of internal threats to basic public order and restoration and maintenance of minimum essential political, security, and economic conditions within victim states combined might constitute the new 'major combat operation' for US land forces."[49] Barnett believes that the US Army needs to promote and sustain regional security by not just engaging "military and insurgent forces," but also by concentrating "on economic, cultural, and sociopolitical structures and issues."[50] Author Carl Schramm argues: "The United States' armed forces are uniquely positioned to contribute to world peace and prosperity by means other than actual force. And if they apply the ideas [of expeditionary economics], they could start a revolution in thinking about economic growth."[51]

Such an approach constitutes "unified action:" the synchronization of government and nongovernment efforts with military operations. Despite their reluctance to undertake this mission, a former undersecretary for Personnel and Readiness concluded that to prevent future wars, the US military must engage in peacebuilding.[52] Although controversial, a strong case can be made that a military lead for the US government holds merit.

How a Military Lead Works

The military often leads peacebuilding efforts when there are no other viable options. Since US military forces have enjoyed some success in this role, an expectation persists that they should lead in peacebuilding for practical or expedient reasons. In past and current operations, the US military took the lead in rebuilding operations because civilian agencies lacked adequate resources or the capability to do so. This happened in Bosnia where the military Stabilization Force (SFOR) had to expand its mission to assist international organizations in typically civilian endeavors. The military recognized that SFOR was "moving into the area of nation building but saw no alternative if SFOR was ever going to withdraw."[53]

The DoD has been able to gather the resources and authorities needed for soft power problems, and has the leadership and processes to tackle complex operations. The military could lead when civilian organizations lack the necessary means to succeed, as in Bosnia, because it is well organized and resourced. The military's leadership is especially needed when security is so bad that civilian organizations cannot function, and yet to meet national goals, economic development and governance must progress.[54] Because of its practical merits and past experience, the military's leadership of US government efforts could further security, economic development, and improved governance in Africa.

Military leadership of US government efforts in Africa could not be a "go it alone" affair, however. Military lead would require the support of the whole US government, intergovernmental organizations (IGOs), and nongovernmental organizations (NGOs), just as civilian organizations sometimes need the capabilities of the military.[55] The pantheon of participants in a military-led effort would remain the same as in a civilian one, but their relationships would change to allow military personnel to organize, plan, and execute the effort. US military units have shown they are able to execute primarily civilian responsibilities, with limited or full assistance from host governments and US or international agencies.[56]

Nonetheless, difficulties exist because of the steep learning curve for such activities, even when using reserve component forces with consummate civilian skills. The lag in learning can be costly, too, as demonstrated by initially fitful civil-military efforts in Iraq. The US military has learned much from these economic and governance functions, is better able to integrate the expertise of other agencies to achieve common peace and prosperity goals, and is consciously codifying their experience for when it is needed again.[57]

Addressing the Problems of Military Lead

There are organizations that resent the military taking a lead role, or that are unable to cooperate with the military in this manner.[58] NGOs may be the most difficult case because they are independent and governed by international impartiality principles; also, they often prefer to work at the operational and policy levels. Their participation is essential because compared to military organizations, NGOs tend to be more focused, faster to respond, more experienced in their fields, and more likely to remain longer to ensure continuity.[59] The barriers between these two sides might be overcome by a focus on common goals; reluctant NGOs might join with US forces if projects were coordinated through UN or US civilian agencies.

An integrated approach towards a common goal could coordinate agencies under military leadership, and could result in a comprehensive approach that combines host governments, international organizations, NGOs, agencies of other countries, and private entities. Such unified action could create a community based upon a common understanding of a situation, a shared purpose, and an agreed level of cooperation.[60] The main challenge is that the use of military forces is "inherently political" in contrast to the "morally autonomous" traditional humanitarian efforts; a distinction that complicates, if not dooms, such cooperation despite good intentions on both sides.[61]

Unified action is a broad link between US government efforts and those of the agencies of other countries, NGOs, and the private sector, but it is a relatively weak link because of sometimes diverging national and organizational interests. Given shared national security goals, US government agencies should strive for a more demanding level of coordination and a greater unity of effort. While difficult to achieve, unity of effort is one of the key requirements for stability and peace operations. It requires multi-level support from participants to succeed, whether under military or civilian lead.[62]

Every presidential administration since President John F. Kennedy has tried to institutionalize unity of effort within the executive branch. In 2005, the Bush administration emphasized interagency cooperation in stability operations through National Security Presidential Directive 44 (NSPD-44), which built upon the Clinton administration's Presidential Decision Document 56, *Managing Complex Contingency Operations*, in order to better coordinate efforts in Iraq and Afghanistan under the DoS. As has been argued throughout this volume, promoting interagency cooperation was a driving force behind the creation of AFRICOM.

These presidential decisions could be revised to allow a DoD lead in Africa. NSPD-44 requires other agencies to build their capabilities to participate in stability operations and, as an extension, peacebuilding, which would make interagency coordination more effective.[63] To enhance cooperation and understanding under military leadership, all participants could together train, plan, and share procedures and terms.[64] Envisioning this type of cooperation, FM 3-07 was originally written in 2008 to resurrect the concept of stability operations specifically using input from nonmilitary sources in order to serve as a common reference.[65] Such exercises and training are second nature to military forces, which is another advantage to a military lead scheme: better preparation under practiced military tutelage. Planning and integration are required to improve the whole of government approach, which has remained elusive despite cooperative efforts otherwise.

To make such a military-civilian hybrid work would require systemic changes in the US government. To start, the military should develop dedicated nation assistance specialists with broad backgrounds in the methods and roles of related government and nongovernmental agencies, and judiciously assign such officers to appropriate government staffs.[66] Select military units may need to specialize and to perform assigned functions to support and interact with other government organizations or NGOs. Reserve units, with diverse civilian expertise, or civil-military units may be best suited for these new lead and support roles. Modern operations, however, have shown that stability operations and nation assistance should not be confined to specialists, although specialists are needed. Training for all units should include skills and considerations that support immediate or follow-on tasks to achieve stability, but with an eye to economic development and governance enhancement. This training requires a different mindset than combat operations training.[67] Such integration of the DoD and other government agencies under one command would require statutory changes; revisions to legal authorities were necessary for the less ambitious integration of military and nontraditional missions now attempted by AFRICOM.[68]

As other chapters in this volume discuss, the US government is making changes in order to strengthen the reconstruction role of some civilian agencies. If a standing cadre of security, economic, and governance professionals is needed, then US government agencies with smaller personnel authorizations should seek larger authorizations to allow regular training and contingency preparation.[69] Such an expansion would solve the staffing problem experienced in the more modest experiment of integrating interagency personnel into AFRICOM.

While other authors in this volume have argued that the ongoing civil-military imbalance should be addressed by increasing the size of the civilian agencies, one could look at it as a rationale for proposing a solution where the military leads. The military could efficiently balance the strapped assets of other departments. The fear, however, is that such "continued growth in military capability in these areas [would become] self-reinforcing, accelerating the downward spiral of civilian capacity in favor of more expedient military solutions."[70] One argument, therefore, is that the US military should lead other US government resources, and indirectly non-US or civilian personnel only until the DoS and others build a "more modern and expeditionary Foreign Service" as envisioned in the 2010 House *Foreign Relations Authorization Act.*[71] It is worth stressing that this solution should work in tandem with host nation support whenever possible to reinforce capacity building and continuity.[72] Under many conditions, a US military lead role in stability and security operations that assist in economic and governance problems might be attractive. However, the many necessary modifications to military and other government institutions suggest that the military's leadership role might be an undesirable option.

Drawbacks of Military Leadership

Just because professional military forces could lead efforts in Africa does not mean that they should. Despite the merits of a military lead in a unity-of-effort approach, current Western democratic values do not easily tolerate a military organization directing economic development and governance aid, what many label "securitization." Western countries probably would refuse to overthrow centuries of successful military subordination for the uncertain prospects of speeding improvements in Africa. Moreover, no donor country has significant interests at stake to warrant such a dramatic departure, as countries arguably undertook during the Marshall Plan.

The changes needed to make a military lead option viable may reinforce military organizations at the expense of other departments, and thus some DoS and USAID officials fear AFRICOM is taking the lead on US efforts in Africa.[73] As evidence of the military's ascendency, critics note that the DoD's share of official US aid money has grown from 3 to 22 percent in the past decade, while USAID's share has dropped from 65 to 40 percent.[74] Correcting the imbalance of resources and personnel available for nonmilitary organizations is necessary regardless of what organization is leading.[75]

Another danger of overemphasizing military capabilities is that military personnel will be used in situations where their presence is not appropriate.[76] Legally there are problems with the military taking the lead in economic and governance missions. US laws governing government organizations' foreign missions would need to be revised to permit the military's changing role, and the military's budget would need to be increased to allow it to conduct economic and governance missions.[77] Even if these steps were taken, international law would remain an obstacle because it limits military forces to providing security and order in economic development projects.[78] Thus, domestic factors and traditional expectations make a military lead of US government development efforts an awkward option.

Military forces have the capability to organize, lead, and assist in complex foreign development and governance issues. They could assume a lead role through various existing structures; military forces might oversee the sharing of resources, processes, and training needed to make cooperation more effective. However, the military's deep resources, established processes, and can-do attitude could overwhelm cross-discipline efforts if the military were in the lead. Critics of this approach fear that continued over-reliance on the military eviscerates the organizations that specialize in these roles, sets a poor example of civil-military relations for the people these efforts are meant to help, and violates the US public's expectation that the military should not lead civilian organizations in most cases. Given the realities of the situation, another option is to reverse the positions and adequately resource civilian institutions to lead with appropriate military support.

Should the Civilians Lead?

Because AFRICOM is perceived by some as becoming the proconsul of US government affairs in Africa, a more appropriate US government civilian institution like USAID could assume this role through adequate resourcing and support. Many Africans, suspicious of any increased military role, wonder why the leadership of the US government's assistance efforts is not given to an already existing institution that specializes in promoting development and is more acceptable locally and internationally.[79] USAID has been active throughout Africa for decades and is respected for its work. While the previous chapters have argued that military involvement in such activities is controversial, they have not critically analyzed the argument that civilian institutions do a better job. Thus, this chapter next analyzes the advantages and disadvantages of a civilian lead.

Why a Civilian Lead

Whole of government leadership under USAID offers the advantages of that organization's longstanding expertise in development issues and focus on long-term solutions—neither of which are inherent in military efforts. To implement this would require substantial changes in how US foreign policy is created and structured. The current US political system brings both military and civilian efforts together only at the chief executive level. Since long-term African affairs, like development, rarely rise high enough in the national interest to demand coordination by the US president, competition over goals and resources occurs at lower levels and inhibits cross-agency cooperation (as bureaucratic offices fight to preserve and then extend their authorities).[80]

The National Security Council (NSC) coordinates the US government departments in common foreign policy for the president, but development and governance issues in places such as Africa rarely receive sufficient attention at this level either.[81] The tools by which the US and other governments can assist Africans towards peace and prosperity already exist, but need to be properly structured and resourced. The military is an important element needed by a civilian-led effort because of the military's contacts with similar organizations in African countries, effective resources, security expertise, and experience in complex operations. These are the same strengths that would allow a military lead, but here they would be utilized under USAID direction, oversight, and strategy. The process to attain national security goals in Africa should synchronize civilian and military capabilities toward "soft power to promote participation in government, spur economic development, and address the root causes of conflict," the comprehensive approach advocated by ADRP 3-07, *Stability*.[82]

The NSPD-44 is a presidential directive that sets the State Department, within the executive branch, as the lead agency responsible for coordinating and leading "US government efforts to prepare, plan for, and conduct reconstruction and stabilization activities ... to include balancing civilian and military activities."[83] This mission includes improving the US government's institutional capacity to intervene successfully before security problems arise.[84] Given the will to assist, the NSPD-44 mandate is broad enough to incorporate improving conditions in Africa to achieve stabilization and security through economic development and better governance.

Addressing the Problems of Civilian Lead

Over a decade ago, an effort in Haiti under USAID's lead synchronized civilian and military stabilization and reconstruction activities with mixed results.[85] The Haiti mission demonstrated such an arrangement could work, but that USAID needed more resources, greater expertise, and better planning and executing abilities. These lessons were relearned in Iraq and Afghanistan, and by 2007, the State Department formed the Office of the Coordinator for Reconstruction and Stabilization (renamed the Bureau of Conflict and Stabilization Operations in 2011) to "promote the security of the United States through better coordination, planning, and implementation of reconstruction and stabilization activities." This approach makes diplomacy and development by the US government "more agile, responsive, and complimentary."[86] These are steps in the right direction to help the civilian component plan, execute, and lead stability efforts.

These changes strengthen the roles of development and governance in achieving stability and security, and show the importance of these roles in foreign policy. Although many processes are in place to improve development and governance efforts, in the civilian world there is no clear authority in charge of regional efforts, as there are no civilian counterparts to a regional combatant commander. Various bureaus and offices spread throughout the foreign policy bureaucracy each have the lead on their own operations, which are not subject to any coordination body outside the US ambassador in each country. One option would be to appoint an equivalent diplomatic proconsul, "a regional super ambassador with clear authority to integrate all US Government activities in a region."[87] Another way to enhance unity of effort is to create a "Standing Regional Security Council composed of senior representatives from all of the national security departments and agencies," perhaps as a sub-division of the NSC or within the State Department's regional bureaus.[88] These options might enable USAID to play a stronger role in security through long-term economic development and governance.

US government and international civilian organizations have the mandate and experience needed to help Africans improve their situation. The US and other militaries should play their expected role in enforcing security and stability directly and indirectly through economic development and good governance, though firmly under overarching civilian oversight. To avoid the perception that a robust AFRICOM might overstep this preferred order requires that the existing system of procedures and proposals between civilian and military organizations be reinforced and improvements hastened. NSPD-44 clearly designates the State Department as the overall lead in stability and peace operations, but both the DoS and USAID need more resources and backing to meet this charge. In support of its lead mission, changes should be made to fully use assets that are available to the State Department and USAID. To streamline this effort, all US government assets and procedures should be coordinated.

Finally, the designation of a lead entity or person for regional affairs could balance resources and efforts within the US government, and help coordinate actions with other governments, NGOs, and IGOs. As this chapter has shown, for practical reasons and to honor long-held democratic traditions, consolidating economic development and good governance efforts under a civilian agency lead is a viable way to attain US national interests in security and stability in Africa and other regions of the world.

Conclusion

In this chapter, I traced the roles and responsibilities of US government agencies in African policy, outlined how needed change is happening, and suggested what could still be done. Rather than advocating new policies, I concluded that the US government is starting down a promising track with Africans to confront political and economic malaise, although these efforts seem to be weakening with the end of efforts in Afghanistan and the curtailing of federal government budgets. Since long-term security and stability rest on economic development and proper governance, these latter two elements must be addressed to meet the goals of peace and relative prosperity for Africa. Both governance and development must be tackled together, and military forces can play an important part.

The US military has a role to play in establishing these favorable conditions in Africa, and the founding of AFRICOM focuses and coordinates military efforts. The current method for military forces to promote stability and security is either by directly intervening, as during peace operations or, preferably, by enabling host forces to play their role in security while supported by US theater engagement activities. Although important, these traditional activities have a limited influence on the root causes of instability, and therefore military forces' roles and responsibilities could be expanded.

One potential option would be to broaden AFRICOM's role and place it at the lead of US government interagency efforts. Although the US military has performed such a role throughout history, directly involving the military in sustained development efforts or leadership of a larger effort to rebuild tottering states would be a departure from the norm that Africans, the US public, and the international community might not tolerate. Military leadership also would counter NSPD-44 and require many changes to implement. The possible gain to national interests from a more peaceful and prosperous Africa does not justify the precedent and organizational disruption such additional responsibilities entail.

Therefore, the good that the military offers in terms of countering violence and establishing order and efficient delivery of economic and political development is best employed under civilian control—whether that control unifies the efforts of US government organizations or actions with the international community. The US government should continue its emphasis on civilian leadership through improved manning, resources, and processes; and greater integration of military-civilian efforts. Africa needs outside assistance to better its situation, and strengthening the roles and responsibilities of civilian lead agencies will help.

Although I have argued that the military should remain subordinate to civilian agencies, the military's role in attaining security and stability remains important. Military forces should first focus on security, and then address the necessary parts of stabilization and peacebuilding—putting into place the structure for proper governance and a viable economy required by a functioning state. Within the US government then, the military should complete appropriate security and stability enforcement tasks, and judiciously support development and governance roles under the strong leadership of properly outfitted professional civilian agencies before a crisis. Military personnel lack the depth of knowledge in the crucial disciplines that promote long-term security and stability. For this reason, they should defer to civilian professionals, and support them to serve US interests and the needs of Africans. It is time for Africans to interact with the global community as equals, and the present course puts them on that much delayed path.

Notes

Note: The opinions expressed in this chapater are my own and do not represent official statements or positions of the United States government, Department of Defense, or any of its organizations.

[1] *High Level Regional Consultative Meeting*, 2.

[2] Dobbins, "Guidelines for Nation Builders," 25.

[3] United Nations Secretariat, *United Nations Peacekeeping Operations*, 29-30.

[4] Denoeux, *Development Assistance and Counter-Extremism*, iii-iv and 14-15.

[5] Harlow, "Army Unveils New Stability Operations Manual."

[6] West Africa Network for Peacebuilding (WANEP), *An Assessment of the ECOWAS Mechanism*.

[7] Harrison, *The Central Liberal Truth*, 48.

[8] Ott, *A Guide to Economic Growth*, 1.

[9] United States Joint Forces Command, *The Joint Operating Environment 2008*, 12-19.

[10] Department of the Army Headquarters, *Stability Operations*, Foreword. Although FM 3-07 has been superseded by Army Doctrine Reference Publication 3-07 in August 2013, the sentiment expressed here by LTG William Caldwell is still very relevant, as are the few other references to this document in this chapter.

[11] The five were Benin, Tanzania, Rwanda, Ghana, and Liberia; they were selected as examples in Africa "where democracy is advancing, where economies are growing, and leaders are meeting challenges...." The White House, "Trip to Africa February;" and Garland, "U.S.-Africa Policy and Florida."

[12] Chairman Joint Chiefs of Staff, *Stability Operations*, vi.

[13] Siegl, "Clarity and Culture," 99.

[14] Schadlow, *Organizing to Compete in the Political Terrain*, 3-4; see also chapter three in this volume for a more detailed review of the military's involvement in nation building.

[15] Department of the Army Headquarters, *Stability*, 1-1 to 1-2 and 1-9 to 1-10.

[16] United States Department of Defense, *Peace Operations*, GL-5.

[17] Department of the Army Headquarters, *Stability*, 1-14.

[18] Department of the Army Headquarters, *Stability*, 1-1, 2-4 to 2-6; Department of Defense, *Peace Operations*, GL-5.

[19] Moyo, "Why Foreign Aid Is Hurting Africa;" Kaplan, "West African Integration;" and Mistry, "Reasons for Sub-Saharan Africa's Development Deficit," 666.

[20] Moyo, "Why Foreign Aid Is Hurting Africa;" and Kaplan, "West African Integration," 84-85.

[21] United Nations, *Towards Human Resilience*, 153.

[22] Barnes, "Global Flows: Terror, Oil, and Strategic Philanthropy," 6.

[23] Department of the Army Headquarters, *Stability*, 1-10.

[24] Crane, "Phase IV Operations: Where Wars Are Really Won," 20.

[25] Department of the Army Headquarters, *Stability*, 1-2 to 1-3.

[26] Department of the Army Headquarters, *Stability Operations*, vii.

[27] Ward as quoted in Malan, "AFRICOM: Joined-Up Geographic Command," 1.

[28] United States Department of Defense, *Joint Operations*, V-15.

[29] Risio, "Security Cooperation MAGTF," 18.

[30] Copson, *Africa Backgrounder*," 19.

[31] Department of State, "Fact Sheet: African Contingency Operations," and Dempsey, "The Transformation of African Militaries," 387-391.

[32] Department of Defense, *Joint Operations,* V-15 to V-16.

[33] Garcia, "Achieving Security Cooperation Objectives," 105-6.

[34] Palmer, "Legal Impediments," 83.

[35] Department of Defense, *Joint Operations*, V-14.

[36] Ibid.

[37] Department of the Army Headquarters, *Stability*, 1-2, , 3-4 and 3-9.

[38] Ulriksen, "Deployments for Development?" 560.

[39] Delevingne, "Controversy Dogs Creation of U.S. Military Command," 3.

[40] Handy, "African Contingency Operations," 59.

[41] Doe and Nyanseor, "AFRICOM: A Model."

[42] Basilotto, *A Revisionist View of Nation Assistance in Africa*, 7.

[43] Palmer, "Legal Impediments," 84.

[44] Department of the Army Headquarters, *Stability*, 1-2; and Department of Defense, *Joint Operations*, V-10 and V-14.

[45] Siegl, "Clarity and Culture in Stability Operations," 101.

[46] Cole, "An Open Door," 6; and Schramm, "Expeditionary Economics," 94.

[47] Birtle, *U.S. Army Counterinsurgency*, 238; and Department of the Army Headquarters, *Stability*, 1-1.

[48] "Bush's Unfinished Africa Legacy," *The Christian Science Monitor,* 8.

[49] Cole, "An Open Door," 7.

[50] Barnett as quoted in Siegl, "Clarity and Culture," 99-100.

[51] Schramm, "Expeditionary Economics," 97.

[52] Crane, "Phase IV Operations," 12.

[53] Ibid., 5-6.

[54] Ibid., 12-13.

[55] Department of the Army Headquarters, *Stability*, v.

[56] Siegl, "Clarity and Culture," 102.

[57] Delevingne, "Controversy Dogs Creation of U.S. Military Command," 2.

[58] Van Baarda, "A Legal Perspective of Cooperation," 102-6.

[59] Abiew, "NGO-Military Relations in Peace Operations," 26-29; see more detailed discussion in chapter three of this volume.

[60] Department of the Army Headquarters, *Stability*, 1-3 to 1-4.

[61] Abiew, "NGO-Military Relations in Peace Operations," 28.

[62] Cavaleri, *Easier Said Than Done*, 14.

[63] Department of the Army Headquarters, *Stability Operations*, 1-13 to 1-14. As the stability efforts in Iraq have ended, and those in Afghanistan are waning, this mandate for other agencies to build up their own stability operations capabilities is also waning under the pressure of budget cuts. This may again indicate that military lead stability operations in the future may be the only viable option if such actions again become a national priority.

[64] Anderson and Wallen, "Preparing for Economics in Stability Operations," 97.

[65] Cole, "An Open Door," 5, and Harlow, "Army Unveils New Stability Operations Manual." FM 3-07, *Stability Operations*, was the first update to stability operations concepts by the US military since FM 31-23, *Stability Operations*, was published in 1972 at the end of the US involvement in Vietnam. FM 3-07 is the foundation upon which current US Army stability operations doctrine, Army Doctrine Publication (ADP) 3-07, *Stability*, and ADRP 3-07, *Stability*, are derived.

[66] Basilotto, "A Revisionist View of Nation Assistance in Africa," 28; and Anderson and Wallen, "Preparing for Economics in Stability Operations," 96.

[67] Crane, "Phase IV Operations: Where Wars are Really Won," 11.

[68] Hockmuth, "AFRICOM: More Questions than Answers," and Palmer, "Legal Impediments to USAFRICOM Operationalization," 84.

[69] Anderson and Wallen, "Preparing for Economics in Stability Operations," 96.

[70] Hicks, "Africom: Vision and Prospects," 2.

[71] Schadlow, *Organizing to Compete in the Political Terrain*, 9.

[72] Morelli and Ferguson, *Low Intensity Conflict*, 23.

[73] McCrummen, "Report: U.S. Africa Aid is Increasingly Military," A-10.

[74] Refugees International, *Report Challenges Militarization*, 1.

[75] US Joint Forces Command, *The Joint Operating Environment 2008*, 47.

[76] Pincus, "U.S. Africa Command Brings New Concerns," A-13.

[77] Palmer, "Legal Impediments to USAFRICOM Operationalization," 83-84.

[78] Department of the Army Headquarters, *Stability,* 2-12, and 2-17.

[79] Pittman, "Support Missions in Africa Face Suspicion."

[80] Schraeder, *United States Foreign Policy Toward Africa*, 1-7.

[81] Anderson and Wallen, "Preparing for Economics in Stability Operations," 92.

[82] Harlow, "Army Unveils New Stability Operations Manual" and Department of the Army Headquarters, *Stability*, Introduction, and 1-4 to 1-5.

[83] Department of the Army Headquarters, *Stability Operations*, B-1.

[84] Flavin, "New Doctrine for a New Era," 2.

[85] Crane, "Phase IV Operations: Where Wars Are Really Won," 4.

[86] Clinton, "Town Hall Meeting to Announce; also see Chapter 3 of this volume for a detailed account of strengthening the role of civilian government agencies in stabilization and reconstruction.

[87] Hicks, "Africom: Vision and Prospects," 3.

[88] Ibid., 2-3.

10

Effectively Integrating Security and Development

G. William Anderson

As many of the authors in this volume have argued, effective collaboration between the US Agency for International Development (USAID) and the Department of Defense (DoD) should be a critical element of the US government's (USG's) approach to security, governance, and development in Africa. While recent initiatives have expanded USAID and DoD collaboration, broader opportunities exist for a more integrated approach to security and development between USAID and the DoD, under Department of State coordination. If the US government moves to accelerate initiatives that have already begun over the medium-to-long term, the US can prevent or mitigate crises and conflicts in Africa's weak and fragile states and address cross border tensions more successfully.

In a period of budget reductions, using available resources as efficiently as possible is even more essential. A more integrated USG approach in Africa at both interagency and multilateral levels will help support African economic growth and poverty reduction; accelerate African progress in reaching its Millennium Development Goals; reduce the number and intensity of conflicts; and blunt the growth of violent extremism among vulnerable populations, such as disenfranchised and unemployed youth in fast-growing mega-urban centers.[1] Such progress will serve both US security objectives and African development and security goals.

As many of the previous chapters focused on the DoD-DoS relationship, this chapter explores four principal questions about the DoD-USAID dynamic. First, what is the potential for USAID and DoD collaboration in Africa; (2) what are the challenges facing DoD/USAID coordination; (3) what are the risks some see in a closer USAID and DoD relationship; and (4) what can be done now to improve cooperation between USAID and DoD in Africa? The chapter argues that increased collaboration is both possible and necessary. USAID development assistance has a major role to play in comprehensive security and justice sector reform, in combatting violent extremism, and in preventing future crises. Formulating a cohesive USG conflict and crisis prevention strategy supported by an interagency framework with clear authorities, roles, and responsibilities are prerequisites for effective conflict prevention in Africa over the long term.

The Potential for USAID and DOD Collaboration in the Field

The 2010 US *National Security Strategy*, the 2010 *Quadrennial Diplomacy and Development Review (QDDR)*, and the World Bank's *World Development Report 2011: Conflict, Security, and Development,* emphasize the interdependence between security and development.[2] To quote former Secretary of Defense Robert Gates, "You can't have development without security, and you can't have security without development."[3] Development assistance organizations cannot operate effectively without a minimal level of security. Successful security and justice sector reform (SJSR), in which both USAID and the DoD play major roles, is necessary to transform local institutions in fragile or conflict-prone states over the long-term. Over time, providing "citizen security, justice, and jobs" through legitimate institutions can both deter and mitigate violence.[4] US agencies pursuing US national security objectives cannot achieve those objectives without a foundation of broad-based development, which provides long-term stability.

For some time, current policy discussion has emphasized employing all elements of national power to address conflict and crisis situations.[5] The 2010 National Security Strategy urged the "integration of skills and capabilities within our military and civilian institutions, so they complement each other and operate seamlessly." Although US forces are not currently deployed in a combat role on the African continent, the United States faces challenges and opportunities in Africa that require all its civilian and military capabilities.[6] Half of the forty-seven fragile states identified by the Development Assistance Committee's International Network on Conflict and Fragility (INCAF) lie in Africa.[7] Current conflicts in the Central African Republic and South Sudan, which have resulted in tens of thousands of internally displaced people, and other crises in Mali and Nigeria illustrate some of the challenges fragile states face. Moreover, the Ebola epidemic in West Africa has required a major US and multinational response.[8]

Pursuing US diplomatic, development, and security objectives in Africa, including more effective crisis prevention, requires cooperation with international partners, host governments, the private sector, and civil society.[9] The USG has been embarking on efforts to improve coordination across various agencies, as well as to pursue a more expansive view of security. First, the 2010 *QDDR* recommended changes to enable civilian agencies like USAID and the State Department to lead conflict response and prevention efforts, including more integrated security and justice sector reform.[10] Second, the policy guidelines of the 2013 US Security Sector Assistance Policy make clear that US security sector assistance should complement overall US foreign assistance objectives, enhance interagency and multilateral collaboration, promote sustainable economic development, and undergo rigorous monitoring and evaluation.[11] The goal of these changes is to more effectively pursue a developmental approach to security, both for Americans and Africans.

What Would Effective DoD/USAID Collaboration Look Like?

Effective USAID and DoD collaboration in Africa would reflect several crucial characteristics. As a prerequisite, USAID and DoD staff would exhibit a high level of mutual understanding of what each agency brings to the table in financial resources, capabilities, and field assets. Second, each agency would possess knowledge of the other agency's regional and bilateral activities in each African country where both agencies are active. Experienced field staff with multi-year assignments would be encouraged, through career and other incentives, to build long-term relationships aimed at improved coordination. Third, and based on this broader understanding, USAID's Africa Bureau, United States Africa Command (AFRICOM), US Special Operations Command (SOCOM), and other relevant parts of the DoD would plan together at both regional and country levels, ensuring that long term strategies and specific programs were complementary. Fourth, joint coordination of program implementation would develop from collaborative program design. Fifth, as more monitoring and evaluation of program results were undertaken jointly, both agencies could shape DoD security cooperation and USAID development assistance to exploit each agency's comparative advantages.

Recent Advances

Over the past two years, USAID and the DoD (especially SOCOM and AFRICOM) have pursued a joint effort to identify crucial factors of resilience and drivers of conflict and instability in the Sahel aimed at preventing future crises in that region. The steps taken by USAID and the DoD, and lessons learned from this effort point the way toward more creative, interagency approaches.

The Sahel effort began in October 2012 with a meeting between USAID Administrator Rajiv Shah and SOCOM Commander Admiral William McRaven. During this meeting Administrator Shah shared detailed, layered GIS mapping of the Sahel with overlays of conflict, rainfall patterns and related climate changes, environment, food security, infrastructure, and other factors. A joint desk study, based on USAID's Conflict Assessment Framework (CAF), and two interagency workshops in 2013 followed. The second interagency workshop in June 2013 led to identification of priorities and gaps in the Sahel that then helped focus the effort on more specific Sahelian subregions.

In January 2014, USAID and the DoD decided to test development hypotheses developed from the preceding 15 months of analysis on how critical drivers of instability and resilience would interact through a DoD simulation called a "Development Game." After two planning meetings in January and February 2014, the game took place in May 2014. A large number of senior leaders and field staff from multiple bureaus within USAID, SOCOM, AFRICOM, State, and others participated. The games' two moves included multiple funding scenarios and resulted in creative, outside-the-box recommendations on how the US should move forward in the Sahel in a joint interagency fashion to reduce risk, strengthen resilience, and avert future crises and violent conflict. This two-year effort reflects the first three of the five principle for effective USAID/DoD collaboration, and, as efforts continue, promises to include joint program implementation, monitoring, and evaluation as well.

In addition, an "African Strategic Dialogue" took place February 19-20, 2014, during the intensive Sahel effort. Hosted by AFRICOM in Stuttgart, Germany, the two-day meeting assembled over 100 senior leaders from the Departments of State and Defense and from USAID, including many senior managers from the field, "to discuss how to align desired outcomes with US foreign policy objectives, and develop a unified strategic approach" to Africa.[12] According to AFRICOM Commander General David M. Rodriguez,

> We developed this forum as a way to discuss our respective policies and perspectives, and to help us determine our priorities. With that information, we can better leverage everyone's capabilities and determine future funding and programmatic decision-making cycles.[13]

Combined with the two-year Sahel joint planning effort, the African Strategic Dialogue event marks significant progress toward more effective collaboration in strategic and program planning for the Sahel and for Africa as a whole. Although this combined effort is impressive, it remains to be seen whether senior leaders from USAID, State, and the DoD participating in these events will ensure that the current momentum will continue to accelerate.

What Opportunities do USAID and DOD Offer Each Other for Effective Collaboration?

DoD

The potential for fruitful collaboration between USAID and the DoD is substantial. The principal contribution that the DoD and AFRICOM can make to USAID's foreign assistance efforts in Africa lies in the security sector through a range of security cooperation programs. These programs are mostly aimed at building professional militaries that are accountable to civilian governments, respect international human rights standards, are regarded by local populations as protectors, and contribute to regional peacekeeping missions.[14] USAID and its NGO partners cannot make much of a difference in people's lives without accountable governance, which includes militaries that local populations respect rather than fear. Building more professional and accountable militaries is an important aspect of comprehensive security and justice sector reform, which integrates the capabilities of "the military, the police, the justice system, and other governance and oversight mechanisms," including legislatures and civil society.[15]

The DoD carries out a range of security cooperation programs through AFRICOM and its more than 1,000 headquarters staff based in Stuttgart, service component military personnel stationed elsewhere in Europe, and additional DoD staff assigned to embassies in Africa. The principal long-term DoD staff in-country include Defense Attaché Offices (DAOs) and Offices of Security Cooperation (OSCs). AFRICOM does not yet have long-term OSC staff posted in all African countries where a fully staffed USAID mission or office exists. In the absence of an OSC, the DAO is responsible for security cooperation. In such circumstances, the DAO will usually limit its activities to a few high priority programs. These usually consist of sales, often through loans, of US military weapons systems and training of local military contacts at DoD training facilities.

Despite the widespread impression that the DoD has colonized American diplomatic outposts and foreign policy towards Africa, the DoD does not in fact have a large presence in Africa. Outside a few large personnel concentrations in Africa like the Combined Joint Task Force-

Horn of Africa (CJTF-HOA) based in Djibouti and larger numbers of DoD personnel who participate in major exercises or emergency assistance such as the 2014 Ebola Response, the number of DoD long-term field staff in each embassy are generally much smaller than USAID mission staff and the networks of implementing partner staff executing USAID-funded assistance activities. Although USAID field staff have some knowledge regarding overall DoD capabilities, it is unlikely that USAID headquarters staff in Washington are fully informed of the full range of DoD's security cooperation programs. USAFRICOM also has a liaison officer stationed in USAID's Office of Civilian-Military Cooperation in Washington to ensure coordination and communication with the Command.

USAID
USAID contributes to US national security objectives in its capacity to strengthen weak and fragile states by building accountable governance institutions over the long term and addressing major issues such as food security and climate change. Further, by improving delivery of improved health and education services and by helping accelerate inclusive economic growth that provides jobs for unemployed youth and reduces poverty, USAID assistance supports stability and helps prevent conflict. Former Secretary of Defense Robert Gates made this point in 2010 when he argued that "development is a lot cheaper than sending soldiers."[16] USAID-funded assistance actually covers more than 47 of the 53 countries in the AFRICOM area of operation, which includes North Africa.[17] USAID implements its assistance programs through 28 bilateral missions and offices; one senior development advisor (assigned to the Combined-Joint Task Force, Djibouti); 3 regional USAID missions dealing with West, East, and Southern Africa; and 2 regional programs based in Africa for the Sahel and Central Africa. The regional missions and programs support regional organizations like the African Union (AU) and ECOWAS as well as cross-border trade, infrastructure, river basin programs, and conflict early warning systems.[18]

Established in 2005, a robust USAID Office of Civilian-Military Cooperation (CMC) currently shepherds an expanding USAID/DoD relationship worldwide. CMC places USAID liaison officers in all five DoD regional combatant commands and DoD liaison officers in USAID/Washington. Four experienced USAID officers, one at general officer/flag rank, presently serve at AFRICOM Headquarters: (1) a senior development advisor who sits within the Commander's Action Group, (2) a deputy development advisor, (3) a foreign service officer (FSO) who serves in a dual-hatted role as chief of health and humanitarian activities, and (4) a humanitarian assistance advisor/military, who focuses on disaster relief and preparedness. The Office of Civilian-Military Cooperation also has a staff member who works alongside the AFRICOM liaison officer helping to provide coordination in planning, policy, and training/outreach between USAID staff at the COCOM and USAID regional and technical bureaus. USAID's Africa Bureau and its field staff manage billions of dollars of assistance, much of which is aimed at strengthening institutions critical for citizen security, and therefore of direct relevance to DoD and USG objectives of security and stability.

Directly relevant to DoD security cooperation programs, USAID can quickly field assessment teams for strategic planning, to design programs to address all aspects of development, including conflict or crisis situations, to provide immediate assistance, and to evaluate assistance programs. USAID can provide operational guidance and leadership through the Office of Foreign Disaster Assistance (OFDA) and Office of Transition Initiatives (OTI), both of which can mobilize teams in days to fund and manage the disaster relief or crisis mitigation efforts in which DoD personnel are often involved.

On a strategy and plans level, USAID's approach to addressing violent extremism, insurgency, and similar issues in pre-conflict situations and the underlying analysis that led to this strategy demonstrate how and where development assistance contributes most effectively to USG counter-insurgency and stabilization efforts.[19] USAID bilateral and regional missions house strong planning, implementation, and evaluation capabilities across all development sectors. These capabilities also address cross-cutting areas, such as youth, gender equality, climate change, and conflict prevention, response, and mitigation.

The USAID regional missions in Ghana, Kenya and South Africa, along with the Joint Sahel Programming Cell in Dakar, Senegal, provide legal, procurement, and financial accountability backup to USAID sub-Saharan bilateral missions. They also support regional initiatives in collaboration with the African Union and other African regional institutions, through which they can help to link the DoD to these regional bodies. Finally, USAID representatives to the international donor and NGO communities in Europe and Asia constitute established channels of communication that could help connect AFRICOM with these donor organizations and NGO networks. The chapter in this volume by Crawford and Zwicker demonstrated limits of this approach when undertaken directly by AFRICOM itself.

What Are the Current Challenges Facing DoD/USAID Collaboration?

Cooperation between USAID and the DoD at regional and country levels in Africa has been expanding gradually since AFRICOM's creation in 2008. Until recently, improvements in collaboration centered on specific areas, such as disaster response, pandemic preparedness, HIV/AIDS prevention, and regional counter-terrorism programs such as the on-going Trans-Sahara Counter-Terrorism Partnership (TSCTP). In the last two years, however, the pace of coordination among USAID, the DoD, and the State Department has quickened, evidenced by the two-year Sahelian effort discussed in the beginning of this chapter.

Several complementary efforts have increased this momentum. These include the African Strategic Dialogue (February 2014); assignment of a planner from the SOCOM component of AFRICOM (or SOCAF) to the USAID regional mission in Ghana in 2014; more frequent visits of AFRICOM senior leaders to USAID/Washington and of USAID/Africa Bureau senior leaders to AFRICOM; and the participation of the USAID assistant administrator for Africa in one of AFRICOM's major exercises in Niger in 2014. This coordination with respect to Africa programs seems to be leading the way: the Office of Civilian-Military Cooperation notes that USAID hosts more General Officers from AFRICOM than from any other DoD regional command.[20] Finally, in early 2014 USAID, State, and the DoD established joint interagency strategies for the Trans-Sahara Counter-Terrorism Partnership and the Partnership for Regional East Africa Counterterrorism (PREACT).[21] These interagency approaches address some of the criticisms raised by Andrea Walther-Puri in her chapter on security sector assistance and the TSCTP. Thus, recent events point clear to a period of broader and deeper USAID/DoD collaboration in Africa that extends to State Department and other agencies.

Nevertheless, maintaining the momentum of these recent advances in interagency cooperation in Africa requires perseverance by senior leaders of key departments and agencies in Washington, Stuttgart, and the country teams to continue to address a number of obstacles and perceived risks, both at macro and micro levels. These include the need to continue progress toward "joint" strategic and program planning at global, regional, and country levels and greater mutual understanding of USAID and DoD strategies, programs, resources, field presence, and capabilities, especially at regional and country levels. Senior leaders must continue to emphasize expanded collaboration and target stronger career incentives on interagency assignments and efforts.

AFRICOM must fight for additional funding to support new OSCs in the five remaining countries with USAID missions/offices but without long-term DoD staff who can build enduring relationships with USAID field staff. Otherwise, former Secretary of Defense Robert Gates' 2010 description of the United States' interagency tool kit as "still a hodgepodge of jury-rigged arrangements constrained by a dated and complex patchwork of authorities, persistent shortfalls in resources, and unwieldy process" will remain true and continue to thwart efforts for greater USAID/DoD collaboration.[22] The perceived risks of closer DoD/USAID cooperation, including apprehension by NGOS and the wider development community that the DoD will take over a greater share of US foreign assistance, can also obstruct expanded USAID/DoD partnership at more practical levels.

Finally, two underlying issues remain that will ultimately block long-term progress towards greater USAID/DoD collaboration. First, in the long run, prevention is more important than response. The United States government has made little or no progress since 2001 in shifting emphasis from crisis response to conflict prevention. In such an effort, USAID and the State Department have clear comparative advantages and more flexible capabilities. Second, as noted by several chapters in this volume, restoring the capabilities of US civilian foreign affairs agencies that were gutted in the 1990s after the end of the Cold War is essential to rebalancing our national security toolkit successfully.[23] Unless rectified, the continuing lack of experienced personnel and effective programming systems in USAID, State, and other US civilian foreign affairs agencies will continue to hamper expanded cooperation.

Common Issues Reported by Senior USAID Officers in the Field

Difficulties reported by USAID mission directors in the field over the last several years have primarily related to the DoD's ponderous bureaucracy and to challenges with community-level projects funded under the DoD's Humanitarian Assistance Program (HAP). The huge difference in scale between the DoD's $100,000 to $200,000 village projects versus USAID's national health or education programs totaling tens of millions of dollars makes USAID field staff question the tradeoffs in time spent working with and assisting DoD community project teams. Additionally, at times there have been embarrassing glitches when the DoD engages in humanitarian assistance efforts without coordinating with USAID. For example, one senior USAID officer described a ribbon-cutting ceremony for an intensive care unit (ICU) in a major city refurbished by the DoD. Because USAID health staff in-country had not been adequately engaged in project planning, the ICU was completely empty with no medical equipment, supplies or personnel at the time this high-profile ceremony took place, such that publicity exposed the DoD handing over the empty shell of a care unit.[24] Now that USAID staff brief deploying DoD Civil Affairs Teams, including contacts in the field, problems with coordination of DoD HAP activities should have diminished.

Moving Toward Joint Programming

The fundamental problems that have inhibited effective USAID/DoD collaboration in the past have been low levels of collaborative program planning, execution, monitoring, evaluation, and learning from experience at strategic, regional, and country levels. Since both USAID and the DoD engage in planning and implementing programs at multiple levels with similar planning approaches, major opportunities exist for more coordinated and even joint planning. At present, USAID staff assigned to AFRICOM headquarters and in the field provide more input and comments to Theater Campaign and Security Cooperation plans at both regional (theater) and country levels. They also contribute substantially to the design, parameters, and assumptions of major exercises. As long as this occurs early in the DoD planning process, USAID personnel at AFRICOM can "reach back" to appropriate technical staff in USAID/Washington for their health, education, or role of law expertise.

Similarly, USAID's African missions develop five-year regional and bilateral strategies and programs in multiple development sectors, including areas such as youth skills training and employment, conflict early warning, food security, and community resilience that are directly relevant to AFRICOM regional security plans and broader USG foreign policy objectives. Reportedly, USAID's Africa Bureau and its regional and bilateral missions are now engaging DoD field and COCOM staff more regularly in such strategic planning as well. On monitoring and evaluation, there is less evidence of movement toward joint efforts. According to recent GAO reports, the DoD's monitoring and evaluation systems for regional programs like TSCTP and PREACT as well as other security cooperation programs are in early stages of development.[25] This is not unique to AFRICOM; the DoD's lack of evaluation and monitoring processes and metrics for its non-kinetic programs is well known.

USAID's senior development advisor and other staff assigned to AFRICOM are available to help drive forward an array of collaborative actions, such as facilitating visits by USAID mission directors and other field staff to brief AFRICOM and service component staff on their programs and receive similar briefings from AFRICOM and other DoD staff. To do so requires that the AFRICOM commander and other senior leaders see such efforts as one of their top priorities. Current events suggest such a priority exists, for the DoD (specifically AFRICOM and SOCOM) and USAID, at least. The challenge will be to maintain that priority through changes of command in Stuttgart and changes of senior leadership in USAID.

Although slow in coming, interagency coordination of the two major interagency counterterrorism programs for which the State Department's Bureau of African Affairs has management responsibility (TSCTP and PREACT) has improved. The guidelines of the new US security sector assistance policy under Presidential Policy Determination (PPD) 23, which urge greater interagency collaboration as well as more "rigorous analysis, assessments, and evaluations of impacts and results" of security cooperation" may have contributed to these improvements.[26] PPD-23 has also identified the Interagency Security Sector Assessment framework (ISSAF), developed through USAID leadership in 2010, as the standard assessment framework for PPD-23 implementation.[27]

The first joint strategy for TSCTP was approved in January 2014 and a similar joint strategy for PREACT in 2013, which means it is too early to assess their effectiveness addressing the concerns raised by Andrea Walther-Puri in Chapter 5. Management of these two interagency programs also now benefits from quarterly update meetings at the deputy assistant secretary level. Nevertheless, monitoring and evaluation of these two programs remain at a more basic level. Although USAID, State, and the DoD have undertaken some monitoring and evaluation of their individual TSCTP activities, no comprehensive, joint evaluation of the overall TSCTP program has occurred.[28] With broader collaboration, USAID's extensive experience with such systems could help AFRICOM establish stronger evaluation systems compatible with existing USAID monitoring efforts.

Regarding assistance to professional militaries in Africa, it has not been clear whether AFRICOM (or the DoD, more generally) uses a systematic assessment and planning approach for what is, in fact, a long-term capacity and institution building effort. The usual approach would include a defense sector assessment tool or other form of analysis to assess the existing problems in an African military followed by a formal planning process for the overall defense sector and its components or sub-sectors. The Defense Reform Initiative Program (DIRI) focuses on defense sector evaluations prior to applying US assistance tools, rather than after the implementation of those programs.[29] Given USAID's long experience in capacity development in Africa, AFRICOM and its service components would clearly benefit from USAID's lessons and best practices, some of which would likely apply to defense sector institution building.

Who's On First? Expanding Mutual Awareness and Understanding

Since its creation in 2007, DoD leaders and staff have become more familiar with both how USAID works in general, and the full range of capabilities possessed by USAID bilateral and regional missions in Africa. Several years ago, one experienced USAID mission director in Africa referred to the DoD's "total lack of understanding about what USAID does and how we work."[30] That lack of understanding by DoD is less prevalent now. USAID's CMC office offers a broad menu of both online and instructor-led training that acquaints USAID staff on working with the military and vice versa.[31] Further, OFDA continues to deliver annually a Joint Humanitarian Operations Course (JHOC), preceded by a required online prerequisite, to all regional commands, their service components, and other functional commands. Thus, opportunities for USAID and DoD staff to learn about how the other agency works and what it can contribute have begun more plentiful in recent years.

Three questions remain. First, whether strong incentives will spur the staff of each agency to learn about each other as well as to work together in more innovative ways. Second, whether USAID's training for military audiences, and especially for AFRICOM and other regional command staff, provides participants with a complete picture of the resources, capabilities, programming processes, implementation modalities, and field presence to enable DoD staff to understand the potential for collaboration. Third, whether training on the DoD for USAID provides the same understanding of what the DoD brings to the table.

Continuing to expand mutual awareness and understanding by the DoD of civilian agencies like USAID and State and vice versa is essential in effectively integrating security and development. Without a clear grasp of the full range of capabilities and resources that the DoD and USAID both bring to the table, it is extremely difficult for each party to see how best to complement the efforts of the other.

Maintaining Senior Leader Commitment to Expanded Collaboration

Contacts among USAID and DoD leadership have increased substantially over the last two years. Will this current commitment survive changes in USAID, AFRICOM, and SOCOM leadership? Two of the three principals—USAID's Africa Bureau assistant administrator and SOCOM's commander—have now moved on. To what degree have the advances in USAID/DoD collaboration been institutionalized in either USAID or SOCOM? Without a number of complementary changes in incentives, establishing clear expectations for staff on priorities is a job for senior leadership. When priorities and expectations are clear, members of the organization will usually act according to their boss's lead, once the rationale is explained and if staff are not overwhelmed with other priorities.

Incentives for Interagency Postings

In the past, weak incentives often discouraged both DoD and USAID officers from pursuing interagency assignments. At present, the Bureau of Democracy, Conflict, and Humanitarian Assistance (which oversees the Office of Civil-Military Coordination) does not have data on the onward assignments of USAID senior development advisors after their COCOM assignments. Anecdotally, it seems that USAID SDAs are moving on to senior-level assignments, such as mission directors. But building a clear story based on facts would be more convincing. In addition, specific USAID promotion precepts—such as requiring interagency or similar "nontraditional" assignments before consideration for senior management positions—are needed to enhance incentives for bidding on SDA assignments. Similar signals are needed for DoD staff as well, in particular the message that assignments working in or with USAID, State, or other US government agencies will support promotions and the eligibility of DoD officers for general officer or flag rank.

Nobody's Home in USAID: Rebuilding Civilian Capabilities

Another fundamental obstacle for effective collaboration between USAID and the DoD has been the weakness of USAID, the State Department, and other US civilian foreign affairs agencies. Several chapters in this volume have already discussed these trends, so here I focus on the implications of these trends and what has been done to address them. From 1990 until 2008, USAID lost more than 40 percent of its staff, even though foreign aid budgets and the number of USAID missions were increasing, especially during the last Bush administration. As staffing declined, USAID's capabilities in program planning, implementation, and evaluation degraded to a dangerous level. In 2006, the agency lost its Washington-level budgeting and policy planning capability to the new Foreign Assistance Bureau (the F Bureau) in the State Department. Those functions were not reestablished at USAID until 2011. Over the same two-decade period, the State Department suffered similar but less extreme staffing losses and benefited from a substantial boost in hiring under Secretary of State Colin Powell.[32]

Since 2008, USAID has begun to rebuild its staffing levels and technical capabilities by hiring approximately 850 new Foreign Service staff under the Development Leadership Initiative (DLI). Following the arrival of Administrator Rajiv Shah in early 2010, the agency embarked on a series of ambitious reforms known as "USAID Forward." Under this reform effort, USAID has reconstituted basic programming systems, trained staff in these systems, reestablished budget and policy offices, and issued a comprehensive agency policy framework for 2011 to 2015.[33]

Nevertheless, rebuilding technical staff with program expertise will continue for several years, assuming adequate funding levels. In addition, although USAID's human capital and program management capabilities are rapidly improving, its overall weakness over more than ten years has meant that its ability to engage robustly with the DoD at all levels, play its appropriate role in the field, and protect its prerogatives has suffered. This weakness has compromised the achievement of US security, foreign policy, and development objectives in Africa and other regions. Current budget pressures could again cripple USAID and the State Department and reverse current efforts to rebuild civilian capabilities, especially in USAID.[34]

Ignoring Conflict Prevention (Versus Preparing for Crisis Response)

Prevention of crises, such as recent conflicts in Mali, the Central African Republic (CAR), and South Sudan, should command high priority for the DoD, USAID, and State. Both the DoD and USAID pay some attention to conflict prevention in their work at the country level and regional levels. Two of the three USAID Africa regional missions work on conflict early warning and mitigation with regional African organizations like the African Union and ECOWAS. One of AFRICOM's "Four Cornerstones" is the "prevention of future conflicts."[35] In Washington, USAID's Office of Conflict Management and Mitigation (CMM) pioneered the development of a conflict assessment framework, which has become an interagency tool of State's Bureau of Conflict and Stabilization Operations (CSO). CMM has also published a series of nine toolkits addressing land, women, and youth, with concrete options for addressing causes of conflict. Recent research suggests that assuring food security for vulnerable regions and populations, in which USAID enjoys strong capability, plays a major role in preventing violence.[36]

Notwithstanding the creation of the Bureau of Conflict and Stabilization Operations in the State Department, no coherent US government strategy to prevent crises and conflicts exists.[37] Other than the over-committed National Security Council (NSC) in the White House, no federal department or agency possesses a clear leadership role for conflict and crisis prevention, has authority to act within the Executive Branch, or can commit the US in the international community.[38] Despite multiple references to conflict prevention in the 2010 *National Security Strategy* and the *QDDR*, discussion on conflict in both these documents refers mostly to response in conflict situations, not prevention of them.

The *World Development Report 2011* concludes that "Building capable and legitimate institutions to deliver citizen security, address injustice, and create employment is key to breaking . . . cycles of violence," and that this process takes a generation.[39] Building legitimate institutions in fragile states requires the commitment of local governments, private sector and civil society combined with help from the international community. This means that in addition to specifying clear interagency roles and responsibilities, a coherent USG conflict and crisis prevention strategy must also engage bilateral and multilateral partners. Until it has its own house in order, the USG will lack credibility in the international community on multilateral prevention efforts.

"These Folks Don't Talk or Act Like Me:" *Conceptual Constraints to Collaboration*

In spite of major similarities, USAID and the DoD differ in language, style, and culture. As Jessica Piombo explores in Chapter 3, for USAID the term "humanitarian assistance" means short-term assistance to populations afflicted by natural disasters or other emergencies. For the DoD, the same term means community assistance projects, such as schools, health clinics, water, and sanitation projects. For USAID, these types of assistance are often part of longer-term assistance programs in education and health.[40] Through these programs, USAID focuses on poverty reduction, promoting resilient, democratic societies, and thereby advancing US security and prosperity.[41] DoD focuses on state-level security threats, response to which usually favors quick results. Therefore, much of DoD's engagement at the country level consists of short-term teams arriving to conduct military exercises, training, or quick-impact community projects.

USAID missions maintain a large country footprint, the majority of which are Foreign Service Nationals. Most USAID staff have substantial cross-cultural, area, and language expertise. The number of DoD staff in individual OSCs is quite small compared to total USAID mission staff. Furthermore, aside from the few regionally-trained Foreign Area Officers, most of these field staff lack country expertise and cultural sensitivity. This increases USAID's burden of working with the DoD on community projects and other security cooperation activities that might complement USAID assistance.

USAID's preferred operating style is to examine problems to be addressed, and then build agreement for solutions among local stakeholders. The DoD tends to respond quickly to a perceived problem, a style which could be described as "Don't just stand there; do something!" When not engaging with USAID staff, the DoD's "action first" style can result in community, ethnic, or religious tensions and unsustainable projects.[42] While some DoD community assistance projects may be aimed at countering threats versus long-term sustainability, USAID and State should normally have the determining voice in deciding whether negative impacts of DoD projects on diplomatic or development objectives outweigh their potential contribution to security objectives. Finally, USAID uses empirically-based strategic and program planning, including in-country assessments and problem analyses. While the DoD has many experienced planners, it usually employs top-down strategic planning derived from theater campaign and security cooperation plans. Although improving, DoD's planning systems for humanitarian assistance and security cooperation remain less robust than USAID's revamped planning systems in the areas of systematic assessment, strategic planning and project design, monitoring and evaluation, and learning.

None of these differences by themselves prevents expanded collaboration between USAID and the DoD in Africa. But their cumulative effects complicate and constrain cooperation. Effective collaboration requires that each party understand how the other works, its objectives, and its language. Disagreements on approaches to problems must surface early and be resolved transparently, even if issues have to be raised to higher-level decision-makers in both agencies. Effective collaboration requires effort, training, and sufficient time working together.

Concerns and Risks of Closer USAID/DoD Cooperation

Concerns about greater collaboration between AFRICOM and USAID radiate from within and outside the US government. They include concerns about the militarization of US foreign assistance; uncoordinated security and justice sector reform efforts; the risk of the DoD assuming more responsibility for nonmilitary foreign assistance; and the hazards for the United States if it fails to link security and development efforts in Africa effectively.

Apprehensiveness from NGOs and the Development Community

In spite of the 2005 "Guidelines for Relations Between US Armed Forces and Nongovernmental Humanitarian Organizations in Hostile or Potentially

Hostile Environments" worked out between the DoD and InterAction (the principal US-based NGO consortium for disaster response and relief NGOs), NGOs and the larger development community fear that greater collaboration in Africa between the DoD and USAID may mean one more step toward the militarization of US foreign assistance.[43] They suspect that more DoD community assistance projects will be uncoordinated with USAID, poorly designed, and unsustainable, and in some cases will exacerbate ethnic, religious, or regional tensions. NGOs also fear that aid workers operating in conflict-prone environments may be threatened if DoD humanitarian assistance teams operate in the same areas as their staff.

While these are serious concerns, those who raise these points often are not aware that the total volume of USG economic assistance resources allocated for Africa dwarf the funding for the DoD's African security cooperation programs. AFRICOM's budget for all security cooperation programs in Africa totaled less than $500 million for fiscal year (FY) 2010.[44] By comparison, total US economic assistance committed to Africa in 2010 was $6.9 billion and rose to $7.2 billion in FY 2011. Even though AFRICOM's overall security cooperation budget has grown marginally since 2011, fears by NGOs and the larger development community that the DoD's security cooperation and related assistance budget for Africa will overwhelm civilian-managed economic assistance are exaggerated.

AFRICOM's funding for humanitarian or community assistance programs, which tend to be hot buttons for critics of DoD foreign assistance, totaled less than $15 million in 2010. Compared to USAID assistance budgets in health, education, food security, water, and other sectors, AFRICOM funding for community projects in 2010 represented a tiny proportion of total US economic assistance to Africa – less than one quarter of one percent. Nevertheless, it is true that the DoD civic assistance teams have had problems in the design, placement, and sustainability of community assistance projects in Africa.[45] In addition, DoD objectives for access and influence in particular geographic areas may conflict at times with USAID's impact and sustainability objectives. If activities in the same area work at cross purposes, this can complicate USAID relationships with host country partners.[46]

On a positive note, current DoD guidance for civic assistance programs directs AFRICOM and DoD field staff to consult with USAID in the early stages of programs to identify and design activities and to "seek concurrence from the USAID mission director prior to the chief of mission ... for approval."[47] USAID field and Washington staff agree that coordination with the DoD has improved on community assistance activities of all kinds.[48] Although as noted earlier, USAID officials have experienced problems in coordinating with DoD OSC staff and civil affairs teams on individual projects, past experience also demonstrates that this can be done successfully.

Two examples demonstrate how USAID concerns with AFRICOM community assistance projects can be often dealt with by robust engagement with the DoD. In both of these cases, senior USAID and State Department officers managed the relationship with AFRICOM with positive results. In one case in a remote Sahelian town, DoD teams worked with USAID and the State Department on a joint community project. The DoD provided a substantial quantity of vegetable seeds and USAID provided farmer training and a new water pump. The US ambassador visited the town with USAID and the DoD several times to support the townspeople who had initiated the project.[49] A second case involving interagency collaboration on an East African project aimed at easing cross border pastoralist tensions. The US ambassador and USAID insisted on limiting AFRICOM's civil affairs teams to security issues, which required a high level of labor-intensive oversight. The USAID mission's current five year Country Development and Cooperation Strategy included a specific objective for whole of government work to bring peace and security to the same region with AFRICOM's civil affairs teams focused on security issues.[50]

Risk of Uncoordinated USAID and DoD Assistance Efforts in Fragile States

If budget pressures intensify, the political will of the executive branch and Congress to continue to rebuild USAID and other civilian foreign affairs agencies over the long term may ebb. If the US government cannot stay the course to rebuild these institutions, Congress and the executive branch may again ask the DoD to take responsibility for a larger share of US foreign assistance. If asked, the DoD will accept. The costs will be great, however. First, the DoD is simply not a development agency, as this and other chapters in this volume have argued at length. The DoD lacks the capability, skills, and modes of operation to plan and implement long term development assistance and, especially, to develop sustainable institutional capacity outside of the defense sector.[51] As former Secretary of Defense Robert Gates admitted in a public roundtable with Secretary of State Hillary Clinton and USAID Administrator Rajiv Shah, development is "not our [DoD's] core competency."[52] Second, having the DoD take on a greater responsibility in economic assistance could degrade the DoD's effectiveness in responding to the security challenges it is designed to address. Finally, greater DoD involvement in economic assistance will also send a troubling message to the international community of creeping militarization of US foreign assistance.

What to Do Now to Expand DoD/USAID Collaboration

Over the last several years, USAID/DoD collaboration in Africa has improved in several major dimensions as discussed earlier. These successes may open the way for a range of important actions that can now be taken by the DoD and USAID to accelerate effective collaboration in Africa.

Senior leaders in these agencies should continue to work together to improve coordination in areas of complementarity. State, the DoD, and USAID could synthesize and use the lessons from evaluations and reviews of TSCTP overall and of individual agency evaluations of assistance to counter violent extremism, to engage youth constructively, and to provide other related assistance in West and East Africa. In planning, the DoD and USAID together with State should involve each other in strategic and project planning as well as joint monitoring and evaluation in priority areas of mutual interest. To improve coordination on community projects, USAID should utilize "robust engagement" to make sure that the DoD's community projects are consistent with broader US government development objectives. AFRICOM and USAID's Africa Bureau, including USAID missions in Africa, should expand their efforts to increase their mutual awareness and understanding of what each agency brings to the table.

To encourage staff from both agencies to link up creatively, the DoD and USAID should strengthen organizational and personnel incentives for interagency collaboration versus bureaucratic competition. The DoD should also create OSCs with long-term staff in the remaining countries with USAID missions or offices which lack OSCs. Finally, AFRICOM should continue to detail AFRICOM or service component staff with appropriate experience for the year-long assignments to each of the three USAID regional missions and the Sahel Joint Planning Cell. When these DoD staff return to Stuttgart, they would be expected to educate AFRICOM headquarters and field staff on (1) the full range of USAID regional missions' capabilities, resources, and field presence and (2) how AFRICOM could exploit and utilize the capabilities of USAID regional missions and planning groups capabilities to help achieve DoD objectives and vice versa.

Senior Leaders Should Continue to Expand Collaboration

Part of the process of change is establishing new ways of doing things. If new patterns of actions are repeated by many over time, they can create new institutional habits. In this case, senior USAID and DoD leaders can model new ways of working and direct their subordinates to follow their lead. For example, when AFRICOM's commander, either deputy, or any of their Directorate commanders travel to a country with a USAID mission or

Office, they could routinely include in their itineraries time to work with USAID staff. This would enable them to receive briefings on USAID programs relevant to AFRICOM objectives; visit relevant USAID project sites; or participate in NGO or donor community roundtables arranged by the USAID country director. Key DoD field staff in that country would normally attend all these events.

When the USAID assistant administrator for Africa (AA) or one of his/her deputy assistant administrators travel to the field, they could schedule one- to two-day visits in Stuttgart on their outward or return leg for discussions on TSCTP implementation, on next steps in the joint Sahel effort, or on other US government priorities in Africa. All USAID staff stationed in AFRICOM would attend those meetings. Similarly, when USAID African mission directors (or their deputies) travel to or from Washington, they should know that their AA expects them to visit AFRICOM either coming or going to engage their AFRICOM (and service component) colleagues on top priority regional issues.

When the AFRICOM commander invites US ambassadors from Africa to Stuttgart to discuss regional security and development priorities, they could invite all USAID mission directors to such sessions as equal partners with ambassadors. When USAID organizes Africa mission director or technical officer conferences, the USAID conference organizers could invite relevant AFRICOM colleagues. When supervisors in either USAID's Africa Bureau or AFRICOM are approving work objectives and performance measures for their USAID and the DoD staff, they could normally include at least one work objective for the coming year aimed at expanding collaboration with the other agency or fashioning innovative ways of working with or complementing the efforts of the other agency.

These are just examples of simple, specific actions that USAID Africa Bureau and AFRICOM senior leaders and staff can take. When multiplied, adapted, and improved by large number of people, these patterns of actions, together with other changes, can lead to improved security and better food security, health care, and education for local people. Based on recent experience with several significant initiatives to expand cooperation, USAID's assistant administrator for Africa and the AFRICOM commander should also emphasize the priority for expanded collaboration at AFRICOM headquarters, USAID missions and offices, and in country teams. This could begin with a joint decision message to their respective AFRICOM and USAID senior staff that would support and follow up on the December 17, 2013 official message from Major General Charles Hooper, then director of AFRICOM's Directorate of Plans and Programs (J-5) to AFRICOM staff in Africa, which stated in part:

> One of the biggest assets to our team are the members from the United States Agency for International Development (USAID) located on the continent. I want you to get to know your USAID counterpart(s) in your AOR [Area of Operation]. Find areas of mutual cooperation for our security cooperation programs or other areas of mutual activities. I solicit any ideas you may have to connect USAID and AFRICOM programs to generate more synergy to meet U.S. National interests.[53]

A command-level follow-up message would state that the AFRICOM Commander and the USAID AA/AFR endorse Major General Hooper's message and expect to see immediate and continuing progress in expanding DoD/USAID collaboration in Africa in coordinated programming and in other areas. Such a joint message would announce actions to improve personnel incentives to bolster this effort. The AFRICOM commander could assign his two deputies and other senior leaders to supervise progress and emphasize the importance of this initiative to DoD field staff on his country visits. USAID's AA/AFR would act similarly with regard to his or her senior staff in Washington and with African mission directors. Both the AFRICOM dommander and the USAID AA/AFR could schedule periodic meetings with their respective senior staff (perhaps quarterly in the first year) to track progress and annual joint meetings to celebrate innovative approaches and successes.

Learn from Experience

AFRICOM, USAID, and the State Department have a wealth of lessons learned through TSCTP in North and West Africa and PREACT in East Africa (also involving CJTF-HOA) focused on the interrelated areas of security, governance, and justice sector reform and as well as in combatting violent extremism and insurgency. As the two-year joint Sahel effort and development simulation game have demonstrated, USAID development assistance has a major role to play in comprehensive security and justice sector reform, in combatting violent extremism, and in preventing future crises.[54] Other individual agency evaluation of TSCTP and PREACT components exists as well as the results of the recent 2013 interagency review and recent academic research.[55]

USAID and the DoD both have provided substantial assistance over long periods in a number of other fragile states in Africa, including Ivory Coast, Uganda, Nigeria, Liberia, and Guinea. The recent whole of government Ebola Response effort, which USAID led and in which the DoD and the Centers for Disease Control (CDC) played major supporting roles, will generate a series of new lessons for USAID, the DoD, the CDC, and State collaboration in major epidemics. A serious joint effort by USAID, the DoD, and the State Department to synthesize the results and lessons learned from all these experiences over the last 10-15 years in Africa would provide a foundation for future policy and programming.

In areas of successful DoD/USAID collaboration, such as disaster assistance; pandemic planning, preparedness, and response; and HIV prevention and supportive care, USAID, the DoD, and the State Department could similarly evaluate jointly results by country, synthesize best practices, and advance collaboration accordingly.

Deploy Staff to Strengthen Field Partnerships

USAID and the DoD cannot build collaborative relationships if they don't have partners to work with over time. None of the concrete suggestions for increasing cooperation will work without strong relationships. Therefore, USAID country directors should place a high priority on developing creative partnerships within embassy teams. They could request that an AFRICOM staff officer or planner be assigned to their missions for a year or more and expand joint strategic planning, program design and evaluation with DoD staff in-country. AFRICOM has already detailed one of its planners to the USAID West Africa regional mission in Accra. It should follow this action by detailing planners for at least a year to USAID regional offices in South Africa, Kenya, and Senegal. Similarly, each regional USAID mission could detail one of their program staff to appropriate offices in AFRICOM headquarters.

In their interagency detail assignments, DoD and USAID detailees return to their home organizations understanding much more about the resources, capabilities, and elements of programming of the other agency. They should be required to then work across agencies to develop possible initiatives for expanded cooperation. AFRICOM and USAID detailees would also be expected share their experience and recommendations with senior management in AFRICOM and in the USAID regional missions where they are assigned. Clearly, once strong incentives are in place, there are myriad ways to build innovative ways of working more collaboratively.

Strengthen Personnel and Career Incentives

None of these efforts to increase collaboration and coordination will happen in a sustained manner unless organizational and career incentives support such actions. Most people in organizations behave most of the time in ways that support their career interests. Although command advocacy of broader collaboration is a necessary step, USAID and DoD staff, including active duty military personnel with a more clearly defined top-down chain of command, will look skeptically at statements by leaders directing expanded collaboration unless they see evidence that promotions, desirable onward assignments, awards, and higher pay follow interagency assignments and expanded efforts to broaden cooperation. To strengthen incentives for coordination, AFRICOM and USAID leaders could revise eligibility requirements for senior leadership positions to include long-term interagency assignments, in a way similar to DoD's requirement that a joint assignment in a combatant command or similar organization is required for promotion to the O-6 rank of colonel or Navy captain.

Coordinate Programming

Both the DoD's and USAID's assistance programs start with planning. Each agency undertakes strategic and project planning at several levels. USAID and the DoD have significantly increased the level of engagement of the other agency in their strategic and program planning. In both regional and country security cooperation plans, AFRICOM could increase the engagement of USAID regional and bilateral mission staff in conferences and earlier in the planning process. USAID regional and bilateral missions could invite more AFRICOM headquarters and field staff to participate earlier and more often in the development of USAID's five-year Regional and Country Development Cooperation Plans (RDCSs and CDCSs) as well as in project designs, which bring their strategies to life. The State Department's new strategic planning processes, which include developing multi-year Integrated Country Strategies (ICS) and a Security and Justice Strategy for each country team, could gradually shift to joint planning in Africa involving all agencies at post, with a focus on collaborative planning among the State Department, USAID, and the DoD.

Yet, planning is only one step in programming. It must be followed by program execution, monitoring, evaluation, and learning from experience. Broadened DoD/USAID partnerships are essential in these other stages as well. Each of these steps includes feedback loops that affect other stages of planning. Joint program monitoring and evaluation leads to greater awareness of each agency's relative strengths and weaknesses.

Employ Robust Engagement

As a tool in effective coordination and coordinated planning, USAID mission management and staff should engage robustly in insisting that the DoD coordinate its activities with USAID strategies and projects. This applies to OSC staff assigned to their countries, to short-term civil-affairs teams who design and implement community activities and conduct exercises, and to AFRICOM headquarters and service component staff. Robust engagement means that the USAID mission director and her/his staff and the US ambassador and his/her staff routinely scrutinize DoD activities from planning to execution, raise issues when appropriate, and challenge DoD plans and actions on the aspects that do not meet standards of interagency coordination or sustainability. Such assertive action is expected and generally welcomed in the DoD's bureaucratic culture, both by DoD field staff as well as by senior AFRICOM staff. If the USAID mission director does not succeed in obtaining needed adjustments to a DoD activity, she or he should raise the issue to the ambassador. If such interventions do not work, then the USAID director and the ambassador should jointly raise their issues with AFRICOM leadership and their respective Africa Bureau superiors in Washington.

Looking Ahead: Confronting Underlying Issues

Much can be done under existing authorities by leaders in the DoD and in USAID to maintain current momentum and accelerate coordination. With the right signals from their agency heads, vigorous collaboration in Africa that extends beyond the joint effort for the Sahel could emerge as a consistent pattern—perhaps in the Ebola response and especially in the long-term public health efforts in West Africa. As these patterns of action breed better results, they could blaze a trail for other DoD regional commands and USAID regional Bureaus to follow.

At the same time, achieving both US development and security objectives in Africa over the longer term will occur only if two crucial underlying issues are addressed: (1) if US conflict and crisis prevention efforts in Africa improve in effectiveness, and (2) if rebuilding of US civilian foreign affairs agencies, especially USAID and State Department, continues.

Enhancing US Conflict Prevention Capabilities

Formulating a cohesive USG conflict and crisis prevention strategy supported by an interagency framework with clear authorities, roles, and responsibilities are prerequisites for effective conflict prevention in Africa over the long term. Prevention allows sustainable development efforts to continue and, as former Defense Secretary Gates quipped, it's "a lot cheaper than sending soldiers."[56] Focusing on prevention in Africa is crucial because Africa's high number of fragile states and exposure to droughts in the Sahel, the Horn of Africa, and elsewhere make the continent more vulnerable to conflict.

Preceding fundamental changes in Washington, more effective US government crisis prevention in Africa can occur through improved coordination between the DoD and USAID under the aegis of the State Department. Efforts to counter violent extremism under TSCTP, PREACT, and the Sahel joint planning effort have made progress. Existing efforts should expand to other priority countries and subregions in Africa. Building on the lessons of the Sahel experience, AFRICOM/SOCOM, USAID, and State should develop integrated plans to (1) identify and address drivers of conflict; (2) accelerate inclusive development, especially for vulnerable groups like marginalized and unemployed youth groups; (3) identify more effective ways of combatting violent extremism insurgency; (4) strengthen accountable governance through legitimate institutions; and (5) hasten comprehensive security and justice sector reform.

The problems faced by the US and international actors in Africa include new challenges. These include the lower degree of certainty and agreement among international and local stakeholders regarding how to effect change in interrelated social, political and economic systems already affected by climatic shifts. In concert with local and international actors, planners from multiple US agencies will have to devise more robust planning approaches appropriate for greater complexity. Moreover, implementation approaches will require much more adaptability than is currently possible under existing laws and regulations.[57]

For this effort, USAID would draw on its Africa Bureau and specialized Washington staff in the Bureau for Democracy, Conflict, and Humanitarian Assistance. State would draw on its Bureaus of Africa, Conflict and Stabilization Operations, International Narcotic and Law Enforcement, and Counterterrorism. AFRICOM would call upon its relevant headquarters and field staff, supported by specialized personnel from SOCOM. Joint monitoring systems and evaluations should draw key lessons from interagency programs such as TSCTP and PREACT and from conflict-prone settings like northern Uganda, Mali, and northern Nigeria. Such analysis should include local scholars and researchers currently carrying out evaluative research on CVE, capacity building in fragile states, and the interrelated areas of justice, security sector reform, governance, and rule of law.

Engagement with the European Union's (EU's) special representative for the Sahel, and with like-minded EU member states, will add a necessary multilateral dimension to the US government conflict prevention strategy.[58] The EU implements a strategy for security and development in the Sahel through three capacity-building missions in Niger, Mali, and Libya, and a military training mission in Mali.[59] The EU maintains an overall interest in cooperation on security and development in Africa under the US-EU Development Dialogue.

To initiate an effective interagency effort with unity of command, purpose, and effort, the president should formally designate a lead federal department or agency for conflict and crisis prevention; provide necessary authority; and request sufficient resources for that new responsibility. To obtain funding both in the budget and from Congress under current political dysfunction, the Administration will have to mount a vigorous civil-military effort to justify such resources on the basis of US national security, foreign policy, and development objectives. This effort would require joint Congressional testimony (preceded by extensive private consultations with the House and Senate) before the two foreign affairs and Armed Services committees and the two State/Foreign Operations Appropriations Subcommittees. Those testifying together would include at least: (1) AFRICOM and SOCOM commanders, (2) the USAID administrator accompanied by AAs for Africa and DCHA; and (3) deputy and under secretaries of state with assistant secretaries for Africa, Counter-Terrorism, INL, and CSO. Barring such a full court press, no effective, integrated effort to prevent future conflicts and crises in Africa can occur.[60]

Rebuilding and Maintaining Civilian Foreign Affairs Agencies

Ultimately, USAID's success in playing its requisite role in conflict and crisis prevention, including building a strong collaborative relationship with AFRICOM, SOCOM, and DoD field staff in Africa requires sufficient, experienced USAID field staff of appropriate rank such that DoD COCOM commanders and their subordinates view USAID as a credible partner on the ground. Continuing US political gridlock and budget austerity threatens the ability civilian foreign affairs institutions to maintain their current capabilities, never mind to rebuild their organizations. The political struggle over budget levels will be fought in Washington, but, as discussed in relation to effective conflict and crisis prevention, the DoD, USAID, and the State Department must strive to protect civilian agency budgets for Africa. Restoring the capabilities of civilian agencies that were systematically degraded in the 1990s is a long-term process. Without sustained rebuilding of these agencies and reshaping them to meet more complex problems, the United States will not achieve its security, development, or diplomatic objectives in Africa or elsewhere.[61]

Conclusion

We must not lose the opportunity for more integrated USG engagement in Africa. Although significant progress has been made in recent years, obstacles and risks persist that hamper closer USAID-DoD collaboration that could lead to swifter achievement of US objectives in Africa. Opportunities exist to remove remaining obstacles and manage risks to promote expanded DoD-USAID collaboration. Effective collaboration in appropriate areas between USAID and AFRICOM consistent with US diplomatic goals is a cardinal building block of a "joint" US government approach to security and development in Africa. Through this more integrated approach, the United States can fashion more effective models for preventing crises and conflicts in Africa as well as in other regions. A more focused approach in Africa for crisis response and conflict prevention, both on US government interagency and multilateral levels, can yield great benefits. Reduced conflict will enable African government and nongovernment leaders and institutions to reap the benefits of the impending demographic transition; accelerate inclusive growth and poverty reduction; strengthen accountable justice and governance; and block the growth of violent extremism among vulnerable populations. While improving the lives of tens of millions in Africa, these changes will also serve fundamental US interests of security and prosperity.

Notes

Note: This chapter is an updated and expanded version of an article that appeared in *The Fletcher Forum of World Affairs* 38, no. 1 (Winter 2014).

[1] Sala-i-Martin and Pinkovskiy, *African Poverty is Falling.*

[2] The White House, *National Security Strategy 2010*; Department of State, *Quadrennial Diplomacy and Development Review*; and The World Bank, *World Development Report 2011.*

[3] Remarks during a panel discussion between Robert M. Gates, Hillary Clinton, Timothy Geithner, Rajiv Shah, and Daniel Yohannes at the US Global Leadership Coalition Annual Conference, Washington, DC., September 28, 2010: www.usglc.org/2010/09/28/the-administrations-new-global-development-policy-a-roundtable-discussion (accessed March 15, 2015).

[4] The World Bank, *Conflict, Security, and Development.*

[5] Hunter et. al., *Integrating Instruments of Power and Influence.*

[6] Ham, "Posture Statement of U.S. Africa Command" (2012).

[7] OECD, *Fragile States 2013: Resource Flows and Trends in a Shifting World*. The International Network on Conflict and Fragility (INCAF) is a sub-committee of the Development Assistance Committee (DAC) of the OECD, which includes all major aid donors. Additional information is available at www.oecd.org/dac/incaf/resourceflowstofragilestates.

[8] The White House, "Fact Sheet: U.S. Response to the Ebola Epidemic in West Africa."

[9] Stares and Zenko, *Enhancing U.S. Preventive Action*, vii.

[10] U.S. Department of State, *Quadrennial Diplomacy and Development Review*. Some of these are summarized in chapter three of this volume.

[11] The White House, "Fact Sheet: U.S Security Sector Assistance Policy."

[12] Owolabi, "Africa Strategic Dialogue."

[13] Ibid.

[14] Ward, "Posture Statement of U.S. Africa Command."

[15] Ibid.

[16] Gates, "Helping Others Defend Themselves."

[17] The additional 11 countries without fully staffed USAID missions but with USAID-funded programs and USAID-hired staff in-country are the following: Cameroon, Central African Republic, Chad, Djibouti (senior development advisor only), Lesotho, Libya (OTI), Mauritania, Sierra Leone, Somalia, Swaziland, and Tunisia. Finally, an additional 6 West African countries receive USAID assistance through regional programs in health, education, trade, and other areas managed by the USAID West African regional mission in Ghana. See US Department of State, *Congressional Budget Justification, Foreign Operations, FY 2012*.

[18] USAID has official presence with full-time US Direct Hire staff in 30 countries in the AFRICOM AOR. The largest presence are USAID Missions with USAID Offices having smaller numbers of American and Foreign Service National (local) staff. The three regional missions are in countries with fully-staff bilateral missions: Ghana, Kenya, and South Africa. Similarly, the two regional programs—Sahel and Central African Program on the Environment—are housed in bilateral missions as well: Senegal and the DRC, respectively.

[19] USAID, *The Development Response to Violent Extremism and Insurgency*.

[20] E-mail from Beth Cole, director, USAID Office of Civil-Military Cooperation (CMC), March 9, 2014.

[21] U.S. Government Accountability Office (GAO), *Combatting Terrorism: U.S. Efforts in Northwest Africa*, 20.

[22] Gates, "Helping Others Defend Themselves."

[23] Gates, Landon Lecture.

[24] These points are drawn from a series of e-mails and interviews with senior USAID officers posted in Africa from October 2010 – April 2012.

[25] Adams and Williams, "A New Way Forward," 7; Department of State, "Report on Security Capacity Building," 31. Note that the chair of the committee

writing this DoS report was Dr. William Perry, former Secretary of Defense. See also GAO, *Combating Terrorism: U.S. Efforts in Northwest Africa*, 22-23

[26] The White House, "Fact Sheet: U.S. Security Sector Assistance Policy."

[27] USAID, *Interagency Security Sector Assessment Framework.*

[28] GAO, *Combating Terrorism: U.S. Efforts in Northwest Africa*, 23.

[29] Department of Defense Office of Inspector General, *Defense Institution Reform Initiative.*

[30] E-mail from senior USAID official in Africa, 2010.

[31] USAID, "USAID Office of Civilian-Military Cooperation Training."

[32] "An Interview with Donald Steinberg," 161-162.

[33] USAID, *USAID Policy Framework: 2011-2015.*

[34] Anderson, "A Make or Break Moment for U.S. Foreign Policy."

[35] AFRICOM, "Cornerstones."

[36] Simmons, "Harvesting Peace," 35-41.

[37] Stares and Zenko, *Enhancing U.S. Preventive Action*, 19.

[38] Earle et al, *Concept Plan (CONPLAN) 4242 Lessons Learned Study*, 51, 55, 56.

[39] World Bank, *World Development Report 2011*, 3.

[40] In fact, on the first day of the June 2007, EUCOM-USAID Humanitarian Assistance Partnership Conference in Tunis, the more than 100 USAID, DoD, NGO, and State participants spent much of the first morning discussing what DoD and USAID each meant by the term "humanitarian assistance."

[41] The text of the revised USAID mission reads: "We partner to end extreme poverty and to promote resilient, democratic societies while advancing our security and prosperity." USAID website, http://www.usaid.gov/who-we-are/mission-vision-values (accessed and verified January 29, 2014).

[42] GAO, *Humanitarian and Development Assistance.*

[43] United States Institute for Peace (USIP), *Guidelines for Relations Between US Armed Forces and Non-Governmental Humanitarian Organizations.*

[44] Estimates provided to author in informal communications by AFRICOM, OSD, and other staff.

[45] Bradbury and Kleinman, *Winning Hearts and Minds?*, 63-69.

[46] Informal comments from senior USAID Foreign Service colleagues posted in Africa.

[47] SecDef, "Policy Guidance for DoD Overseas Humanitarian Assistance Program (HAP)."

[48] E-mail from Christian Hougen, USAID Bureau of Policy, Planning, and Learning (PPL), October 20, 2010.

[49]E-mail from the senior USAID officer directly involved in the project with DoD and the US ambassador.

[50] Ibid.

[51] Gates, "Helping Others Defend Themselves."

[52] US Global Leadership Coalition (USGLC), *Roundtable on the Administration's New Global Development Policy*, 4.

[53] Hooper, "Notes from the Flagpole #27."

[54] USAID, *The Development Response to Violent Extremism and Insurgency.*

[55] Warner, "The Trans Sahara Counter Terrorism Partnership," 1; USAID, *Mid-Term Evaluation of USAID's Counter-Extremism Programming in Africa*; Swedberg and Smith, *Mid-Term Evaluation of Three Countering Extremism Programming in Afric*a; and Aldrich, "First Steps Toward Hearts and Minds?"

[56] Panel discussion at US Global Leadership Coalition Annual Conference. Washington, D.C., September 28, 2010.

[57] Hummelbrunner and Jones, "A Guide for Planning and Strategy Development."

[58] The White House, "Joint Statement: U.S.-EU Summit;" Anderson, "The U.S.-EU High-Level Development Dialogue."

[59] Council of the European Union, "Council conclusions on implementation of the EU Strategy for Security and Development in the Sahel."

[60] Anderson, "A Much Needed Shot in the Arm."

[61] Ibid.

11

Pursuing
Multidimensional Security

Jessica Piombo

Beginning with the postulation that security, governance, and development are inextricably linked, the authors of this book have examined security programs of the US government, particularly the US military, that attempt to work across all three sectors. The rationale for involving the military in such nontraditional missions is based on the argument that, when development and security are linked, addressing sources of insecurity requires attention to governance and development as much as it does to "traditional" security institutions like militaries and police forces. In Africa, focusing solely on traditional notions of security may inadvertently undermine the goals of the programs when government institutions are weak, corrupt, or nonexistent—as evidenced in conflict zones such as the Democratic Republic of Congo. Given this, the US military has attempted to create new programs that involve a range of government and nongovernment actors in new security programs that focus on more than just training and equipping African militaries.

In the previous chapters, we have analyzed various aspects of this new, "nontraditional" approach to African security. We examine the design of programs, their execution, and the degree to which various initiatives have fostered coordination across military and civilian agencies. As a secondary focus, we assess how the programs aimed to address the developmental drivers of insecurity, and whether they had an impact. In this regard, we consider the degree to which military-civilian cooperation exists and analyze how interagency approaches contribute to more nuanced security programs and, in some cases, how the lack of these relationships has curtailed the effectiveness of initiatives.

Most of the chapters point to an imbalance between the resources of civilian and military agencies and show that the lack of adequate resourcing for the civilian side has hampered the ability of the programs to comprehensively address the sources and symptoms of insecurity in Africa. Without a comprehensive strategy to engage with their civilian counterparts, interagency approaches have been sporadic. This is critically important, because the authors all argue that the paucity of true interagency processes is one of the key factors preventing the US government from reaching its full potential to reduce insecurity in Africa. When programs were conducted with the full coordination of interagency counterparts, designed in ways to support larger initiatives undertaken by the Department of State and USAID, they were able to produce better results.

The positive development here is that genuine interagency cooperation has been increasing, and recent initiatives (like the Sahel program analyzed in Chapter 10) could set the bar for how to institutionalize cross-agency coordination. If this is to become fully routinized, however, the DoS and USAID (as well as other agencies) will need appropriate infusions of personnel and financial resources. Without this, the small cadre of Africa-focused civil servants will become overwhelmed as the military seeks to coordinate more and more programs. Interagency differences in institutional cultures, operating timelines, planning processes, understanding and definition of key concepts, emphasis on monitoring and evaluation, and priorities of the goals to be pursued will also continue to limit cooperation and collaboration across agencies. These distinctions either need to be minimized by some sort of governmental overhaul, or more realistically, by being acknowledged and built into program design and implementation in an honest fashion.

Regarding concrete improvements in the security situation in sub-Saharan Africa, the authors are mixed in their assessments. Many are skeptical that the US military's programs have brought about measurable improvements in the areas of comprehensive security sector reform, the capacity of African navies to promote maritime security, and shaping the environment through civil-military operations. The US military lacks the tools to create sustained improvements in human capacity and to address developmental drivers of insecurity. That's not its primary mission, nor how military personnel are trained.

This does not mean that the authors believe that the US military should get out of this business; rather, they argue that the DoD should conduct these missions differently. We are divided on whether AFRICOM has moved in the right or wrong direction, in terms both of its interagency orientation and its ability to effect concrete changes that will improve security in Africa, for Africans. Military engagements, particularly civil-military operations, can have positive outcomes for both security and development, but only when undertaken in close concert with civilian agencies like the Department of State and USAID, and with local counterparts. Without this, we argue, positive outcomes will be limited at best.

Clarence Bouchat (Chapter 9) sums up the analyses of the other authors well when he argues that, as currently conceived, US military engagement to enhance African security will not achieve the goals of improving African security and pursuing US national security objectives. Current DoD programs in Africa lack the depth, breadth, and persistence needed to address Africa's security and stability problems. Foreign military engagement is limited in its effects because of general concerns about military involvement in economic and governing affairs. Despite the fact that theater security cooperation programs support security and stability in foreign countries, in part through improving their economic and governing bases, they fall short of their mark. AFRICOM's theater security cooperation program is of minor assistance to combating Africa's real problems, Bouchat concludes. In any strategy used to support stability and security in Africa, this program will be a necessary part, but it is insufficient to achieve a significant lasting impact on its own.

Andrea Talentino (Chapter 2) warns us about several weaknesses in AFRICOM's approach to development. In her assessment, AFRICOM has been pursuing a form of development that fulfills certain formulaic markers of democracy, rather than building a system of government that creates effective states with active citizens who believe in democracy. Without long-term efforts to create mechanisms that connect citizens to government, efforts can ignore, marginalize, and neglect local actors and resources, and in the end contradict what the local population actually needs. Talentino argues that US government policy is not coherent enough to allow AFRICOM to forge a comprehensive effort—an idea also raised by Bouchat. She recommends that the US government be more selective about which countries it partners with to ensure that they have the will and the capacity to make use of US assistance.

Despite these concerns, Talentino maintains that there are small but important mechanisms by which military actors can emphasize the development side within the context of military tasks. The DoD, in particular AFRICOM, can model institutional norms, and by so doing, military actors can reinforce political and social shifts that may already be happening or which may have been encouraged by other programs. AFRICOM's primary weakness, however, is that its military approaches do

not address the root causes of weakness and may actually perpetuate them—
a theme that Dustin Sharp develops in Chapter 4.

In the end, Talentino asserts that AFRICOM is in a position to make a
significant contribution to understandings of development and security. If it
focuses solely on military tasks as its endpoint, however, it will remain a
very familiar example of US approaches to the world. But if it can use
military tasks as a means to fuel other change, then it really could be
different and effective. Carefully choosing which countries to work with can
extend the role of the military to include norm modeling that can encourage
social and political shifts. The problem is that there are many times when
the command is simply told to partner with another military, for reasons that
have little to do with real compatibility and everything to do with US
agendas, UN agendas, the personal interests of policymakers, and perhaps
even media coverage of world events.

Assessing the Record

The analyses set forth in this book collectively present a set of findings and
recommendations for how to address the lines between various actors within
the US government, how to create programs that build on the
complementarities between various actors, and what recurring issues
continually challenge the generation of productive interactions between
these different actors. Throughout the book, we have focused on military
activities and utilized AFRICOM as a microcosm of the broader debates
about the roles of various actors in promoting a more stable and secure
environment within Africa. In the remainder of this final chapter, I review
the major debates surrounding US military involvement in quasi-
developmental activities and reflect on how the information in the book
addresses these critiques.

Reducing Insecurity in Africa

The case studies almost universally conclude that military actors face many
difficulties when they attempt to embrace and operationalize programs that
help to enhance human, rather than state security, for a variety of reasons.
These findings resonate with real world developments: in the years since
AFRICOM was created, some of its initial vision has been realized, while
many of the more developmental and interagency aspects have been scaled
back.

Despite this seemingly negative prognosis, the chapters do note some
success in promoting interagency coordination and advancing new
approaches to security policy, especially in programs like the African

Contingency Operations and Training Assistance (ACOTA) program. Dustin Sharp (Chapter 4) and Andrea Walther-Puri (Chapter 5) point out important synergies between various government agencies that have helped to promote the goals of security sector reform. Similarly, Maureen Farrell and Jessica Lee (Chapter 6) conclude that CMO are most effective in advancing their security-focused objectives when the military works with DoS and USAID as partners—that is, when the military is viewed as a "force multiplier" in carrying out US policy rather than vice versa.

Other case studies raise the question of whether security sector capacity-building efforts are working. Alison Vernon and Margaux Hoar (Chapter 7) find that, even when the US military attempted to train African militaries using nontraditional methods like the APS, it did not necessarily increase the capacity of area navies. They argue that the activities performed by the US military in the APS engagements were successful in the tactical sense that they delivered education and brought African service-people from various countries to work together. The engagements were not sufficient to develop partner capacity in terms of the individuals putting what they learned into practice once back with their navies, however. The authors are also skeptical that the APS thus concretely helped to reduce threats to the maritime sector in Africa. This provides some evidence in support of the critiques that the US might not be achieving long-term results with short-term training and events typical of what occurs in military stabilization or humanitarian operations. Without embedding these training events in a longer-term structure of education and training, they will not build capacity in the partner countries.

Yet, APS missions did have a positive effect on regional, cross-country collaboration. If one shifts the metric for success, APS achieved results: it helped to foster relationships between regional navies, as well as cross-organizational relationships within area governments. Vernon and Hoar stress that the relationships facilitated by APS might lead to a broader understanding of the regional maritime threat environment, and consequently more accurate threat assessments for each country and a deeper understanding of appropriate regional responses. These are concrete improvements to maritime security in West Africa that can be traced to this particular program. APS evidenced the interagency constraints, in this instance because Naval Forces Africa did not adequately reach out to embassy staff to incorporate diplomatic elements into its engagements. In so doing, it limited the ability to use APS as a bridgehead for diplomatic discussions about maritime security that could have changed the policy environment in Ghana.

It is hardly coincidental that the case study authors conclude that the programs experiencing greater success in interagency collaboration are the ones that operate in a more traditional security field, rather than the programs closer to the traditional terrain of development—those involving civil affairs and NGO collaboration. As Maureen Farrell and Jessica Lee demonstrate in Chapter 6, DoD actors face specific constraints that may prevent them from fully pursuing developmental approaches to security. Teresa Crawford and Trina Zwicker (Chapter 8) note that there are similar obstacles with respect to coordinating and including nongovernmental actors in programs and planning processes. While the DoD has recently been given tools to overcome some of these constraints, they appear not be widely known or taken advantage of.

On their side, civilian agencies lack the personnel and budgets to dedicate staff to interacting with the DoD, further reducing collaboration. As several authors note, instead of the original 25 percent of staff coming from the interagency, now AFRICOM plans for only 3 percent civilian staff; and reaching even that figure is unlikely to happen in the constrained fiscal environment since 2012.[1] Within the embassies in Africa, the small number of USAID civilians, in particular, will limit their ability to respond to all the requests for collaboration as the DoD increases its engagement activities. Some have already expressed consternation at the demands for coordination.[2]

Reflecting these realities and as the security situation has changed in Africa (particularly after the military operations in Libya and Mali), the DoD has backed away from some of the more integrated and development-oriented initial goals for AFRICOM. The 2011 change of command from General Ward to General Ham began this trend, but the environment changed even more with the transfer from General Ham to General Rodriguez. Since 2013, the DoD has re-oriented AFRICOM more towards a traditional combatant command.[3] The US military has been engaging in more support operations to African militaries, direct action operations in support of African and American initiatives, and more intelligence, surveillance, and reconnaissance operations across the continent. With the increased operational tempo and the rise of these traditional missions, some of the "softer" defense programs have been de-emphasized. Multiple authors point to this when they discuss the four cornerstones that frame ARICOM's engagement under Rodriguez.

Defense with Development: What role for the US Military?

The first three chapters of this book introduce a set of debates surrounding the US military's role in reconstruction and stabilization activities. The first and most encompassing set of concerns relates to capabilities of the US military to conduct reconstruction operations.[4] The most strident of these focuses on the fact that the US military has not been trained to engage in development work, yet has undertaken projects within this realm. Thus, there are concerns over the design and execution of these projects: the military's approach is not crafted in a way to create local ownership of projects; the military can not devote personnel to a project on a long-term basis; and the time horizon of military engagements is considered woefully short and therefore unable to produce truly developmental outcomes. Better, critics argue, to put more resources into the agencies that know how to develop human capacity, state institutions, and economies—such as the State Department and USAID.

Capacity concerns are voiced about the planning process, implementation, monitoring and evaluation, and how the security rationale of the programs would influence the effect they could have on bringing larger-order improvements to a particular country. In the planning arena, questions arise as to how projects are selected and then planned. Given the security objective of the programs, country needs and priorities are often not condidered when the projects are being planned. Vernon and Hoar's analysis (Chapter 7) bears out this concern: a common shortfall in the APS was the manner in which US Navy officials initiated discussions with the Ghanaians. US actors tended to focus on the US perception of Ghana's security environment and how that impacted the United States' own security concerns in the region, failing to take into account the needs and interests of their partners. This, Vernon and Hoar note, did not lead to productive discussions with the Ghanaians. However, over time APS planners began to move beyond a US-centric focus, which demonstrates that, with experience, military actors can learn from their early mistakes. Framing the discussion in a way that focused on Ghanaian concerns, Vernon and Hoar argue, is far more constructive for the United States in pursuing its own objectives.

Reconstruction and "development" programs are criticized for being conducted in areas of strategic importance, without consideration of population density or economic connection to the rest of the country. This means that funds might be wasted, used in areas marginal to the economy and broader population instead of contributing to broad-based economic development. Here, the criticisms are not without merit: the process for nominating and accepting projects within the military command is based on complex DoD regulations that require justification of the security impact, rather than developmental logic or goals. Needs assessments are secondary to security payoffs, and here, the global war on terror imperative often dominates.

The CJTF-HOA experience shows that this dynamic does influence the distribution and type of projects that are pursued. The counterterrorism imperative that motivates the CJTF-HOA means that projects tend to concentrate in areas with high Muslim populations even if these are not the areas of demographic concentration in a country. In Kenya, for example, most projects focus on the remote areas of Lamu and Garissa, rather than on the Rift Valley or in/around Nairobi where a far greater proportion of the country's population resides. These projects will bring some limited benefits to remote areas, but not broader development to the majority of the Kenyan population, and they cannot have any significant economic impact. This pattern has been replicated across the CTJF-HOA's areas of operation: projects did (and still often do) tend to take place in remote locations considered to be vulnerable to extremism.

On the implementation front, critics question the rationale of who carries out the projects. Delivering humanitarian or developmental assistance is a tool for training: increasing the skills of the US military is the main objective of the programs. Local populations often contribute little to project implementation in the main humanitarian assistance programs, which means that there are few opportunities to transfer skills and build capacity in the local populations. Because of this, the developmentally oriented humanitarian assistance projects contravene one of the fundamental lessons learned from over 50 years of development practice: that a combination of community participation, ownership, and buy-in, along with local capacity building, is the only way to make projects sustainable and to have a long-term impact. Because local populations are rarely involved in the implementation of military reconstruction operations or civil affairs projects, the US military also misses an opportunity to develop ties with the local population. Should a project later require maintenance, the population may not have gained the skills necessary to conduct the work.[5]

Civil Affairs planners and AFRICOM officials often refute these criticisms by arguing that they are inappropriate, since development is not the goal of the programs.[6] Accordingly, when Farrell and Lee were asked to evaluate AFRICOM's civil affairs projects, they were instructed to assess strategic impacts. Thus, they did not examine the developmental or economic impacts of the projects. Using this argument to side-step the criticism is problematic, however, because the programs look like "development," and copy some aspects of social and economic developmental programs. If they don't contribute to lasting change or improvement of any sort, even the "strategic" impact they might have comes into question.

The case studies provide input for answering what role the U.S military should play in this security environment. In Chapter 9, Clarence Bouchat complements the insights from the case studies by postulating that one *could* make an argument that the military should lead interagency reconstruction and "nation building" enterprises. In his provocative discussion, Bouchat does not question whether an interagency approach is necessary; rather, he asks who should lead that effort. Based on the fact that military forces are well versed in the skills of leadership, organization, strategic thinking, and planning for contingencies, Bouchat reasons that the DoD could effectively lead engagements in Africa. In this role military forces might oversee the sharing of resources, processes, and training needed to make cooperation more effective.

In the end, however, Bouchat argues against this course of action, both because of legal and conceptual obstacles and because the military could overwhelm civilian counterparts if placed in the lead. Given the realities of the situation, another (more viable) option is to reverse the positions of military and civilian actors, by which he means to adequately resource civilian institutions to lead—with appropriate military support. US government and international civilian organizations have the mandate and experience needed to help Africans improve their situation. The US and other militaries should play their expected role in enforcing security and stability directly and indirectly through economic development and good governance, though firmly under overarching civilian oversight. Bouchat advocates creating a "proconsul-like" post to oversee regional affairs, similar to a combatant commander in the DoD, to coordinate and streamline across the interagency efforts. The designation of a lead entity or person for regional affairs could balance resources and efforts within the US government, and help coordinate actions with other governments, NGOs, and IGOs.

Critiques of Humanitarian Operations

A second set of concerns focuses on the US military's involvement in disaster relief or complex emergencies, rather than military involvement in reconstruction/development-type activities. Here, the criticisms are most often articulated by nongovernmental organizations (NGOs). Important critiques emerging from the NGO community consider military involvement in humanitarian assistance (HA) missions to be a danger to humanitarian principles and therefore to humanitarian aid workers. As a result, the mission itself could become compromised, which would then threaten the safety of individuals working in the mission, even if they are not military. NGOs are also concerned that military humanitarian assistance missions are dominated by security issues to the exclusion of humanitarian principles. Additionally, since military humanitarian assistance places security and stabilization at the core of its mission, many fear that it will be denied to needy populations if they pose a security risk, or if they are considered to be enemy combatants.[7] A corollary to this objection is that, if military humanitarian assistance is delivered on a partisan basis, the military may only respond to crises that the US government considers important to US national interests.

The case study chapters do not directly respond to the first of these critiques, but they do speak to the last few. Evidence shows that when asked, the military will adjust its programming to move out of the strategically sensitive areas and direct more resources towards areas in greater need. For example, in the wake of the election violence in January 2008 in Kenya, the then-US ambassador to Kenya requested that the CJTF-HOA provide emergency relief in the Rift Valley. Prior to this, CJTF-HOA had only operated in the Lamu and Garissa regions. Initially, the civil affairs teams had considered this a misuse of their resources, since there was little terrorist threat in the Rift Valley.[8]

The members of the civil affairs team changed their perspective on this, however, once they understood how much their assistance was appreciated by the Kenyan government and people—and therefore, how much greater impact the programs could have. By June 2008, when I interviewed civil affairs teams in Nairobi, the group leaders were publicizing their activities to help with postviolence recovery. By the time that Farrell and Lee conducted their research, the fact that the ambassador had to force the CA team into the Rift Valley was not even remembered. Instead, CA teams operating in Kenya's central region was taken as the norm, when in fact this was far from the original operating concept.

In this case, a military asset was re-assigned to work on a humanitarian issue, without regard to the direct security impacts. Similar dynamics occurred in the US Navy's provision of emergency assistance in the wake of the Indian Ocean tsunami in 2004, the Kashmir earthquake in 2005, Haiti in 2010, and multiple other natural disasters. In these instances, military assets were diverted from their primary missions to assist with disaster response, often with laudable results.[9] While there may at times be initial resistance to providing assistance—for the reasons feared by the humanitarian assistance community—when directed by the USG to provide the assistance, the directive was followed. Therefore, there is no little evidence that military provision of humanitarian assistance will be denied to populations who need it, simply because they are not strategically important.

Another final concern is that military forces also often fail to consult NGOs in the planning process when designing a humanitarian intervention. Often, the US military has been unaware (or unappreciative) of the role of HA organizations during relief efforts, which can lead to the military either duplicating other relief efforts or acting in a manner that may be detrimental to the relief operation.[10] In Chapter 8, Crawford and Zwicker provide some evidence that this criticism is at least partially accurate. The command experienced difficulty discovering stable ways to interact with the NGO community.

At the same time, Crawford and Zwicker's chapter shows the critiques to be a bit undeveloped and un-nuanced. The authors point out that the issue is not that the military is unaware that it could or should reach out to NGOs to coordinate efforts. The practice of working with NGOs is not easy, due to the military's own rules and procedures, a lack of systemic support for these efforts, and the difficulty of working with a non-hierarchical and diffuse set of actors such as the NGO community. Based on their experiences and analysis, Crawford and Zwicker argue that AFRICOM has encountered deep challenges when attempting to reconcile the interaction and communication gap between military forces and NGOs. Groups with similar mission sets often failed to create synergy in their activities, organizations, or goals.

Despite these challenges, Crawford and Zwicker find that engagement exists along several fronts: strategic, humanitarian, planning, tactical program implementation, and information/outreach. They also show that AFRICOM has experimented with different methods of interaction, and while it has yet to find a stable solution, it remains committed to finding some way to coordinate with NGOs. Working with USAID and other defense actors as intermediaries simplifies some of the legal hurdles, though these options obviously add an additional coordination dynamic. Finally, AFRICOM does have embedded staff from the Office of Foreign Disaster Assistance at USAID, and as a matter of policy does not engage in any disaster response without working through that representative, so the worst fears in this area are not borne out.

Overall, the chapters by both Vernon and Hoar (Chapter 7) and Crawford and Zwicker (Chapter 8) argue that that Africa Command is interacting with civilian organizations to include NGOs, at a variety of levels, and on a diverse number of issues. Command staff still has some way to go to address the structural issues that limit interaction with NGOs; here Crawford and Zwicker sound a warning note based on internal reorganizations within AFRICOM that occurred in late 2012. Improving structural conditions could include articulation of a clear strategy, deepened understanding of NGOs, broadened outreach to additional NGOs, and improved information sharing between headquarters and field/in-country staff.

Additional Findings and Highlights

There are many insights from these chapters that go beyond responding to the criticisms of military involvement in SSTR and humanitarian operations. Several of the authors discuss how military actors can address the security-development divide and help promote human security. We based our analyses on the assumption that a reconceptualization of security at the human level can move past problems rooted in bad governance, uneven development, exclusion, and human rights abuses perpetuated by regimes and their security forces. While this may hold in theory, many chapter authors noted that in practice it is often difficult— though not impossible— for military actors to embrace and operationalize programs that help to enhance human, rather than state security.

In Chapter 4, for example, Dustin Sharp stresses that, far from being peripheral to the security-development nexus, issues of accountability and impunity for human rights abuses must be brought to the center of thinking and programming in areas of peace operations, development, and security and justice sector reform. In many African countries the security sector itself has too often become a persistent source of insecurity through acts of corruption, extortion, criminality, and various human rights abuses. When such abuses are allowed to go unchecked over time, protectors become predators, operating in some instances with near total impunity.

Here is where development and security overlap. Sharp argues that "the reasons for predatory behavior by traditional security sector actors are complex and include structural factors such as poor salaries and inadequate training. Compounding matters, in many cases security forces do not operate within an architecture of well-functioning checks and balances intended to foster a climate of accountability." The Guinean case that Sharp presents makes it clear why it is necessary to embed the (newly) well-trained militaries within an institutional structure that promotes high standards of behavior and prevents abuse and corruption. Military training, proceeding without corresponding institutional development, will perpetuate insecurity. In turn, this insecurity will then prohibit economic development, creating a continuous negative-feedback loop.

A lack of accountability for corruption and human rights abuses undermines the rule of law and diminishes prospects for advancing develop-ment and security. Given this, security sector reform programs that focus only on building the capacity of security forces will create more problems if they are not embedded in larger-order governance programs. When addressing the security-development nexus in West Africa today, the implications of Sharp's arguments are that international actors must include greater efforts to close this accountability gap in the traditional security sector, and programs must progress in tandem with governance reforms. Thus, in order to create a more secure world for the majority of African citizens, and not just the elites and leaders of their countries, external engagement must focus on developmental and traditional security dynamics.

Perhaps at odds with his colleagues in this book who seem to argue that the military's involvement in nontraditional missions should be curtailed, Sharp uses his analysis to argue for *more* involvement in these activities: "Reorienting defense and security forces along a human security axis might entail forms of military humanitarianism—that is deploying military expertise and skills for development—especially in civil engineering, agriculture, medicine, regional peace support operations, and other internal security challenges." Going forward, building human security requires that the United States and the international community bring issues of accountability and impunity for human rights abuses by security forces to the center of thinking and programming in areas of peace operations, development, and security and justice sector reform.

In Chapter 5, Andrea Wather-Puri focuses on the interagency aspects of security sector assistance and reform. Walther-Puri maintains that chronic imbalances between military and civilian agencies in the USA will lead to unsustainable efforts at security sector reform. She argues that, if they proceed without attendant governance reform and capacity development, these efforts could exacerbate security problems as military capacities are increased. Questions about whether the USA inadvertently contributed to the military coup in Mali in 2012 by providing extensive counterterrorism training drive home this point.[11]

In this sense, if the DoD and AFRICOM focus only on military training, they will not be able to bring about the changes they desire on the ground in Africa: a more secure environment in which African governments are able to take care of their backyards, reduce transnational threats, and enhance the security for their citizens. The nature of the security challenge in Africa demands a comprehensive, integrated approach. Walther-Puri asserts that AFRICOM is not the right tool to bring out security sector development on its own. When brought into a comprehensive approach that is coordinated across multiple government agencies (which themselves are strong and robustly resourced), however, it becomes one part of a larger coherent effort that can bring development and improvement to the security sectors of African countries.

G. William Anderson (Chapter 10) makes a strong case that, because it encompasses developmental as well as traditional security dynamics, reducing insecurity in sub-Saharan Africa will require multidimensional approaches. To be effective in creating a more safe and secure environment in Africa, these programs will require expanded USAID and DoD collaboration. Anderson argues that broader opportunities exist for a more integrated approach to security and development between USAID and the DoD under Department of State coordination. If the US moves to accelerate initiatives that have already begun over the medium- to-long term, it can prevent or mitigate crises and conflicts in Africa's weak and fragile states and address cross-border tensions more successfully. In a period of budget reductions, using available resources as efficiently as possible is even more essential. A more integrated US goverment approach in Africa at both interagency and multilateral levels will help support Africa's economic growth and poverty reduction; accelerate progress toward reaching its Millennium Development Goals; reduce the number and intensity of conflicts; and blunt the growth of violent extremism among vulnerable populations, such as disenfranchised and unemployed youth in fast-growing mega-urban centers.[12] Such progress will serve both US security objectives and African development and security goals.

Final Thoughts

The "developmental challenge" in addressing insecurity in Africa takes two main forms. The first is addressing the economic and governance issues that create human and state-level insecurities. The second is the need to build up the human, institutional and infrastructural capacity within African governments, so that they can appropriately utilize the resources in their security sectors. The collective evidence in this volume has demonstrated that, under the right conditions, the US military can help to build human and institutional capacity, but that it will be most effective at this when the subject of the project remains in a traditional military field: defense sector reform, military professional development, and military-to-military training.

Though we recognize that stability is dependent on the mutually constitutive elements of security, governance, and development, and that productive synergies can be created when various government agencies work together, it remains important that each of these dimensions is best addressed by specific actors. The interconnectedness of these three sectors necessitates that actors work together to create synergistic outcomes—to adopt a "whole of government" approach that goes beyond rhetoric. There are distinct needs for programming and coordination to work across the development-security divide in order to effectively address Africa's deep-seated security challenges. These chapters have shown that despite progress, there is much work that still needs to be done in this realm.

One of the biggest challenges for interagency coordination is the complexity among interagency organizational structures, cultures, time horizons, funding and staffing levels, operating procedures, and mandates. Despite knowledge of these issues, the disjunctures still continue to impair working relationships. Knowing the nature of the coordination problem has yet to translate into enduring and institutionalized solutions within AFRICOM, embassies in Africa, and Washington-based agencies.

Communication problems are particularly damaging to the development of cooperative and synergistic interagency relationships. Differing organizational traits and cultures also create serious challenges when US military, civilian, and nongovernmental actors attempt to cooperate. More productive ends with less waste could be created when various actors make the effort to learn how to work together and alter their processes to facilitate coordination. AFRICOM has seen success in creating cooperation across USG agencies in health programs when the military has consciously sought to modify its programs to more closely align with USAID processes and expectations. In the traditional military realm, the successful Sahel exercise and the initiatives associated with it set another model for interagency collaboration. Both can serve as examples for other programs.

The expansion of the civil affairs and capacity building missions within AFRICOM has been viewed by many as an encroachment into what they consider the exclusive roles of the diplomatic and development communities. There are serious concerns from the Department of State, USAID, and NGOs about the fact that US military personnel are not trained in development or true capacity and institution building, that the DoD does not have the time horizon built into its programs that true development projects require, and that the DoD engages in "developmental" activities for strategic ends. These differences are part of why integration, or at least cooperation and coordination, are necessary to create layered programs that will have lasting effects in truly addressing African security challenges.

The question again arises, however, of who should lead coordination. Some feel that AFRICOM can serve as an essential organization to coordinate and facilitate future US-led stabilization projects in Africa. Others are less convinced, and the inability of AFRICOM's leadership to generate a clear purpose and mission for the command has made it more difficult to find resolution on this. Regardless of the position that one takes on this issue, the fact is that chronic imbalances in human and financial resources between the main US government foreign policy agencies deeply impair the ability to generate cooperative relationships, particularly the development and deployment of programs and the sharing of information. These issues are unchangeable in the short term and must therefore be planned for and worked around, while processes are initiated via executive and legislative channels to remedy the situation in the longer term.

In terms of recommendations, the insights from this volume suggest that a strategy of coordination with differentiation might be the best way to address these challenges. Actors should each work in their areas of expertise and to their comparative advantage, while integrating into an overall coordinated project. The DoD will need to acknowledge where and when other agencies should be in the lead, and develop strategies to support their efforts rather than attempt to replace them. Aligning DoD programs with existing and planned initiatives pursued by USAID and DoS can help to provide a long-term outlook to defense programs, despite personnel and funding fluctuations. Actors that work in this arena need to develop a common lexicon at best, or at minimum a more sustained awareness that terms and concepts are not universal.

On their side, AFRICOM staff could work within the DoD to fix the structural issues that limit interaction with civilians and NGOs. Ultimately, however, the resource imbalance between civilian and military agencies will have to be addressed if sustained cooperation is to occur. Based on their experiences in Iraq and Afghanistan, DoD actors often assume that DoS and USAID personnel do not want to go on assignment with the military or cooperate with military-led programs. Our chapter authors have frequently noted, however, that lack of cooperation is often not an issue of will, but of resources, rules, and career incentives. A better understanding within the DoD of the processes and constraints of civilian agencies would help the various actors find ways to work with or around these potential constraints. On their side, civilian agencies will eventually need to generate career incentives that motivate their staff to accept assignments at AFRICOM and other combatant commands, in order to encourage and facilitate regular exchanges between staffs.

The consistency of coordination challenges revealed in the chapters of this book, along with the identification of some successes in ways of engaging across agencies and with African partners, is important. One might say that none of the findings here are "path breaking" in the sense that those observing government have been aware of them previously. But the consistency of the issues that arose, regardless of the type of program being analyzed, is marked. Given this, it is time to move beyond the rhetoric of noting problems and to identify and to institutionalize ways of engaging productively across the range of governmental and nongovernmental actors to enhance both US and African security at the interstate, national, and human levels. Until there are stable and replicable ways of harnessing all the instruments of US national power to address the security issues in Africa, and to do this in a multidimensional manner, the same lessons will be noted, reported, and subsequently ignored.

Notes

Note: All opinions expressed in this chapter are my own and do not reflect oficial positions of the Naval Postgraduate School or the US government.

[1] Brown, "AFRICOM at 5 Years," 22.

[2] Author's communication with USAID personnel in Djibouti (July 2008), AFRICOM (November 2008), and Monterey, CA (December 2010). William Anderson also notes this frustration in his chapter.

[3] For an extremely skeptical analysis of this, see Turse, "AFRICOM Goes to War on the Sly."

[4] GAO, *Defense Management*, 14.

[5] These findings are augmented and supported by the author's own work evaluating the civil affairs operations of the CJTF-HOA.

[6] Author's interview with a civil affairs team leaders in Nairobi and Djibouti, July 2007.

[7] Abiew, "NGO-Military Relations," 31.

[8] Personal communication with the author, June 2008.

[9] See, for example, Piombo and Malley, "Beyond Protecting the Land and the Sea."

[10] Hinson, *US Military Interaction with Humanitarian Assistance Organizations*.

[11] Whitlock, "Leader of Mali Military Coup Trained in the US"; Lando, "Mali – A Double Tale of Unintended Consequences."

[12] Sala-i-Martin and Pinkovskiy, *African Poverty is Falling*.

Bibliography

10 U.S.C. § 101, et seq. - *Armed Forces.* www.law.cornell.edu/uscode/text/10 (accessed April 30, 2012).

10 U.S.C. §1050a. *Armed Forces.* "African Cooperation: Payment of Personnel Expenses." Added Pub. L. 111–383, div. A, title XII, § 1204(a), Jan. 7, 2011, 124 Stat. 4386. www.law.cornell.edu/uscode/text/10 (accessed April 30, 2012).

Abiew, F.K. "NGO-Military Relations in Peace Operations." *International Peacekeeping* 10, no. 1 (2003): 24-39.

Adams, Gordon and Rebecca Williams. "A New Way Forward: Rebalancing Security Assistance Programs and Authorities." Washington, DC: The Henry L Stimson Center, March 2011.

African Union Panel of the Wise. *Election-Related Disputes and Political Violence: Strengthening the Role of the African Union in Preventing, Managing, and Resolving Conflict.* The African Union Series. New York: International Peace Institute, July 2010.

Aldrich, Daniel P. "First Steps Toward Hearts and Minds? USAID's Counter Violent Extremism Policies in Africa." *Terrorism and Political Violence* 26, no. 3 (2014): 523-546

Allgov. "US Foreign Policy in Africa: Oil and Commandoes." March 24, 2014. www.allgov.com/news/us-and-the-world/us-foreign-policy-in-africa-oil-and-commandoes (accessed July 3, 2014).

Anderson, David A. and Andrew Wallen. "Preparing for Economics in Stability Operations." *Military Review* 88, no. 2 (March-April 2008).

Anderson, G. William. "A Much Needed Shot in the Arm for US Civilian Power." The Hill's Congress Blog. Washington, DC: December 2, 2010. http://thehill.com/blogs/congress-blog

_____. "The U.S.-EU High-Level Development Dialogue: Building on the Legacy of the Marshall Plan." Washington, DC: German Marshall Fund US Policy Brief, June 24, 2011.

_____. "A Make or Break Moment for U.S. Foreign Policy." *DEVEX*, September 8, 2011.

Andrews, Robert and Mark Kirk. *Integrating 21ˢᵗ Century Development and Security Assistance.* Washington: Center for Strategic and International

Studies, January 2008. www.csis.org (accessed November 15, 2010).

Aning, Kwesi. "Are There Emerging West African Criminal Networks? The Case of Ghana." *Global Crime* 8, no. 3 (August 2007): 193–212.

An Interview with Donald Steinberg," *Prism* 3, no. 2 (2014): 157-163.

Associated Press. "Africans Wary of AFRICOM, U.S. Motives." November 5, 2007. www.military.com/NewsContent (accessed May 8, 2012).

Atwood, J. Brian, M. P. McPherson, and Andrew Natsios. "Arrested Development: Making Foreign Aid a More Effective Tool." *Foreign Affairs* 87, No. 6 (2008): 123-132.

Autessere, Severine. *The Trouble with the Congo.* New York: Cambridge University Press, 2010.

_____. *Peaceland: Conflict Resolution and the Everyday Politics of International Intervention.* New York: Cambridge University Press, 2014.

Ball, Nicole, Piet Biesheuvel, Tom Hamilton-Baille and 'Funmi Olonisakin. *Security and Justice Sector Reform Programming in Africa.* DFID Evaluation Working Paper 23. London: Department for International Development, April 2007.

Barnes, Sandra T. "Global Flows: Terror, Oil, and Strategic Philanthropy." *Asian Studies Review* 48, no. 1 (April 2005): 1–23.

Basilotto, John P. *A Revisionist View of Nation Assistance in Africa.* Master's thesis, US Army War College, 1991.

Beebe, Shannon D. and Mary Kaldor. *The Ultimate Weapon Is No Weapon: Human Security and the New Rules of War and Peace.* New York: Public Affairs, 2010.

Beebe, Shannon. "Solutions Not Yet Sought: A Human Security Paradigm for 21st Century Africa." Unpublished manuscript, 2009.

Benjamin, Daniel. "Examining U.S. Counterterrorism Priorities, Strategy Across Africa's Sahel Region." Testimony by Daniel Benjamin, coordinator, Office of the Coordinator for Counterterrorism, to the Senate Committee on Foreign Relations, Subcommittee on African Affairs, November 17, 2009. www.state.gov/j/ct/rls/rm/2009 (accessed September 4, 2014).

Berschinski, Robert G. *AFRICOM's Dilemma: The Global War on Terrorism, "Capacity Building," Humanitarianism, and the Future of U.S. Security Policy in Africa.* Carlisle, PA: US Army War College Strategic Studies Institute, 2007.

Bessler, Manuel and Kaoruko Seki. "Civil-Military Relations in Armed Conflicts: A Humanitarian Perspective." *Liaison* 3, no. 3 (November 2004).

Birtle, Andrew J. *U.S. Army Counterinsurgency and Contingency Operations Doctrine 1942-1976.* Washington, DC: US Army Center of Military History, 2006.

Boutros-Ghali, Boutros. *An Agenda for Peace: Preventive Diplomacy, Peacemaking and Peace-keeping.* Report of the Secretary-General pursuant to the statement adopted by the Summit Meeting of the Security Council on 31 January 1992 (A/50/6-S/1995/1). New York: United Nations, June 17, 1992.

Bradbury, Mark and Michael Kleinman. *Winning Hearts and Minds? Examining the Relationship between Aid and Security in Kenya.* Medford, MA: Feinstein International Center, Tufts University, April 2010.

Brody, Reed. "The Prosecution of Hissène Habré: International Accountability, National Impunity," in *Transitional Justice in the Twenty-First Century; Beyond Truth versus Justice,* edited by Naomi Roht-Arriaza and Javier Mariezcurrena. Cambridge, MA: Cambridge University Press, 2006.

Brzozowske, Brooke. "Week One of Africa Partnership Flight Wraps Up." Accra, Ghana: US Air Forces Africa Public Affairs, March 23, 2012. www.africom.mil/NEWSROOM/Article/8877 (accessed July 14, 2014).

Bush, George W. "2004 State of the Union Address." Washington, DC: January 20, 2004.

Bush, George W. "2005 State of the Union Address 2005." Washington, DC: February 2, 2005.

Byman, Daniel. "Uncertain Partners: NGOs and the Military." *Survival* 43, no. 2 (Summer 2001): 97-114.

Carothers, Thomas." The Rule-of-Law Revival," in *Promoting the Rule of Law Abroad: The Problem of Knowledge,* edited by Thomas Carothers. Washington, DC: Carnegie Endowment for International Peace, 2006.

———. "The Problem of Knowledge," in *Promoting the Rule of Law Abroad: The Problem of Knowledge,* edited by Thomas Carothers. Washington, DC: Carnegie Endowment for International Peace, 2006.

Cavaleri, David P. *Easier Said Than Done: Making the Transition Between Combat Operations and Stability Operations.* Fort Leavenworth, KS: Combat Studies Institute Press, 2005.

Center on International Cooperation. *Annual Review of Global Peace Operations 2013.* Boulder: Lynne Rienner Publishers, 2013.

Chabal, Patrick and Jean-Pascal Daloz. *Africa Works: Disorder as Political Instrument.* Bloomington: Indiana University Press, 1999.

Chairman of the Joint Chiefs of Staff. "Military Support for Stability, Security, Transition and Reconstruction (SSTR) Operations" (CJCS Notice 3245.01). Washington, DC: Combined Joint Chiefs of Staff, May 12, 2006. http://intlhealth.dhhq.health.mil (accessed March 14, 2015).

———. *Civil-Military Operations.* Joint Publication 3-57. Washington, DC: Government Printing Office, 2008.

———. *Joint Operational Planning.* Joint Publication (JP) 5-0. Washington, DC: Government Printing Office, August 11, 2011.

———. *Stability Operations,* Joint Publication (JP) 3-07. Washington, DC: Government Printing Office, September 29, 2011.

Chandler, David. "The Road to Military Humanitarianism: How the Human Rights NGOs Shaped A New Humanitarian Agenda." *Human Rights Quarterly* 23 (2001): 678-700.

———. "The Security-Development Nexus and the Rise of Anti-Foreign Policy." *Journal of International Relations and Development* 10, no. 4 (2007): 362–386.

Chatterjee, Deen K. and Don E. Scheid, eds. *Ethics and Foreign Intervention.* Cambridge: Cambridge University Press, 2003.

Chesterman, Simon. *You, the People: The United Nations, Transitional Administration, and Statebuilding.* New York: Oxford University Press, 2004.

CIVICUS: World Alliance for Citizen Participation, "CIVICUS Civil Society Index Methodology." www.civicus.org (accessed April 30, 2012).

Clinton, Hillary Rodham. "Town Hall Meeting to Announce the Quadrennial Diplomacy and Development Review." Speech at Dean Acheson Auditorium, Washington, DC, July 10, 2009. http://video.state.gov/ (accessed July 8, 2014).

Cole, Beth. "An Open Door." *PKSOI Bulletin* 1, no. 1 (October 2008).

Collier Paul, et. al. *Breaking the Conflict Trap: Civil War and Development Policy.* Washington, DC: The International Bank for Reconstruction and Development/The World Bank, 2003.

_____. "A Worldwide Pact for Security and Accountability in Fragile 'Bottom Billion' States." *Development Outreach* 11, no. 2 (October 2009): 10-12.

Combined Joint Task Force–Horn of Africa. "About the Command." www.hoa.africom.mil (accessed July 20, 2014).

Commander, US Naval Forces Africa. "About Africa Partnership Station." www.c6f.navy.mil (accessed June 25, 2014).

Commander, US Naval Forces Europe-Africa/Commander, US 6th Fleet. "Africa Partnership Station 2012 Begins." Naples, Italy: CNE-A/6th Fleet Public Affairs, Feb 25, 2012. www.navy.mil (accessed June 25, 2014).

Copson. Raymond W. *Africa Backgrounder: History, U.S. Policy, Principal Congressional Actions.* RL30029. Washington, DC: Library of Congress Congressional Research Service, January 5, 2001.

"Cornerstones," AFRICOM website, www.africom.mil/about-the-command/cornerstones (accessed August 2, 2014).

Council of the European Union. "Council Conclusions on Implementation of the EU Strategy for Security and Development in the Sahel." Brussels: Foreign Affairs Council Meeting, March 17, 2014.

Crane, Conrad. "Phase IV Operations: Where Wars Are Really Won." *Military Review* 88, no. 4 (July-August 2008).

Crawley, Vince. "Pentagon Emphasizing Humanitarian Aid, Reconstruction Work." *The Washington File,* February 3, 2006.

Center for Strategic and International Studies. "Post-Conflict Reconstruction: Task Framework." Joint Project of the CSIS and the Association for the United States Army (May 2002).

De Mesquita, Bruce Bueno and George W. Downs. "Intervention and Democracy." *International Organization* 60, no. 3 (Summer 2006): 627-649.

Defense Science Board. *2004 Summer Study on Transition to and from Hostilities.* Washington, DC: Office of the Undersecretary of Defense for Acquisition, Technology, and Logistics, December 2004. www.acq.osd.mil/dsb/ (accessed July 25, 2006).

Defense Security Cooperation Agency. "Fiscal Year 2015 Budget Estimates." Washington, DC: The Defense Security Cooperation Agency, March 2014. http://comptroller.defense.gov (accessed September 2, 2014).

Delevingne, Lawrence. "Controversy Dogs Creation of U.S. Military Command." *Interpress Service*, June 3, 2008.

Dempsey, Thomas A. "The Transformation of African Militaries," in *Understanding Africa: A Geographic Approach,* edited by Amy Krakowka and Laurel Hummel. West Point, NY: US Military Academy, 2009.

Denoeux, Guilain. *Development Assistance and Counter-Extremism: A Guide to Programming.* Washington, DC: USAID, October 2009.

Department of Defense Office of Inspector General. *Defense institution Reform Initiative Program Elements Need to Be Defined.* Report No. DODIG-2013-019. Alexandria, VA: Department of Defense Office of Inspector General, November 9, 2012.

Department of the Army Headquarters. *Counterinsurgency.* Field Manual (FM) 3-24. Washington, DC: December 15, 2006. www.fas.org (accessed February 28, 2013).

_____. *Stability Operations.* Field Manual (FM) 3-07. Washington, DC: US Government Printing Office, October 6, 2008. http://usacac.army.mil (accessed August 13, 2013).

Department of the Army Headquarters. *Stability.* Army Doctrine Reference Publication (ADRP) 3-07 Change 1. Washington, DC: US Government Printing Office, 31 August 2013. http://armypubs.army.mil (accessed May 22, 2014).

Dobbins, James F. "Guidelines for Nation Builders." *Strategic Studies Quarterly* 4, no. 3 (Fall 2010): 15-42.

Dobbins, James, et al., *America's Role in Nation Building: from Germany to Iraq.* Santa Monica, CA: Rand Corporation, 2003.

Doe, J. Kpanneh and Siahyonkron Nyanseor. "AFRICOM: A Model for 'Capacity' Building and Development or Not?" *The Perspective,* November 24, 2007.

Duffield, Mark. "The Liberal Way of Development and the Development-Security Impasse: Exploring the Global Life-Chance Divide." *Security Dialogue* 41, no. 1 (February 2010): 53-76.

Duffield, Mark, Joanna Macrae, and Devon Curtis. "Editorial: Politics and Humanitarian Aid." *Disasters* 25, no. 4 (December 1991): 269-274.

Earle, Caroline R. "Taking Stock: Interagency Integration in Stability Operations." *Prism* 3, no. 2 (March 2012): 37-50.

Earle, Caroline R., with Ashley N. Bybee and Daniel R. Langberg. *Concept Plan (CONPLAN) 4242 Lessons Learned Study.* Washington, DC: Institute for Defense Analyses, December 2009.

Eastwood, Robert and Michael Lipton. "Demographic Transition in Sub-Saharan Africa: How Big Will the Economic Dividend Be?" *Population Studies* 65, no. 1 (2011) 9-35.

Ebo, Adedeji. "Security Sector Reform as An Instrument of Sub-Regional Transformation in West Africa," in *Reform and Reconstruction of the Security Sector,* edited by Alan Bryden and Heiner Hanggi. Munster: DCAF/LIT Verlag, 2004.

Eisenstadt, S. N. *Modernization: Protest and Change.* Englewood Cliffs, NJ: Prentice Hall, 1966.

Ellis, Mark S. "Combating Impunity and Enforcing Accountability as a Way To Promote Peace and Stability–The Role of International War Crimes Tribunals." *Journal of National Security Law & Policy* 2, no. 1 (2006): 111-164.

Englebert, Pierre and Denis M. Tull. "Postconflict Reconstruction in Africa: Flawed Ideas about Failed States." *International Security* 32, no. 4 (Spring 2008): 106-139.

Epstein, Susan B, Alex Tiersky, and Marian Lawson. *State, Foreign Operations, and Related Programs: FY2015 Budget and Appropriations.* P. 2. R43569. Washington, DC: Library of Congress Congressional Research Service, August 15, 2014.

Farr, Samuel S. "From Idea to Implementation: Standing Up the Civilian Response Corps." *PRISM* 2, no. 1 (December 2010): 19-26.

Fearon, James and David Laitin. "Neurotrusteeship and the Problem of Weak States." *International Security* 28, no. 4 (Spring 2004): 5-43.

Ferris, Elizabeth. "Addressing the Gap between Relief and Development." Comments to the Humanitarian Assistance Working Group, Brookings Institution, October 24, 2007. www.brookings.edu/speeches (accessed August 4, 2008).

Flavin, William. "New Doctrine for a New Era." *PKSOI Bulletin* 1, no. 1 (October 2008).

Fletcher, Michael A. "Bush Has Quietly Tripled Aid to Africa." *Washington Post*, December 31, 2006.

Fukuyama, Francis. *State-Building: Governance and World Order in the 21st Century.* Ithaca: Cornell University Press, 2004.

Fund for Peace. "2014 Failed States Index." Washington, DC: The Fund for Peace. http://ffp.statesindex.org (accessed September 29, 2014).

Galtung, Johan. "Violence, Peace, and Peace Research." *Journal of Peace Research* 6, no. 3 (1969): 167-191.

Garcia, Mario V. "Achieving Security Cooperation Objectives through the USECOM Humanitarian and Civic Assistance Program." *The DISAM Journal of International Security Assistance Management* 25, no. 1/2 (Fall 2002-Winter 2003): 105-108.

Garland, Gregory L. "US-Africa Policy and Florida." Presentation by Garland, Public Affairs Chief, African Affairs, to the Tallahassee Kiwanis Club, Tallahassee, FL, March 18, 2008.
http://2001-2009.state.gov (accessed July 7, 2014).

Garrett III, William B., Stephen J. Mariano and Adam Sanderson. "Forward in Africa: USAFRICOM and the U.S. Army in Africa." *Military Review* (January-February 2010).

Gates, Robert M. Landon Lecture at Kansas State University, November 26, 2007. www.defenselink.mil (accessed October 11, 2010).

_____. "U.S. Global Leadership Campaign." Washington, DC; July 15, 2008. www.defense.gov (accessed September 1, 2014).

_____. "Helping Others Defend Themselves: The Future of U.S. Security Assistance." *Foreign Affairs,* 89:3 (May/June 2010).

Gates, Robert M., Hillary Clinton, Timothy Geithner, Rajiv Shah, and Daniel Yohannes. 2010. Panel discussion at US Global Leadership Coalition Annual Conference. Washington, DC. September 28, 2010. http://www.usglc.org.

Ghana Business News. "Ghana Drug Abuse Cases Up 61%." May 23, 2011.

Gheciu, Alexandra. "Security Institutions as Agents of Socialization? NATO and the 'New Europe.'" *International Organization* 59, no. 4 (Fall 2005): 973-1012.

Golub, Stephen. "The Legal Empowerment Alternative," in *Promoting the Rule of Law Abroad: The Problem of Knowledge*, edited by Thomas Carothers. Washington, DC: Carnegie Endowment for International Peace, 2006.

Government Accountability Office. *Foreign Assistance: USAID Needs to Improve Its Strategic Planning to Address Current and Future Workforce Needs.* GAO-10-496. Washington, DC: Government Printing Office, June 2010.

_____. *DoD Needs to Determine the Future of Its Horn of Africa Task Force.* GAO-10-504. Washington, DC: Government Printing Office, April 2010.

_____. *DOD and State Need to Improve Sustainment Planning and Monitoring and Evaluation for Section 1206 and 1207 Assistance Programs.* GAO-10-431. Washington, DC: Government Accounting Office, April 15, 2010.

Griffin, Christopher. "A Working Plan." *Armed Forces Journal* no. 4, (2007).

Ham, Carter. "AFRICOM, Commander's Intent." AFRICOM Homepage, August 2011. www.africom.mil (accessed April 30, 2012).

_____. "AFRICOM Perspectives." Talk presented at CSIS Military Strategy Forum. Washington, DC, October 7, 2011. www.africom.mil (accessed April 30, 2012).

_____. "Posture Statement of US Africa Command," Statement before the US House of Representatives, House Armed Services Committee, 112th Cong., 2nd sess., February 29, 2012.

Harlow, John. "Army Unveils New Stability Operations Manual." *U.S. Army News*, October 6, 2008.

_____. "Army Unveils New Stability Operations Manual." *DISAM Journal of International Security Assistance Management* 30, no. 4 (December 2008): 105-107.

Harrison, Lawrence E. *The Central Liberal Truth.* New York: Oxford University Press, 2006.

Herbst, Jeffrey. "Economic Incentives, Natural Resources, and Conflict in Africa." *Journal of African Economies* 9, no. 3 (October 2000): 270-94.

Herman, Johanna, Olga Martin-Ortega and Chandra Lekha Sriram. "Beyond Justice Versus Peace: Transitional Justice and Peacebuilding Strategies," in *Rethinking Peacebuilding: The Quest for Just Peace in the Middle East and the Western Balkans*, edited by Karin Aggestam and Annika Björkdahl. London: Routledge, 2012.

Hernandorena, Carlos. "U.S. Provincial Reconstruction Teams in Afghanistan, 2003-2006: Obstacles to Interagency Cooperation," in *The Interagency and Counterinsurgency Warfare: Aligning and Integrating Military and Civilian Roles in Stability, Security, Transition, and Reconstruction Operations*, edited by

Joseph R. Cerami and Jay W. Boggs. Carlisle, PA: Strategic Studies Institute, January 2008.

Hettne, Bjorn. "Development and Security: Origins and Future." *Security Dialogue* 41, no. 1 (2010): 31-52.

Hewitt, J. Joseph, Jonathan Wilkenfeld and Ted Robert Gurr, with guest editor Birger Heldt. *Peace and Conflict 2012.* Boulder, CO: Paradigm Publishers, 2012.

Hicks, Kathleen H. "Africom: Vision and Prospects." Statement before the Committee on Oversight and Government Reform's Subcommittee on National Security and Foreign Affairs, US House of Representatives, July 23, 2008. http://csis.org/testimony (accessed July 8, 2014).

High Level Regional Consultative Meeting on Financing for Development and Preparatory Meeting for the Third UN Conference on LDCs: Annotated Agenda. Addis Ababa: Economic Commission for Africa and Organization of African States, November 2000. www.uneca.org (accessed July 6, 2014).

Hinson, David R. "U.S. Military Interaction with Humanitarian Assistance Organizations During Small-Scale Contingencies." Research Report, Maxwell Air Force Base, Alabama, April 1998. www.au.af.mil (accessed August 15, 2013).

Hirschman, Albert O. *The Strategy of Economic Development.* New Haven, CT: Yale University Press, 1958.

Hockmuth, Catherine MacRae. "AFRICOM: More Questions than Answers." *Aviation Week and Space Technology*, December 17, 2007.

Hooper, Charles. "Notes from the Flagpole #27." Stuttgart, Germany: US Africa Command, December 17, 2013.

Houngnikpo, Mathurin. "Small Arms and Big Trouble," in *African Security and the African Command: Viewpoints on the US Role in Africa*, edited by Terry Buss et al. Sterling, VA: Kumarian Press, 2011.

_____. *Africa's Militaries: A Missing Link in Democratic Transitions.* Africa Security Brief no. 17. Washington, DC: Africa Center for Strategic Studies, 2012.

Human Rights Watch. *The Perverse Side of Things; Torture, Inadequate Detention Conditions, and Excessive Use of Force by Guinean Security Forces.* New York: HRW, August 2006.

_____. *Dying for Change, Brutality and Repression by Guinean Security Forces in Response to a Nationwide Strike.* New York: HRW, April 2007.

_____. *"My Heart Is Cut": Sexual Violence by Rebels and Pro-Government Forces in Côte d'Ivoire.* New York: HRW, August 2007.

_____. *Arbitrary Killings by Security Forces, Submission to the Investigative Bodies on the November 28-29, 2008 Violence in Jos, Plateau State, Nigeria.* New York: HRW, July 2009.

_____. *Bloody Monday: The September 28 Massacre and Rapes by Security Forces in Guinea.* New York: HRW, December 2009.

_____. *"Everyone's in on the Game": Corruption and Human Rights Abuses by the Nigeria Police Force.* New York: HRW, August 2010.

_____. "Côte d'Ivoire: Lethal Crime Wave, Security Vacuum." Press Release,

March 5, 2012. www.hrw.org (accessed March 18, 2013).

_____. "Guinea: High-Level Charges in 2009 Massacre." July 3, 2013.

Hummelbrunner, Richard and Harry Jones. "A Guide for Planning and Strategy Development in the Face of Complexity." London, UK: Overseas Development Institute Background Note, March 2013. http://www.odi.org

Hunter, Robert E., Edward Gnehm, and George Joulwan. *Integrating Instruments of Power and Influence: Lessons Learned and Best Practices.* Arlington, VA: RAND Corporation.

Huntington, Samuel P. *Political Order in Changing Societies.* New Haven: Yale University Press, 1968.

Hurwitz, Agnès and Kaysie Studdard. *Rule of Law Programs in Peace Operations.* New York: International Peace Academy, August 2005.

International Crisis Group. *Stopping Guinea's Slide.* Africa Report no. 94. Dakar/Brussels: ICG, June 14, 2005.

_____. *Guinea: Military Rule Must End.* Africa Briefing no. 66. Dakar/Brussels: ICG, October 16, 2009.

_____. "Congo: A Stalled Democratic Agenda." Africa Briefing no. 73. Nairobi/Brussels: ICG, April 8, 2010.

_____. *Guinea: Reforming the Army.* Africa Report no. 164. Dakar/Nairobi/Brussels: ICG, September 23, 2010.

International Peace Academy. *The Security-Development Nexus: Research Findings and Policy Implications.* New York: International Peace Academy Program Report, 2006.

Irish, H. Allen. "A 'Peace Corps with Guns:' Can the Military Be a Tool of Development?" in *The Interagency and Counterinsurgency Warfare: Aligning and Integrating Military and Civilian Roles in Stability, Security, Transition, and Reconstruction Operations*, edited by Joseph R. Cerami and Jay W. Boggs. Carlisle, PA: Strategic Studies Institute, January 2008. www.strategicstudiesinstitute.army.mil (accessed September 12, 2013).

Issa, Jahi and Salim Faraji. "Revisiting and Reconsidering AFRICOM." Ghanaweb, July 12, 2009. www.ghanaweb.com (accessed May 8, 2012).

Joint Warfighting Center. *Joint Task Force (JTF) Commander's Handbook for Peace Operations.* Fort Monroe, VA: Joint Warfighting Center, June 16 1997.

Kansteiner III, Walter H. "Rising U.S. Stakes in Africa." Washington, DC: Center for Strategic and International Studies, May 2004.

Kaplan, Seth. "West African Integration: A New Development Paradigm?" *The Washington Quarterly* 29, no. 4 (Autumn 2006): 81-97.

Karl, Terry Lynn. *The Paradox of Plenty: Oil Booms and Petro States.* Berkeley: University of California Press, 1997.

Keenan, J. "US Militarization in Africa: What Anthropologists Should Know About AFRICOM." *Anthropology Today* 24, no. 5 (October 2008): 16–20.

Kelly, Terrence K., Ellen E. Tunstall, Thomas S. Szayna, and Deanna Weber Prine. *Stabilization and Reconstruction Staffing: Developing U.S. Civilian Personnel Capabilities.* Santa Monica: Rand Corporation, 2008.

Kissi, Edward. "Beneath the International Famine Relief in Ethiopia: The

United States, Ethiopia, and the Debate over Relief Aid, Development Assistance, and Human Rights." *African Studies Review* 48, no. 2 (September 2005): 111-132.

Lamb, Guy. "Parading US Security Interests as African Security Policy." *Contemporary Security Policy* 30, no. 1 (April 2009): 50-52.

Lando, "Mali – A Double Tale of Unintended Consequences." *Huffington Post*, January 15, 2013.

Lederer, Marc. "Being There Matters: Growing Partnerships." *Navy Live Blog* (April 11, 2014). http://navylive.dodlive.mil (accessed May 23, 2014).

Lee, Jessica and Maureen Farrell. "A Study of US Civil Affairs in East Africa, November 2009-July 2010." Unpublished report for CJTF-HOA, September 2010.

Lele, Sharachchandra M. "Sustainable Development: a Critical Review." *World Development* 19, no. 6 (1991): 607-621.

Lerner, Daniel. *The Passing of Traditional Society: Modernizing the Middle East.* Glencoe, IL: The Free Press, 1958.

LeSage, Andre. "The Evolving Threat of al Qaeda in the Islamic Maghreb." *Strategic Forum* no. 268 (July 1, 2011).

LeVan, Carl A. "The Political Economy of African Responses to the U.S. Africa Command." *Africa Today* 57, no. 1 (Fall 2010): 3-23.

Carmichael, Wade. "AFRICOM Supports Tunis Assistance Center for Muscular Dystrophy." *AFRICOM Dialogue,* February 1, 2012. www.africom.mil (accessed April 30, 2012).

Linz, Juan and Alfred Stepan. *The Breakdown of Democratic Regimes.* Baltimore: John Hopkins University Press, 1978.

Lischer, Sarah Kenyon. "Winning Hearts and Minds in the Horn of Africa." *Harvard International Review* (March 2007).

Logan, Justin and Christopher Preble. "The Case Against State's Nationbuilding Office." *Foreign Service Journal* (November 2006): 51-56.

Lowe, Mark. "Protecting Hydrocarbon Wealth." *Maritime Security Review*, 23 Oct 2013.

Malan, Mark. "AFRICOM: Joined-Up Geographic Command or Federal Business Opportunity?" Testimony before the Subcommittee on National Security and Foreign Affairs, Committee on Oversight and Government Reform, US House of Representatives, July 23, 2008. ww.refintl.org/policy/testimony (accessed July 7, 2014).

Mani, Rama. "Exploring the Rule of Law in Theory and Practice," in *Civil War and The Rule of Law: Towards Security, Development, and Human Rights*, edited by Agnès Hurwitz with Reyko Huang . Boulder, Co.: Lynne Rienner Publishers, 2008.

Mansfield, Edward D. and Jack L. Snyder. *Electing to Fight: Why Emerging Democracies Go to War.* Boston: MIT Press, 2005.

Marais, Jana and Eduard Gismatullin. "Tullow Delays $3.4 Billion Ghana Oil Field Ramp Up on Well Flow." *Bloomberg News*, November 2, 2011.

Mathews, Jessica. "Redefining Security." *Foreign Affairs* (Spring 1989): 162-177.

McCrummen, Stephanie. "Report: US Africa Aid is Increasingly Military." *Washington Post,* July 18, 2008, A-10.

McFate, Sean. *Securing the Future: A Primer on Security Sector Reform in Conflict Countries*. Washington, DC: US Institute for Peace Press, 2008.

MercoPress. "Joint Global Efforts to Stop IUU Fishing." May 20, 2014. http://en.mercopress.com (accessed June 8, 2014).

Miles, Donna. "Defense Science Review Board Report Recommends New Focus on Stabilization, Reconstruction." *American Forces Press Service,* January 25, 2005.

Miller, Josh. "Obama Pushes More Hires at USAID, State Department." Washington, DC: Devex. February 3, 2010. www.devex.com (accessed February 5, 2012).

Mistry, Percy S. "Reasons for Sub-Saharan Africa's Development Deficit that the Commission for Africa Did Not Consider." *African Affairs* 104, no. 417 (October 2005): 665-678.

Moeller, Robert. "The Truth about AFRICOM." *Foreign Policy* (July 21, 2010).

Morelli, Donald and Michael M Ferguson. *Low Intensity Conflict: An Operational Perspective*. Fort Monroe, VA: US Army Training and Doctrine Command, Office of the Deputy Chief of Staff for Doctrine, April 4, 1984.

Morrison, J. Stephen and Jennifer G. Cooke. *U.S. Africa Policy Beyond the Bush Years*. Washington, DC: Center for Strategic and International Studies, 2009.

Moyo, Dambisa. "Why Foreign Aid Is Hurting Africa." *Wall Street Journal*, 21 March 2009.

Musah, Abdel-Fatau. *West Africa: Governance and Security in a Changing Region*. New York: International Peace Institute, February 2009.

Nathan, Laurie. "AFRICOM: A Threat to Africa's Security." *Contemporary Security Policy* 30, no. 1 (April 2009): 58-61.

Navy News Service. "Africa Partnership Station." www.navy.mil/local/aps/ (accessed July 26, 2013, link no longer active).

Ndlovu-Gatsheni, Sabelo and Victor Ojakorotu. "Surveillance Over a Zone of Conflict: AFRICOM and the Politics of Securitisation in Africa." *The Journal of Pan-African Studies* 3, no. 6 (March 2010): 94-110.

Newman, Edward, Roland Paris, and Oliver Richmond, editors. *New Perspectives on Liberal Peacebuilding*. Tokyo: UN University Press, 2009.

Nhamoyebonde, Tichaona. "AFRICOM—Latest U.S. Bid to Recolonize Continent." *Global Research*, January 7, 2010.

O'Donnell, Guillermo and Philippe C. Schmitter. "Transitions from Authoritarian Rule: Tentative Conclusions About Uncertain Democracies," in *Transitional Justice: How Emerging Democracies Reckon with Former Regimes*. Vol I, edited by Neil J. Kritz. Washington, DC: United States Institute for Peace Press, 1995.

O'Donnell, Guillermo and Philippe C. Schmitter. *Transitions from Authoritarian Rule*. Baltimore: John Hopkins University Press, 1986.

O'Neill, William G. *Police Reform in Post-Conflict Societies: What We Know and What We Still Need to Know*. New York: International Peace Academy, April 2005.

OECD. *Fragile States 2013: Resource Flows and Trends in a Shifting World.* OECD-DAC International Network on Conflict and Fragility, 2012. www.oecd.org.

Office of the Coordinator for Reconstruction and Stabilization. "Post Conflict Reconstruction Essential Tasks." Washington, DC: Office of the Coordinator for Reconstruction and Stabilization, US Department of State, April 2005. www.state.gov (accessed July 26, 2006).

Oliver P. Richmond, ed. *Palgrave Advances in Peacebuilding: Critical Developments and Approaches.* New York: Palgrave MacMillan, 2010.

Organization for Economic Cooperation and Development. *Security System Reform and Governance.* DAC Guidelines and Reference Series. Paris: OECD, 2005. www.oecd.org (accessed September 1, 2014).

Ott, Mary C. *A Guide to Economic Growth in Post-Conflict Countries.* Washington, DC: Economic Growth Office, Bureau for Economic Growth, Agriculture, and Trade, USAID, 2009. http://pdf.usaid.gov (accessed July 7, 2014).

Owolabi, Olufemi. "Africa Strategic Dialogue United DoD, DoS in Whole of Government Approach." Stuttgart, Germany: AFRICOM Public Affairs, February 25, 2014.

Owsley, Steve. "Pandemic Disaster Response Exercise Wraps up in Ghana." Stuttgart, Germany: AFRICOM Public Affairs, February 14, 2012. www.africom.mil (accessed April 30, 2012).

Palmer, Jeffrey S. "Legal Impediments to USAFRICOM Operationalization." *Joint Forces Quarterly* 51, no. 4 (4th Quarter 2008): 79-85.

Paris, Roland and Timothy D. Sisk eds. *The Dilemmas of Statebuilding: Confronting the Contradictions of Postwar Peace Operations.* New York: Routledge, 2009.

Paris, Roland. *At War's End.* Cambridge: Cambridge University Press, 2004.

Patrick, Stewart. "Failed States and Global Security: Empirical Questions and Policy Dilemmas." *International Studies Review* 9, no. 4 (Winter 2007): 644-62.

Perito, Robert. *Integrated Security Assistance: The 1207 Program.* Special Report 207. Washington, DC: United States Institute for Peace Press, July 2008.

Pham, J. Peter. "AFRICOM Stands Up." *World Defense Review.* October 2, 2008. http://worlddefensereview.com/pham100208.shtml (accessed May 8, 2012).

Phillips, Matthew. "US Oil Imports From Africa Are Down 90 Percent." *Bloomberg Business Week*, May 22, 2014.

Pickering, Jeffrey and Ezmet Kisangani. "Political, Economic, and Social Consequences of Foreign Military Intervention." *Political Research Quarterly* 59, no. 3 (September 2006): 363-376.

Pincus, Walter. "Pentagon Recommends 'Whole-of-Government' National Security Plans." *Washington Post,* February 2, 2009.

Pincus, Walter. "US Africa Command Brings New Concerns." *Washington Post,* May 28, 2007.

Piombo, Jessica. "Civil-Military Relations in the Horn of Africa," in *Understanding Complex Military Operations: A Case Study Approach*, edited by Karen Guttieri, Volker Franke and Melanne A. Civic. New York: Routledge, 2014.

Piombo, Jessica and Michael Malley. "Beyond Protecting the Land and the Sea: The Role of the U.S. Navy in Reconstruction," in *Naval Peacekeeping and Humanitarian Operations: Stability from the Sea*, edited by James J. Wirtz and Jeffery A. Larsen. London and New York: Routledge, 2008.

Pittman, Todd. "Support Missions in Africa Face Suspicion." *Air Force Times*, November 13, 2007.

Ploch, Lauren. *Africa Command: U.S. Strategic Interests and the Role of the U.S. Military in Africa*. RL34003. Washington, DC: Library of Congress Congressional Research Service, July 6, 2007.

_____. *Africa Command: U.S. Strategic Interests and the Role of the U.S. Military in Africa*. RL34003. Washington, DC: Library of Congress Congressional Research Service. July 21, 2011. www.fas.org (accessed May 8, 2012).

Pramod, Ganapathiraju, et al. "Sources of Information Supporting Estimates of Unreported Fishery Catches (IUU) for 59 Countries and the High Seas." *Fisheries Centre Research Reports 2008* 16, no. 4 (2008).

Price, Heather. "The Future of S/CRS—What's in a Name?" *Journal of International Peace Operations* 6, no. 5 (March-April 2011).

Przeworski, Adam and Fernando Limongi. "Modernization: Theories and Facts." *World Politics* 49, no. 2 (January 1997): 155-183.

Pugh, Michael. "Military Intervention and Humanitarian Action: Trends and Issues." *Disasters* 22, no. 4 (December 1998): 339–351.

_____. "The Challenge of Civil-Military Relations in International Peace Operations." *Disasters* 25, no. 4 (December 2001): 345–357.

Putman, Diana. "Addressing African Questions about the Legitimacy of U.S. Africa Command (AFRICOM)," in *Understanding Africa: A Geographic Approach*, edited by Amy Krakowka and Laurel Hummel. West Point, NY: US Military Academy and Carlisle, PA: US Army War College, 2009.

Rajagopal, Balakrishnan. "Invoking the Rule of Law: International Discourses." *William and Mary Law Review* 49, no. 4 (2008): 1347-1376.

Refugees International. *Report Challenges Militarization of U.S. Foreign Aid, Calls for U.S. Africa Policy Reforms*. Washington, DC: Refugees International, July 17, 2008. www.commondreams.org (accessed July 8, 2014).

Reno, William. *Warlord Politics and African States*. Boulder, CO: Lynne Rienner Publishers, 1999.

Rice, Condoleezza. Remarks at Georgetown School of Foreign Service, January 18, 2006. www.unc.edu (accessed May 18, 2012).

Rice, Susan. "Africa and the War on Global Terrorism; Hearing Before the Subcommittee on Africa of the Committee on International Relations, House of Representatives." House Committee on International Relations, Subcommittee on Africa, November 15, 2001. http://commdocs.house.gov (accessed September 2, 2014).

Rice, Xan. "Deficit Fears Cast Shadow on Ghana's Economic Star." *Financial Times*, October 31, 2013.

Rietjens, Sebastiaan J.H., Hans Voordijk and Sirp J. De Boer. "Co-ordinating Humanitarian Operations in Peace Support Missions." *Disaster Prevention and Management* 16, no. 1 (2007): 56-69.

Risio, Chuck. "Security Cooperation MAGTF–Fighting the Long War." *Leatherneck* 91, no. 5 (May 2008): 18-22.

Clinton, Hillary Rodham. "Remarks with Reporters in the Correspondents' Room." Washington, DC, January 27, 2009. www.state.gov (accessed October 3, 2010).

Rodriguez, David M. "Posture Statement of US Africa Command." Stuttgart, Germany: March 5, 2014. www.africom.mil (accessed June 25, 2014).

Rodriguez, David M. "Statement of General David M. Rodriguez, USA, Commander, United States Africa Command, Before the House Armed Services Committee Posture Hearing 5 March 2014." Washington, DC: House Armed Services Committee, March 5, 2014. http://docs.house.gov (accessed July 10, 2014).

Rogin, Josh. "165 House Republicans Endorse Defunding USAID." *Foreign Policy* (January 16, 2011).

Ross, Michael. "The Political Economy of the Resource Curse." *World Politics* 51, no. 2 (January 1999): 297-322.

Rotberg, Robert. *When States Fail: Causes and Consequences*. Princeton, NJ: Princeton University Press, 2003.

Russell J. Handy. "African Contingency Operations Training Assistance: Developing Training Partnerships for the Future of Africa." *Air and Space Power Journal* 17, no. 3 (Fall 2003): 57-64.

Sala-i-Martin, Xavier and Maxim Pinkovskiy. *African Poverty Is Falling ... Much Faster Than You Think*. Cambridge, MA: National Bureau of Economic Research, 2010.

Salih, M. A. Mohamed. "A Critique of the Political Economy of the Liberal Peace: Elements of an African Experience," in *New Perspectives on Liberal Peacebuilding*, edited by Edward Newman, Roland Paris, and Oliver Richmond. Tokyo: United Nations University Press, 2009.

Schadlow, Nadia. *Organizing to Compete in the Political Terrain*. Carlisle Barracks, PA: Strategic Studies Institute, July 2010.

Schaefer, Brett. "Creating an Africa Command." WebMemo #1349 on Africa. Washington, DC: The Heritage Foundation, February 9, 2007. www.heritage.org (accessed May 8, 2012).

Schneider, Mark. "Placing Security and the Rule of Law on the Development Agenda." *Development Outreach*. Washington: Work Bank Institute, October 2009.

Schraeder, Peter J. *United States Foreign Policy Toward Africa: Incrementalism, Crisis, and Change*. Cambridge: Cambridge University Press, 1994.

Schramm, Carl J. "Expeditionary Economics." *Foreign Affairs* 89, no. 3 (June 2010).

Secretary of Defense. "Policy Guidance for DoD Overseas Humanitarian Assistance Program (HAP)." Washington, DC, November 18, 2009.

Sedra, Mark. "Security Sector Reform in Afghanistan: The Slide towards Expediency." *International Peacekeeping* 13, no. 1 (March 2006): 94-110.

Serafino, Nina. *Peacekeeping/Stabilization and Conflict Transitions: Background and Congressional Action on the Civilian Response/Reserve Corps and other Civilian Stabilization and Reconstruction Capabilities.* RL32862. Washington, DC: Library of Congress Congressional Research Service, April 26, 2010.

_____. *Security Assistance Reform: 'Section 1206': Background and Issues for Congress.* RS22855. Washington, DC: Library of Congress Congressional Research Service, January 13, 2012, updated December 8, 2014.

_____. *Global Security Contingency Fund: Summary and Issue Overview.* Washington, DC: Government Accountability Office, April 4, 2014.

Shabazz, Saeed. "Africa Continues to Reject US Military Command." FinalCall.com News, January 14, 2008 (accessed May 8, 2012).

Siegl, Michael B. "Clarity and Culture in Stability Operations." *Military Review* 87, no. 6 (November/December 2007).

Simmons, Emmy. "Harvesting Peace: Food Security, Conflict, and Cooperation." *Environmental Changes and Security Program Report* 14, no. 3. Washington, DC: Woodrow Wilson International Center for Scholars, 2013.

Stares, Paul B. and Micah Zenko. *Enhancing U.S. Preventive Action.* Center for Preventive Action, Council on Foreign Relations. New York Council on Foreign Relations, 2009.

Stavridis, James and Evelyn N. Farkas. "The 21st Century Force Multiplier: Public-Private Collaboration." *The Washington Quarterly* 35, no. 2 (Spring 2012): 7-20.

Stern, Maria and Joakim Öjendal. "Mapping the Security-Development Nexus: Conflict, Complexity, Cacophony, Convergence." *Security Dialogue* 41, no. 1 (February 2010): 5-29.

Stevenson, Jonathan. "AFRICOM's Libya Expedition: How War Will Change the Command's Role on the Continent." *Foreign Affairs*, May 9, 2011.

Stimson Center. "State Department Establishes New Bureau of Conflict and Stabilization Operations." Washington, DC: The Stimson Center, November 22, 2011.

Stone, Paul. "DoD Considers Creating Stability and Reconstruction Force." *American Foreign Press Service,* December 20, 2003. www.globalsecurity.org (accessed July 25, 2006).

Swedberg, Jeffrey and Lainie Reisman. *Mid-Term Evaluation of Three Countering Extremism Projects.* Washington, DC: USAID, February 22, 2013.

Swedberg, Jeffrey and Steven Smith. *Mid-Term Evaluation of USAID's Counter-Extremism Programming in Africa.* Washington, DC: USAID, February 1, 2011.

Tate, M. L. *The Frontier Army in the Settlement of the West.* Norman, OK: University of Oklahoma Press, 1999.

The Christian Science Monitor. "Bush's Unfinished Africa Legacy." February 14, 2008.

Torres, Stefanie. "Africa Partnership Flight." Ramstein, Germany: US Air Forces Africa Public Affairs, January 3, 2012. www.usafe.af.mil (accessed July 14, 2014).

Tuckey, Beth. "Congress Challenges AFRICOM." *Foreign Policy in Focus*, July 22, 2008. http://fpif.org (accessed May 8. 2012).

Turse, Nick. "AFRICOM Goes to War on the Sly." *Foreign Policy in Focus*, April 14, 2014. http://fpif.org (accessed March 15, 2015).

Ulriksen, Stale. "Deployments for Development? Nordic Peacekeeping Efforts in Africa." *International Peacekeeping* 14, no. 4 (August 2007): 553-568.

UN Secretary-General. *The Rule of Law and Transitional Justice in Conflict and Post-Conflict Societies.* UN Doc. S/2004/616. New York: United Nations, August 23, 2004.

Unger, Noam. "Opinion: The QDDR: Following Through on Civilian Power?" Washington, DC: The Brookings Institution, December 16, 2010. www.brookings.edu (accessed June 4, 2012).

United Nations. *Towards Human Resilience Sustaining MDG Progress in an Age of Economic Uncertainty.* New York: UN Development Programme, October 2011. www. undp.org (accessed July 7, 2014).

_____. *Millennium Development Goals Report 2014.* New York: United Nations Headquarters, 2014. www.un.org (accessed July 14, 2014).

United Nations Development Program. *Human Development Report, 1994.* New York: United Nations, 1994. http://hdr.undp.org (accessed March 21, 2009.

United Nations Office on Drugs and Crime. *Drug Trafficking as a Security Threat in West Africa.* New York: United Nations, November 2008.

_____. *World Drug Report 2011.* New York: United Nations, June 2011.

United Nations Secretariat. *United Nations Peacekeeping Operations Principles and Guidelines.* Capstone Doctrine. New York: Department of Peacekeeping Operations, January 18, 2008. http://pbpu.unlb.org (accessed July 7, 2014).

United States Africa Command. "Fact Sheet: The New Strategy toward Sub-Saharan Africa." Washington, DC: The White House and US AFRICOM Public Affairs, June 15, 2012. www.africom.mil (accessed July 3, 2014).

_____. "Fact Sheet: United States Africa Command." Stuttgart, Germany: US AFRICOM Office of Public Affairs, April 15, 2013. www.africom.mil (accessed July 14, 2014).

_____. "About the Command." www.africom.mil/about-the-command (accessed September 25, 2014).

United States Agency for International Development. *Interagency Security Sector Assessment Framework: Guidance for the US Government.* Washington, DC: USAID, October 1, 2010.

_____. *The Development Response to Violent Extremism and Insurgency.* Washington, DC: USAID Bureau for Policy, Planning, and Learning, 2011.

_____. *USAID Policy Framework: 2011-2015.* Washington, DC: USAID, September 2011.

_____. "USAID Office of Civilian-Military Cooperation Training." Washington, DC: USAID Office of Civilian-Military Cooperation.

_____. "The Office of Crisis Surge Response Staff." Washington: DC, USAID.

United States Joint Forces Command. *The Joint Operating Environment 2008.* Suffolk, VA: Center for Joint Futures, 2008.

US Congress. *National Defense Authorization Act for Fiscal Year 2006* (Public Law 109-163, STAT. 3457). Washington, DC: Government Printing Office, January 6, 2006.

US Congress. *Foreign Assistance Act of 1961.* (Public Law 87-195; 75 Stat. 424, enacted 22 U.S.C. 2151 et seq). http://legcounsel.house.gov/ (accessed September 25, 2014).

_____. *National Defense Authorization Act for Fiscal Year 2006* (Public Law 109-163, STAT. 3457). Washington, DC: Government Printing Office, January 6, 2006.

US Congress House Committee on Oversight and Government Reform, Subcommittee on National Security and Foreign Affairs. *AFRICOM's Rationales, Roles and Progress on the Eve of Operations.* Washington, DC, July 15, 2009. www.africom.mil (accessed October 13, 2010).

US Congress Senate Committee on Foreign Relations. "Exploring the US Africa Command and a New Strategic Partnership with Africa." Hearing Before the Subcommittee on African Affairs of the Committee on Foreign Relations, S. HRG. Washington, DC, August 7, 2007.

US Department of Defense. "QDR Execution Roadmap: Building Partnership Capacity." Washington, DC: Deputy Secretary of Defense, US DoD, May 22, 2006. www.hsdl.org (accessed September 4, 2014).

_____. *DoD Decision Directive 1404.14: DoD Civilian Expeditionary Workforce.* Washington, DC: US Department of Defense, January 23, 2009. www.dtic.mil (accessed September 1, 2014).

_____. *Joint Operations.* JP 3-0. Washington, DC: Office of the Chairman of the Joint Chiefs of Staff, August 11, 2011.

_____. *Peace Operations.* JP 3-07.3. Washington, DC: Government Printing Office, August 1, 2012.

_____. "Defense Budget Priorities and Choices, Fiscal Year 2014." Washington, DC: US Department of Defense, April 2013. www.defense.gov (accessed August 2, 2014).

US Department of Defense. *Defense Institution Reform Initiative (DIRI) Factsheet.* October 18, 2013.

_____. *Fiscal Year 2015 Budget Estimates.* Washington, DC: Defense Security Cooperation Agency, March 2014.

US Department of State. *Foreign Operations Budget.* Washington, DC: US Department of State, May 22, 2009. www.state.gov (accessed November 15, 2010).

_____. *International Narcotics Control Strategy Report, Volume 1: Drugs and Chemical Control.* Washington, DC: US Department of State Bureau for International Narcotics and Law Enforcement Affairs, March 2010.

_____. *Congressional Budget Justification, Foreign Operations, FY 2012.* Annex: Regional Perspectives. Washington, DC: Department of State, April 2011. www.state.gov.

_____. "State and USAID FY 2013 Budget." Washington, DC: US Department of State, February 13, 2012. www.state.gov (accessed May 2, 2013).

_____. *Report on Security Capacity Building.* Washington, DC: Department of State International Security Advisory Board (ISAB), January 7, 2013.

_____. "African Contingency Operations Training and Assistance (ACOTA) Program: Fact Sheet." Washington DC, Department of State, February 6, 2013. www.state.gov (accessed July 7, 2014).

_____. *Congressional Budget Justification: Department of State, Foreign Operations, and Related Programs, Fiscal Year 2015.* Washington, DC: US Department of State, April 18 2014. www.state.gov (accessed September 1, 2014).

_____. *Congressional Budget Justification Appendix One: Department of State Operations, Fiscal Year 2015.* Washington, DC: Department of State, April 4, 2014. www.state.gov (accessed September 12, 2014).

_____. *Congressional Budget Justification, Appendix II: Foreign Operations, Fiscal Year 2015.* Washington, DC: April 18, 2014. www.state.gov (accessed September 14, 2014).

_____. "Foreign Military Financing Account Summary." Washington, DC: US Department of State, undated. www.state.gov (accessed September 1, 2014).

_____. "Foreign Terrorist Organizations." Washington, DC: US State Department, Bureau of Counterterrorism, undated. www.state.gov (accessed September 1, 2014).

_____. *Foreign Military Training and DoD Engagement Activities of Interest.* Washington, DC: Department of State, undated. www.state.gov (accessed November 15, 2010).

US Department of State, Office of the Spokesperson. "Fact Sheet: Overview of Obama's FY2013 Budget for State and USAID." Washington, DC: US Department of State, February 13, 2012. http://london.usembassy.gov (accessed June 4, 2012).

US Department of State and US Agency for International Development. *Leading Through Civilian Power: The First Quadrennial Diplomacy and Development Review.* Washington, DC: US Department of State, 2010. www.state.gov (accessed February 2, 2011).

US Energy Information Administration. "How Dependent Are We on Foreign Oil?" May 10, 2013. www.eia.gov (accessed June 5, 2014).

_____. "Petroleum and Other Liquids: Country Level Imports." Washington, DC: US Energy Information Administration, July 2014. www.eia.gov (accessed July 3, 2014).

US Global Leadership Coalition. *Roundtable on the Administration's New Global Development Policy.* Washington, DC, September 28, 2010. www.usglc.org (accessed March 15, 2015).

US Government Accountability Office. *Defense Management: Actions Needed to Address Stakeholder Concerns, Improve Interagency Collaboration, and Determine Full Costs Associated with the US Africa Command.* Report to the Subcommittee on National Security and Foreign Affairs, Committee on Oversight and Government Reform, House of Representatives (GAO-09-181). Washington, DC: GAO, February 2009.

_____. *Humanitarian and Development Assistance: Project Evaluations and Better Information Sharing Needed to Manage the Military's Efforts.* (GAO 12-359). Washington, DC: GAO, February 2012.

_____. *Combating Terrorism: State Department Can Improve Management of East Africa Program.* GAO-14-502. Washington, DC: GAO, June 2014.

_____. *Combatting Terrorism: US Efforts in Northwest Africa Would be Strengthened by Enhanced Program Management.* GAO-14-518. Washington, DC: GAO, June 2014.

US Institute of Peace. *Guidelines for Relations between US Armed Forces and Non-Governmental Humanitarian Organizations in Hostile or Potentially Hostile Environments.* Washington, DC: USIP Press, 2007.

"U.S. Launches Civilian Rapid Response Force for World Hotspots." Agence France-Presse, July 16, 2008.

Van Baarda, Ted A. "A Legal Perspective of Cooperation between Military and Humanitarian Organizations in Peace Support Operations." *International Peacekeeping* 8, no. 1 (Spring 2001): 99-116.

Van de Walle, Nicolas. "U.S. Policy Towards Africa: The Bush Legacy and the Obama Administration." *African Affairs*, 109, no. 434 (2010).

Ward, William E. "Posture Statement of US Africa Command." Statement Before the US Senate, Senate Armed Services Committee, Statement of General 111th Cong., 2nd sess., April 7, 2011. www.africom.mil.

Ward, William. "AFRICOM Posture Statement: Ward Updates Congress on US Africa Command." Washington, DC: USAFRICOM Public Affairs Office, March 13, 2008. www.africom.mil (accessed July 8, 2014).

Ward, William. "Opening Remarks," AFRICOM Theater Security Cooperation Conference. Stuttgart, Germany: November 15, 2010.

Ward, William. "Posture Statement of US Africa Command." Stuttgart, Germany: USAFRICOM, March 9, 2010. www.africom.mil (link no longer active).

Warner, Lesley Anne. "The Trans Sahara Counter Terrorism Partnership: Building Partner Capacity to Counter Terrorism and Violent Extremism." CRM-2014-U-007203-Final. Arlington, VA: CNA Corporation Center for Naval Analyses, March 2014.

Weber, Max. *Essays in Sociology.* Edited and trans. by H.H. Gerth and C. Wright Mills. Oxford: Oxford University Press, 1946.

West Africa Network for Peacebuilding (WANEP). *An Assessment of the ECOWAS Mechanism for Conflict Prevention and Good Governance.* Accra, Ghana: WANEP, undated. www.wanep.org (accessed October 10, 2009).

Wheeler, Victoria and Adele Harmer, eds. *Resetting the Rules of Engagement, Trends and Issues in Military-Humanitarian Relations.* Humanitarian Policy Group Report 2. London: Overseas Development Institute, March 2006. www.odi.org.uk (accessed April 30, 2012).

White House. "NSPD-44: Management of Interagency Efforts Concerning Reconstruction and Stabilization." Washington, DC: The White House, December 7, 2005. www.fas.org (accessed February 28, 2013).

_____. *National Security Strategy.* Washington, DC: The White House, March 2006. http://georgewbush-whitehouse.archives.gov (accessed May 18, 2012).

_____. "Trip to Africa February 15-21, 2008." Washington, DC: The White House, undated. http://georgewbush-whitehouse.archives.gov (accessed July 7, 2014).

_____. *National Security Strategy.* Washington, DC: The White House, May 2010. www.whitehouse.gov (accessed March 7, 2013).

_____. "US National Strategy for Counterterrorism." Washington, DC: The White House, June 2011. www.whitehouse.gov (accessed July 20, 2014).

_____. "Fact Sheet: US Security Sector Assistance Policy." Washington, DC: Office of the Press Secretary, the White House, April 5, 2013. www.whitehouse.gov (accessed March 10, 2015).

_____. *Budget of the US Government, Fiscal Year 15.* Washington, DC: Office of Management and Budget, March 4, 2014. www.gpo.gov (accessed September 1, 2014).

_____. "Joint Statement: US-EU Summit." Washington, DC: Office of the Press Secretary, the White House, March 26, 2014. www.whitehouse.gov (accessed March 14, 2015).

_____. "Fact Sheet: Security Governance Initiative." Washington, DC: Office of the Press Secretary, the White House, August 6, 2014. www.whitehouse.gov (accessed September 1, 2014).

_____. "Fact Sheet: US Response to the Ebola Epidemic in West Africa." Washington, DC: Office of the Press Secretary, the White House, September 16, 2014. www.whitehouse.gov (accessed March 10, 2015).

Whitlock, Craig. "Leader of Mali Military Coup Trained in the US." *The Washington Post,* March 24, 2012.

Winslow, Donna. "Strange Bedfellows: NGOs and the Military in Humanitarian Crises." *The International Journal of Peace Studies* 7, no. 2 (Autumn/Winter 2002): 35-54.

Wood, Sara. "Africa Command Will Consolidate US Efforts on Continent." American Forces Press Service, February 7, 2007. www.defense.gov (accessed January 21, 2012).

World Bank. *Report on Fisheries Sub-Sector Capacity Building Project, Ghana.* Report No. 26166. Washington, DC: World Bank, June 27, 2003.

_____. *World Development Report 2011: Conflict, Security, and Development.* Washington, DC: The International Bank for Reconstruction and Development/The World Bank, May 26, 2011.

World Health Organization. *Environmental Health in Emergencies and Disasters: A Practical Guide* (2002). www.who.int (accessed September 12, 2013).

Yamamoto, Donald. "The Growing Crisis in Africa's Sahel Region." Testimony by Acting Assistant Secretary Donald Yamamoto, Bureau of African Affairs, US Department of State to the House Subcommittees on Africa, Global Health, Global Human Rights; International Organizations and Terrorism, Nonproliferation, and Trade; and Middle East and North Africa; Washington, DC, May 21, 2013. www.state.gov (accessed September 1, 2014).

The Contributors

G. William Anderson is visiting professor of practice at Virginia Tech's School of Public and International Affairs. He is also a principal and founding member of the Modernizing Foreign Assistance Network, a reform coalition of international development and foreign policy practitioners, policy advocates and experts, and private sector organizations. A former USAID senior foreign service officer, he served in Senegal, the Democratic Republic of Congo, Tanzania (as deputy USAID mission director), and Eritrea (as USAID mission director) and also as the director of the Office of East and South Asia in USAID's Asia Near East Bureau and, in July 2006–July 2008, as the USAID senior development advisor at the US European Command in Stuttgart, Germany.

Clarence J. Bouchat is a retired US Air Force officer, a senior researcher with the US Army Peacekeeping and Stability Operations Institute, and adjunct professor of strategy and Africa regional studies at the US Army War College. He served in 2006–2007 as part of the Security Sector Reform team in Liberia that reconstituted the country's Ministry of Defense.

Teresa Crawford has more than a decade of experience working with civil society organizations to help them make better use of information and information technology in their work. In 2006–2009, she was director of the Advocacy and Leadership Center at the Institute for Sustainable Communities, building a robust training and capacity-building program for conflict and stabilization operations with a focus on collaborative advocacy and transformational leadership. She is the cofounder of IPKO, the first postwar Internet service provider in Kosovo, and now serves on the board of the IPKO Foundation.

Maureen Farrell is a specialist on sub-Saharan African security issues with extensive on-the-ground experience. She currently is a regional program manager for the Anti-Terrorism Assistance program in the State Department's Bureau of Counterterrorism, providing policy oversight and coordination for the implementation and evaluation of counterterrorism capacity-building training for law enforcement in Africa. Previously, she served as one of the founding members of the Socio-Cultural Research and Advisory Team at the Combined Joint Task Force–Horn of Africa.

Margaux Hoar is a senior research scientist and project director at CNA Corporation, a nonprofit research and analysis organization located in Arlington, Virginia, and also serves as scientific advisor to the Marine Corp's Training and Education Command. Her major focus of analysis has been Marine Corps and Navy training issues, including those of time, balance, irregular warfare, and the use of simulation. In addition, she has been extensively involved in the analysis of Navy engagement operations.

Jessica Lee, an analyst with Booz Allen Hamilton, formerly was a member of the Social Science Research Center in US Africa Command (Knowledge Development). Dr. Lee was one of the founding members of the Socio-Cultural Research and Advisory Team at the Combined Joint Task Force–Horn of Africa, where she conducted research on topics related to civil affairs activities in the Horn of Africa.

Jessica Piombo is associate professor in the Department of National Security Affairs at the Naval Postgraduate School (NPS), where her teaching and research focus on political transitions and postconflict governance; mechanisms to manage ethnic conflict; US foreign policy toward Africa; the US military's role in reconstruction and stabilization; and international peace negotiations in Africa. She is author of *Institutions, Ethnicity and Political Mobilization in South Africa* and coeditor of *Interim Governments: Institutional Bridges to Peace and Democracy?* and *Electoral Politics in South Africa: Assessing the First Democratic Decade*.

Dustin Sharp is assistant professor at the Kroc School of Peace Studies at the University of San Diego, where he teaches courses on transitional justice and international human rights law. His research examines the role of law in postconflict reconstruction, transitional justice, and the intersection of economic development and human rights. He also focuses on the political and human rights dynamics of sub-Saharan Africa. In partnership with the Institute for Peace and Justice at the University of San Diego, Professor Sharp leads the West African Human Rights Training Initiative, a capacity-building program focusing on local human rights organizations in Côte d'Ivoire, Guinea, Liberia, and Sierra Leone.

Alison Rimsky Vernon is a senior research analyst at the Center for Naval Analyses, where her projects have included studies of US civil-military relations, interagency cooperation during military operations, and the role of humanitarian operations in the war on terror. She has also directed efforts to examine the African Partnership Station in West-Central Africa and East Africa.

Andrea Walther-Puri currently serves as an Obxtek, Inc., fully embedded contractor with the US Department of State. In her role as counterterrorism programs coordinator, she manages military counterterrorism cooperation and related security assistance in 19 countries throughout the Sahel, Maghreb, and East Africa, with a specific focus on strategic planning, program management, and monitoring and evaluation. Formerly, she worked within the Bureau of Counterterrorism, where she provided policy and programmatic oversight for the Department of State's Antiterrorism Assistance Program in Africa, Europe, the Arabian Peninsula, and the Middle East.

Trina Zwicker, at present with the United States European Command Cyber Directorate, served as branch chief for United States Africa Command for more than three years. She has an extensive background in international economic and community development.

Index

accountability: dependence on political will, 67; mechanisms of, 69; as public good, 78; role of civil society in building, 77–78; rule of law reform and, 65, 73, 74, 75; in security sector, 75, 76–77

Afghanistan: consequences of lack of development in, 21; Ministry of Defense Advisor (MODA) program in, 96; provincial reconstruction teams (PRTs) in, 46

Africa Center for Strategic Studies (ACSS), 95, 96, 144, 150, 155–158, 160

Africa Contingency Operations Training Assistance (ACOTA), 166, 168, 216–217

Africa Leadership Summit, 96

African maritime security, 121, 122–123, 136

African Strategic Dialogue meeting, 186

African Union (AU), 30

Africa Partnership Flight (APF) program, 148

Africa Partnership Station (APS): activities, 6, 130; deployments, 121, 129–130, 137–138; effectiveness of, 122, 217; in Ghana, 122, 133–134, 148; impact of, 131–132; influence of, 135, 136; international staff, 130; involvement in maritime training, 138; military-civilian projects, 129–130; mission, 6, 133; national maritime policies and, 122; objectives, 129, 131; perception of, 131; priorities, 138; relationship building, 5, 137; shortcomings of, 122; success strategy, 135–136

AFRICOM (United States Africa Command): activities, 5, 6–7, 26; African Strategic Dialogue, 186–187; approach to development, criticism of, 215–216; budget, 142, 159n2, 199; civil affairs projects, 220; civilian organizations and, 223; civilian staff in, 17, 218; civil society and, 143, 154, 156–158; conferences organized by, 157; conflict prevention, 196; conspiracy views of, 18; control over CJTF-HOA, 112; cooperation with local organizations, 146; creation of, 8, 16; criticism of, 17–18, 227; engagement in civil-military dialogues, 31; evolution of, 8, 28; exercises and planning, 147; field-level program implementation, 148–149; first commander, 17; future operations, 32; goals and objectives, 17, 218; Humanitarian and Health Activities (HHA) branch, 145; humanitarian assistance programs, 42, 199; J5 Directorate, 146; mission, 12, 16, 32, 105; non-traditional military activities, 153; outreach programs, 149–150; partnerships, 29, 30, 143; peacetime military engagements, 165–166; perspectives on role of, 16–17, 20; Posture Statements, 24–25, 26, 28; potentials of, 28, 29–31, 32; prevention of drug trafficking in Ghana, 125; priorities of, 25, 27, 28; programs, 7–8, 25–26, 29, 157; Public Information Partnership initiative, 150; Public-Private Partnerships branch, 144, 153;

About the Book

Recent US security policy toward Africa has adopted a multi-dimensional approach—including the use of military assets to promote economic development and good governance—that has raised questions and generated considerable debate. Can actors like the US military develop appropriate methods to address both US and African interests? What blend of civilian and military programs are most likely to produce the best outcomes? And more fundamentally, is the military the appropriate actor to undertake governance and development projects?

The authors of *The US Military in Africa* explore these questions, providing an insightful combination of conceptual analysis and rich case studies.

Jessica Piombo is associate professor in the Department of National Security Affairs at the Naval Postgraduate School.